A Mine of Meaning

A Mine of Meaning
(*Ma'din ul-Ma'ani*)

by
Sharafuddin Maneri

Compiled by
Zain Badr Arabi

Translated by
Paul Jackson, S.J.

FONS VITAE

First published in 2012 by
Fons Vitae
49 Mockingbird Valley Drive
Louisville, KY 40207
http://www.fonsvitae.com
Email: fonsvitaeky@aol.com

Copyright Fons Vitae 2012

Library of Congress Cataloging-in-Publication Data

Maniri, Sharaf al-Din Ahmad ibn Yahy, d. 1380?
 [Ma'din al-ma'ani. English]
 A mine of meaning (Ma'din ul-ma'ani) / by Sharafuddin Maneri;
compiled by Zain Badr Arabi ; translated by Paul Jackson.
 p. cm.
 ISBN 978-1-891785-92-4 (alk. paper)
 1. Sufism--Early works to 1800. I. Arabi, Zain Badr. II. Jackson,
Paul, 1937- III. Title.
 BP188.9.M3513 2011
 297.4--dc23
                    2012013547

CONTENTS

Contents, continued

PREFACE

Sharafuddin Maneri was born in Maner, about thirty kilometres west of Patna, the capital of the Indian state of Bihar. As a young teenager he accompanied Maulana Tau'ama to Sonargaon, capital of Bengal. It is near the modern city of Dhaka in Bangladesh. When he felt satisfied with what he had learned and experienced in Sonargaon he returned to Maner with his young son, Zakiuddin. His father had died in the meantime, so he entrusted his son to the care of his own mother and proceeded to Delhi in search of a spiritual guide. After Nizamuddin Auliya had not agreed to accept him, and after finding Bu Qalandar Panipati too engrossed in God to be a suitable guide, he was on the point of returning to Maner when his brother urged him to visit Najibuddin Firdausi, not far from the Qutb Minar. There was an instant rapport between guide and disciple, and Maneri entrusted himself to the loving guidance of Najibuddin Firdausi until his death. Delhi now had no attraction for him so he set out with a party of travellers who were going to Maner. Before reaching his destination, however, he left the party and entered the jungle of Bihiya in order to devote himself wholly to the quest of God. After some time he moved to a cave in the Rajgir Hills, where a number of Hindu and Jain ascetics lived. The Buddha had also visited these hills many centuries previously.

When it became common knowledge that He had emerged from the jungle and was living in a cave in Rajgir, the local people began to pester him to write petitions on their behalf. This annoyed him, because he wanted to spend his time with God, but Sheikh Zada Chishti pointed out to him that he should help bear the burdens of the people. He never forgot this advice, and "bringing comfort to hearts" became not only a favourite phrase of his, but also set the tone of his life, both complementary to, and expressive of, his worship of God.

Hence, when a number of people began to come to him from Bihar Sharif, about thirty kilometres away, for spiritual guidance, he readily acceded to their requests. In order to make things easier for them he volunteered to go to Bihar Sharif for the Friday prayer and stay until all those who wanted to consult him had done so. He would then return to his cave. A small hut was built for him to stay in while he was in Bihar Sharif.

Gradually his sojourns became longer until he finally had to take up residence in a hospice built for him the governor, Majd ul-Mulk, on orders from Muhammad bin Tughluq, the Sultan of Delhi. As long as he could manage to do so, he used to go for a long walk once a month. Finally, his legs gave out and he could no longer walk. He had to be carried in a palanquin. He died in the evening of 2nd January 1381, and was buried the following day.

As is clear from this very brief account, Maneri was a recognized scholar; had trodden the Sufi Path; and had experienced the solitude of the jungle and a semi-secluded life in a cave. He also became aware of, and practised, "bringing comfort to hearts." Countless people called on him for guidance or attended his teaching assemblies. He was held in the highest regard by one and all.

Although he was a very learned man, his teaching was, so to say, filtered through the prism of his own experience, especially in spiritual matters, of which he was a master. Only one other Sufi, Gesudaraz (d.1322) of the Sultanate Period, 1206-1526, left behind a comparable literary heritage.

His basic text, *The Hundred Letters,* was a collection of a hundred letters written to Qazi Shamsuddin in 1346-47and contained a thorough exposition of the Sufi Path. Some twenty-two years later a second collection of 150 letters, published as *In Quest of God,* and written to various people, focussed on the individual needs of the respective recipients and form a complement to his first collection. The present work was the first record of what he taught in the assemblies he conducted, re-arranged topic wise. At least seven more such records followed, but they remained in chronological order, the typical format of such works. In this work, *A Mine of Meaning,* Maneri combines the roles of a spiritual guide and a religious teacher.

Paul Jackson, S.J.

INTRODUCTION TO *MA'DIN UL-MA'ANI*

Ma'din ul-Ma'ani [A Mine of Meaning] belongs to the *malfuz* genre of Sufi Literature. This genre was developed in India by the early Chishti Sufis. Indeed, it was *Fawa'id ul-Fu'ad* [Counsels for the Heart], an account of what transpired in the assemblies of the renowned Sufi, Nizamuddin Auliya (d. 1325), between the years 1307-22, that popularised this form of literature. It was a direct result of the reluctance of the early Chishti Sufis to put pen to paper themselves. The compiler of the work was Amir Hasan Sijzi, a noted Delhi poet. It was a common practice for Chishti Sufis to hold assemblies in which the master would speak on various topics or answer questions. It was a sort of free-flowing tutorial. The compiler would obviously be a regular participant in the assemblies. The fact that Sijzi was a poet indicates his competence to undertake the task. He would write up an account of what transpired shortly after the assembly while it was still fresh in his memory.

These records were normally chronological in nature. Often the actual date of the assembly was given, and even the time of the day. This is not the format followed in *A Mine of Meaning.* To begin with, no dates are given in the work itself, which was compiled by Maneri's faithful secretary, Zain Badr Arabi. If we turn to *Khwan-i Pur Ni'mat* [A Table Laden with Good Things], however, we discover when the work was completed. *A Table Laden with Good Things* was, in fact, the second *malfuz* compiled by Zain Badr Arabi. He wrote: "After the completion of the first volume of the discourses of the Master, known as *Ma'din ul-Ma'ani,* there was completed, from the 15th Sha'ban 749 [8th November 1348] till the end of Shawwal 751 [30th December 1350], whatever came into the defective hearing and deficient understanding of this Helpless One." Throughout his writing Zain Badr Arabi refers to himself as "this Helpless One."

This information clearly states that the work was completed prior to 8th November 1348. It also indicates the time frame in which Zain produced his second volume. It covered a period of two years. Moreover, it contained forty-seven assemblies, but these varied greatly in length. Nevertheless, the work does act as an indicator of the way Zain worked.

Zain provides another important piece of information regarding the chronology of *A Mine of Meaning.* He was also the compiler of the letters written by Sharafuddin Maneri to Qazi Shamsuddin, the official in charge of the township of Chausa. He wrote: "At various times, from the region of Bihar, in the year 747 A.H. [24th April 1346 to 12th April 1347], he ordered them to be sent to the aforesaid township [Chausa] to the petitioner just mentioned [Qazi Shamsuddin]. This is the collection the servants and attendants who were present in that dwelling place compiled from those letters, arranging them in the following order so that, on the day and hour when grace befriends them, they might put into practice what they have read."

Although Zain refers to "servants and attendants" who were involved in compiling the letters, "arranging them in the following order," it is clear that the bulk of the work was done by Zain himself. *Maktubat-i Sadi* [The Hundred Letters] was a huge literary enterprise. An English translation runs into 424 pages. The letters averaged two a week during the year-long period mentioned. It is difficult to see how Zain could have been involved, to any marked degree, in another literary endeavour at the same time.

In his preface to the present work, Zain clearly states that "he assisted at every assembly, where genuine seekers, dependable disciples and loyal servants were present." Zain's regularity in attending the assemblies is clear. He also goes on to say that "after putting together this compilation, he approached the exalted Sheikh and personally requested him, in the honourable assembly, to go over whatever this servant, mere dust beneath the feet of the dervishes, had committed to writing." Thus, "it was read out in the assembly itself, chapter by chapter, word by word, and letter by letter."

The phrase, "after putting together this compilation" is significant. Clearly, Zain had been recording what had been said and done in the assemblies for some time, perhaps four to six years. This was done in the normal chronological manner. It is possible that Zain had this material at hand when the work on *The Hundred Letters* began. These letters brought home to Zain the benefits of material prepared topic wise, not merely in the necessarily scattered format of a chronological presentation. This could have provided the impetus to put his material into the sixty-three chapters of the present work. Chronology was no longer the organizing factor and was abandoned. It was this 'compilation' that Zain brought before his Master, possibly late in 1347, if he had rearranged his material after completing work on *The Hundred* Letters, with his request that Maneri check what he had written. In chapter 13, devoted to the topic of fasting, after a long discussion on the subject, Maneri commented: "I have written an explanation of this in a letter. For further details it should be consulted." The letter referred to is probably "Letter 33: Fasting," in *The Hundred Letters.*

This aside needs to be read in the context of the following statement in Zain's Preface: "Sometimes, during the reading, he would add a suitable anecdote or example to confirm his teaching." If the material in chapter 13 dates back from a few years previously, and if Zain made his compilation in 1347 and the compilation was read out in the assemblies in 1348, prior to 8th November, Maneri's comment would make sense. It would mean that the reading reminded Maneri of his letter on fasting, which was still quite fresh in his memory. It should be noted that Maneri had an excellent memory, as his reminiscences, for example, clearly indicate.

Granted that Zain was recording Maneri's teaching for several years before the whole project of *The Hundred Letters* was initiated, the question arises as to why he took the trouble of arranging the material topic wise and having it checked by Maneri. *The Hundred Letters* was a rich mine of spiritual meaning. Zain's basic motive was his unshakable conviction of the enduring worth of Maneri's teaching. It had to be recorded for posterity. Added to this was the desire of any author to see his work "in print," so to say. Zain did not want his efforts to go to waste. There is also the different focus of *A Mine of Meaning* when compared to *The Hundred Letters.* While the latter work focussed on the Path to God, the former ranged over a wide spectrum of topics, from minute details regarding the correct way of reciting ritual prayers to deep mystical insights. There was, as it were, "something for everybody" in this work. The two works complemented each other. Moreover, the *Letters* were addressed to Qazi Shamsuddin, an experienced disciple, while the present work contains answers to a wide variety of questions from participants of varied backgrounds, experience and interest.

A word of explanation seems appropriate about the English rendition of the title. Although the work itself is in Persian, the title is in Arabic. There is nothing unusual about this. Many Persian works have Arabic titles. An author would not hesitate to choose an apt expression for a title to his work if it were in Arabic. A literal translation of the present work would be: *The Mine of the Meanings.*

This is where there is a clash between the constraints of Arabic grammar, specifically in what is called "the construct state," and the English use of the definite and indefinite articles. *A Mine of Meaning* is meant to convey in English the sense of the original Arabic title. The singular 'meaning' has been preferred to the plural. Undoubtedly the sixty-three-chapter work is replete with 'meanings.' The work itself, however, is like a multi-coloured bed cover. Various coloured threads of wool have been carefully woven together to form a pattern. The whole purpose of the cover, however, is to keep a person warm. We might say that the whole purpose of this literary work is to enable the reader to remain 'warm' in the knowledge of the multiform relationship that exists between us human beings and God.

A Mine of Meaning certainly broadens this 'knowledge.' Even more importantly, however, it leads us into a deeper sense of God. This is because Maneri, besides being a scholar, was a person who lived in the presence of God. It is this 'sense' that is conveyed in the work. It touches people deeply. It is this impact-laden dimension, rooted in Maneri's personal experience, that favours the use of the singular, 'Meaning.'

The Translation

Anyone who has attempted to translate from one language to another knows that there is no such thing as 'the' translation of sentences other than of the most basic ones. One has only to go through the various English versions of the most translated books in the world, the Bible and the Quran, to see this for oneself.

The first point that needs to be examined in a translation such as the present one is the actual text as found in manuscript form. The original *Ma'din ul-Ma'ani* was completed by November 1348. This manuscript is not known to be extant. A current translator has to be content with later manuscripts. The older the manuscript, the more reliable it should be. Unfortunately, no old manuscript copy of the work was available during this translation. Three texts were used: a printed version dated 1884; a manuscript dated 1754; and a photocopy of an undated manuscript. All three have mistakes. The advantage of having three copies is that the mistakes, by means of comparing the three texts, can usually be rectified. Two will often be in agreement in a wording which makes good sense. It is rare for all three to differ. A choice then has to be made in the particular context.

There is also the question of the guiding principles involved in the translation itself. As far as anecdotal material is concerned, a certain amount of liberty can be taken to ensure that the story 'flows.' This type of translation is often referred to as "dynamic equivalence."

Translating terms used for various movements in Muslim ritual prayer, for example, has proved quite challenging. English terms have been utilized, as this is a translation into English. Often a short phrase is needed to convey the sense of a particular Arabic or Persian term.

Great care has been exercised in translating theological and spiritual material. The twin demands of fidelity and comprehensibility have both to be respected by the translator. In a number of places the language may seem difficult. This has to be expected, as the original text often poses very real challenges for a person who can read with competence the original Persian. This is usually because of the nature of the material being presented.

A word has to be said about the poetry found quoted in *A Mine of Meaning.* To begin with, an effort has been made to give it poetic form in English without attempting to produce genuine poetry, with rhyme and rhythm. This seems a far more accurate way of presenting poetry than by rendering it in ordinary prose form. At the very least, it has a poetic look about it. Moreover, poetry is much more suggestive than explicative, specially the type of poetry enjoyed and quoted by Maneri. The format chosen in this translation is more attuned to the suggestive dimension of poetry than to explanatory prose.

The poetry is, of course, more difficult to translate than prose. No attempt has been made to trace the poetry. Sometimes the poet's name is given. A similar remark can be made about prose quotations. Those from the Quran, however, have been identified and the reference given. The Footnotes will be of interest to some readers, while others may prefer to ignore them completely.

The Participants

It is worth reflecting on the variety of people present at the assemblies. All would have had an interest in the Sufi Path to God as enunciated and lived by Sharafuddin Maneri. This statement reflects Maneri's own preference for "discipleship through association" rather than "discipleship through instruction." This is an example of the adage, "values are caught, not taught." In fact, however, a lot of teaching is involved, as *A Mine of Meaning* itself amply illustrates.

Some of those present would have been beginners, novices who were setting out along the Sufi Path. In Maneri's scheme of things, this would normally entail a period of three years. Maneri speaks of this is Letter 5, "Searching for a Spiritual Guide," in *The Hundred Letters.* "When a novice begins to associate with a spiritual guide, he will have to spend three years in three types of training... one year's service on behalf of other people; one year devoted to God; and another year spent in watching over one's own heart." These novices would have been full time in Maneri's hospice and would have attended all the assemblies.

Another group would have consisted of a few senior disciples who also lived full time in the hospice. Zain Badr Arabi, the compiler of *A Mine of Meaning,* was one such person. Other senior disciples, who were chiefly engaged elsewhere, would call in for a short while to be refreshed in spirit by associating with their beloved Master. Some of these would have been scholars who held important posts elsewhere, such as Qazi Shamsuddin, who was in charge of the administration of the township of Chausa. Other officials would have a military background, such as Majd ul-Mulk, the Governor of the province of Bihar. Some of the participants were probably prosperous merchants, such as Khwaja Mahmud Iwaz, who had a large garden not far from Maneri's hospice.

One factor common to all who were present in the assemblies was their knowledge of Persian, for this was the language of the assemblies. In the Western half of the widespread Muslim community such sessions would all have been in Arabic, while comparable gatherings in Christian Europe would have been in Latin. This system allowed people from diverse areas to communicate with one another, either face to face, as in the assemblies, or through correspondence.

The absence of women in the assemblies needs to be noted. This did not mean that they could not make contact with Maneri. This was possible in a semi-private setting, and normally in the local language. In Persian source material from places as far apart as Sonargaon, in modern Bangladesh, to Bihar Sharif and Agra, the local language is referred to as 'Hindavi.' This is a generic term, not a specific one. It indicates the local language, whatever that may have been, as opposed to Persian. Maneri had no trouble quickly mastering the local spoken language, building on his mother tongue that he had acquired in Maner.

Just as there was a variety of people present in the assemblies, so too there was a similar variety among those interested in reading *Ma'din ul-Ma'ani* once it became available. There was a flourishing book trade in the Islamic world at the time of Maneri, due to the widespread availability of paper. Nevertheless, copying took time, and books were expensive. They were prized possessions. Moreover, the more renowned the author, the more the book was valued. This means that, even though Zain Badr Arabi actually wrote *Ma'din ul-Ma'ani,* nevertheless, because it contained the teaching of Sharafuddin Maneri, its value was greatly enhanced.

One important question still needs to be raised. "How faithful is Zain's record of what Maneri actually said?" As a literary form, it does not have the authority of the *Letters* composed by Maneri himself. The subsequent history of these two works shows conclusively that *The Hundred Letters* was a far more popular and widely read work than *Ma'din ul-Ma'ani.* This question, however, has already been answered in this very Introduction. The original text, read out to Maneri in the assemblies, and sometimes corrected by him, or added to by him, was accurate. There can be no doubt about this. It is also worth recalling that Zain had a real mastery over Persian, as his various prefaces amply illustrate.

Relevance

The broadest of all questions is the relevance of the life and teaching of Sharafuddin Maneri, a Sufi Master of fourteenth-century Bihar, for people of the twenty-first century.

To begin with, even 630 years after his death, the fourteen million Muslims of Bihar State in modern India still revere him as their greatest saint. Moreover, his writings were widely studied in madrasas and Sufi hospices throughout the Indian subcontinent. His *Hundred Letters* were read out to Akbar, and Aurangzeb had his own personal copy of the work which he kept with him during his travels. Because of his studies in Sonargaon – probably about eighteen years – Maneri is very well known and revered in Bangladesh. Due to waves of migration from India to Pakistan in the wake of Partition, many devotees now live in Pakistan. Some are also found in the United States, Canada and England.

In the midst of today's violence, fuelled by conflicting ideologies, all claiming to be authentic Islamic teaching, where does a modern Muslim, from Bihar, for example, look for authentic guidance? The basic texts of the Quran and the accepted collections of Traditions are there for all to see, but the interpretations of these texts and the ways of living out a person's faith vary greatly. A Bihari Muslim can safely follow the teaching of Maneri, as expounded in the present work. In addition to the information a reader can pick up, there is also the boon of coming into first-hand contact with Maneri himself, a man totally dedicated to God and to the welfare of his fellow-Muslims. This has both a soothing and reassuring effect on the attentive reader, whoever he or she may be.

For people outside the fold of Islam, yet who wish to benefit from authentic Muslim teaching from a man who was both a scholar and a saint, Maneri has much to offer. In religious discussions, Muslims naturally refer to the Quran, just as Christians refer to the Bible. Within the actual living out of the general categories of Muslims and Christians, however, there are many streams of thought and religious experience. A Dominican priest, for example, who is writing about the challenges faced by contemporary Christians, is almost certain to quote frequently from the writings of Thomas Aquinas, the great Dominican theologian and mystic. He lived in the thirteenth century, a whole century before Maneri. Because of Maneri's significant literary heritage, as well as his reputation for learning and sanctity, he can also be reliably quoted, especially by people from the Indian subcontinent.

One very visible sign of the Sufis throughout the subcontinent is the large number of their tombs. Another not so visible, but of great importance, is the literary heritage found in libraries, such as the Khuda Bakhsh Oriental Public Library in Patna, as well as in private collections. This material is mainly in Persian, as well as in Arabic. Some works have been translated into Urdu, but translations into English are comparatively rare. The most important sign of the influence of Sufis down the centuries, however, lies in the attitudes of heart and mind found in countless Muslims in the subcontinent.

It is convenient to divide the literary material into that of the Sultanate period, 1206-1526, and the Mughal period from 1526 until the changes wrought after 1857, although Sufis continued to flourish even after this political upheaval. The literary output of the Sultanate period is nowhere near as prolific as that from the Mughal period. Moreover scholars, such as Habib and Nizami, warn us about the widespread circulation of spurious *malfuzat*. It is in this context that the writings by and recorded about Maneri (d.1381) are so important. The only other Sufi from the Sultanate period who left a comparable literary heritage is Gesu Daraz (d.1422), who had migrated from Delhi to Gulbarga.

It is in this context that Maneri deserves to be heard. His was an important voice which helped set the tone of the religious life of ordinary Muslims in the subcontinent. The Sufis have left a rich spiritual heritage. It is worth our attention. Moreover, their particular way of experiencing reality was that of living amongst an overwhelming number of people who were not Muslims. These people followed various local religions. Somewhat akin to the term 'Hindavi,' the word covering many of them, 'Hindu,' basically meant that they were followers of the local religion. Although the variety of 'religions' still remains – such as Vaishnavism and Shaivism – nevertheless the term 'Hindu' has taken firm root as an umbrella term.

Although political power in the various places where Maneri lived – Maner, Sonargaon, Delhi, Rajgir and Bihar town – was in the hands of Muslims, the majority of the people were Hindus. It is beyond the scope of this introduction to attempt a detailed account of the interaction that took place, but this ground reality had a definite effect on how Muslims lived out their religion. The evidence that emerges from Maneri's writings shows that he had an accommodative rather than a confrontational attitude towards Hindus.

One final remark can be made about how Maneri frequently, yet unconsciously, shares with us his own experience. He is loath to make any claims or draw attention to himself. Even his reminiscences, mainly from his Sonargaon days, are didactic in nature, rather than autobiographical. A discerning reader, however, can perceive when his teaching about the human spirit's journey towards God is ultimately rooted more in his own personal experience than in any text he may be quoting.

Paul Jackson, S. J.
Patna

A Mine of Meaning
(*Ma'din ul-Ma'ani*)

COMPILER'S PREFACE

In the name of God, the Merciful, the Compassionate[1]

Praise and thanksgiving be to the Lord of Eternity Who poured an abundance of wonderful secret meanings and extraordinary signs of the Divine into the hearts of mystics and of His special ones! From time to time, in accordance with the nobility of the Divinity, which extends to ordinary believers, He gave a sign for the descent upon them from the station of intimate friendship, according to the saying, "The speech of men depends on their capacity to understand," to the abode of ordinary people. Many kinds of wonderful interpretations and paths of sublime hints found passage from ecstatic speech to the ordinary manner of speaking. This enables all in the assembly, so desirous of the pure water of the great river of mystical knowledge and of downpours of oceans of love, to experience refreshment and joy in their lives and spirits. May the seekers who strive heart and soul in their quest experience an increase in their efforts! May those unfortunate ones who, thoroughly ensnared by their selfish souls, have become desirous of the grain of the Simurgh[2] and oblivious to constancy in conduct, tranquillity and noble desires that result from hearing about repentance and conversion, find upright con-

---

1. This is how the compiler of this work, Zain Badr Arabi, begins his Preface. His Persian is highly literary, especially at the beginning, as the reader will perceive from the English translation. Two points merit attention. The first is the writer's obvious command over Persian. This is reassuring. It means we can assume that he had no difficulties, from a linguistic point of view, in understanding what Maneri was saying. The second point to notice is the stark contrast between his literary style and Maneri's pragmatic use of Persian. Maneri's focus is on what he wants to say. Language is the tool he employs to convey his meaning. This fits in well with the very title of the work. It also means that we can accept Zain Badr Arabi's claim to fidelity to Maneri's meaning, and even to his very words.

2. Attar's delightful account of the quest for the fabulous Simurgh in his *Mantiq ul-Tair*, underlies this reference. It means that the quest for the things of this world has supplanted the quest for God.

duct and noble desires coming to birth within themselves! May they be brought out of the dark pit of desire onto the illuminated path of guidance! Some of them have turned out to be models of the correct path.

> Because what is written about them comes from the
> divine threshold,
> They have become numbered among the leaders who
> give guidance.

A hundred thousand greetings, salutations and honourable congratulations be upon the pure tomb of the head of the throne of the Law, the full moon of the firmament, the sun of the constellation of reality, the crown upon the head of the mystics, the chief of the prophets, the one intimate to the secret of "He revealed to His servant what He revealed" (Q53:10), the one breathing the fragrant air of the garden of the station of "at two bows lengths or nearer" (Q53:9),[3] Muhammad, the Apostle of God—the blessings and peace of God be upon him, and upon all of his family members, friends, descendants and followers! May meaning be brought forth from thought, and speech be found flowing from a tongue in an unceasing manner!

After all this thanksgiving and praise of the pure and most exalted Lord, and blessings upon Muhammad, the Chosen One—the peace and blessing of God be upon him[4]—this servant of the dervishes and dust upon their threshold, the compiler of these discourses, which are pearls of meaning and priceless jewels, the helpless Zain Badr Arabi—may God forgive him and wipe away his sins and those of his parents! He is one of the attendants at the threshold of the eminent Sheikh, the famous guide, the manifestation of the sayings of the mystics, the focal point of those who have arrived, the honour of God, of reality, of right guidance, of the

---

3. These quotations refer to the Quranic account of how close Muhammad drew to God during his ascent (*mi'raj*) towards Him.

4. This is the customary expression found after the name of Muhammad. It, as well as other such honorific phrases after the names of special individuals —unless of specific significance—is omitted in this translation.

faith,[5] Ahmad Yahya Maneri.[6] May God bless Muslims with a long life for him and thus prolong for us the blessing of being able to associate with him!

He[7] joined the group and had the felicity of continuously serving the Sheikh. He also assisted at every assembly where genuine seekers, dependable disciples and loyal servants were present. Each one, according to his own state and activities, posed difficulties and questions with regard to the Path; requested explanations concerning the Law; some hints about Reality; and sought disclosure of some of the secrets concerning mystical knowledge. The Revered Master,[8] the sheikh renowned as a nourisher of the faith, responded to the questions posed by proffering clear answers along with full explanations and incomparable hints in pleasing language. Every explanation contained a hundred hidden meanings, and every hint a thousand unassailable nuances. What is desired from every meaning is limitless understanding; from every nuance, endless comprehension; from everything that is understood, countless states; from every state, a delight that cannot be measured; from whatever is comprehended, many stages; and from every stage, information that cannot be contained in this world.

> This mark cannot be seen except by pure eyes:
> A sightless person cannot see the sun.
> If this be so, the blame is with the eyes,
> Just as a fevered tongue cannot taste sugar.

As far as his abilities allowed—with the aid of divine grace and the favour of the Eternal One—he collected what he could remember, in so far as it was possible, by retaining the very words. On ac-

---

5. The word for 'honour' is *sharaf,* and for "the faith" is *al-din* in Arabic. The expression is pronounced as 'Sharafuddin.' This is the spelling utilized in this translation in conformity with conventional Indian usage.

6. 'Ahmad' was the name given to Maneri by his father, Yahya, and 'Maneri' signifies that he is "from Maner," a small township about 25 kilometres west of Patna, the capital of the state of Bihar, India.

7. The reference is to the compiler.

8. This seems an appropriate translation of the original *Bandagi-i Makhdum.* A literal translation of this expression would run something like "the servitude of the served one." This presents a linguistic and cultural barrier. The English expression chosen is meant to convey this sense of respectful devotion.

count of his own weakness and deficiency, however, if he did not retain the very phraseology, yet retained the meaning completely and accurately, he would, of necessity, express the meaning in appropriate language, since the purpose of language is to express meaning.

Moreover, in no way or for no reason did he make any change or alteration in the meaning. If he did not remember the gist of what was said, he would leave some pages blank and, at the next opportunity, put forward his request. After he had been granted the honour of a reply, he would remember what was said and, with the concurrence of the entire assembly, put it in writing.

Even after doing all this, in order to make sure there were no mistakes or omissions, after putting together this compilation, he approached the Exalted Sheikh and personally requested him, in the honourable assembly, to go over whatever this servant, mere dust beneath the feet of the dervishes, had committed to writing.

On account of the perfection of his benevolence he complied fully with the request of this Helpless One, going minutely through the material from the beginning to the end. It was read out in the assembly itself, chapter by chapter, word by word, and letter by letter. In some places where this Helpless One had made a mistake while writing down what had been said, he graciously emended the error.

Sometimes, during the reading, he would add a suitable anecdote or example to confirm his teaching, or an apposite, elegant couplet or quatrain. Any proof or answer adduced in confirmation by the Revered Master was gathered up. He himself used to explain the meaning and also have it included in this volume so that the world and mankind, by studying his excellent discourses, might attain happiness and good fortune from his blameless life.

For this Helpless One[9] it is an occasion for strengthening faith, obtaining forgiveness for sins, and perceiving the Desired of both worlds. The expectations from anyone who reads, hears, sees or writes is that, if the declaration of man becomes the vehicle for abandoning by smoothing over the faults of the one who reveals, by way of justice they should come forward to correct it so that they may be rewarded and recompensed, not showing themselves eager to find fault, for they would then be reproved and scolded.

---

9. This is the expression Zain Badr Arabi uses to refer to himself.

The word of a saintly man is nothing but profitable:
Having a false understanding, however, would be a fault.

Since a righteous seeker, filled with these matters, acquires abundant and limitless meaning as a result of studying this collection, the name *Ma'din ul-Ma'ani* [A Mine of Meaning][10] has been given to it. The work is divided into sixty-three chapters. In each chapter there is a pertinent description, namely, a full exposition to enable the reader to attain his goal quickly—God willing!

---

10. *Ma'din* is more correct than *ma'dan*, which is commonly seen in India. Arabic scholars will notice the choice of the indefinite article, as well as the singular, 'meaning.'

CHAPTER 1
A DESCRIPTION IN CONFIRMATION
OF THE EXISTENCE OF *GOD*[11] AND HIS
ONENESS—EXALTED BE HIS GLORY!

A discussion[12] concerning the existence[13] of the being[14] of *God* arose. The Revered Master—may Muslims enjoy the favour of his long life—said: "Every single particle in the world bears witness to these four things. Firstly, in an ecstatic state, each says: 'I was non-existent. I have not come into existence by myself, for no operation comes into existence from non-existence. This means I have a Creator through Whom I have come into existence. This bears witness to the existence and being of *God*.' Secondly, '*God* Most Exalted is One. If He were not One, He would be two. Conflict would necessarily arise. This is because if one wants to create something and the second does not want to create it, there would be conflict-

---

11. The original is *Haqq*. Various meanings are given for this word, such as "acting justly, uprightly; just, right; truth; reality; the Truth; the true God etc." In this translation '*God*'—in italics—is the normal rendition when the Unique Supreme Being is intended. It carries overtones of "Subsistent Truth" and "Subsistent, Ultimate Reality." It was probably an unconscious choice stemming from Maneri's own profound experience of the incomprehensible 'truth' and 'reality' of the Supreme Being. This is not to say that the word 'Allah,' with its personal, interactive and communicative overtones, is 'supplanted.' It's all a question of 'focus' at the moment of writing. Usually "Most Exalted" is added to *God*. This is a transference of the expression universally added, as a mark of respect, to 'Allah.' This very addition to *Haqq* conveys, but less directly, the overtones mentioned, and justifies the use of 'God' rather than 'Truth' or 'Reality.' On occasion, however, *Haqq*, unaccompanied by "Most Exalted," is more fittingly translated by 'Reality.'

12. *Zikri*. Strictly speaking this means 'remembering.' In Sufi usage it means "remembering God." As always, the context provides guidance in choosing an appropriate English word to convey the intended sense.

13. *Wujud*.

14. *Hasti*.

ing orders. I would not have come into existence. But since I have,
I know that *God* is One—exalted be His glory!' Thirdly, '*God* Most
Exalted is Omniscient. This is because nothing can be brought into
existence unless it is first known.' Fourthly, 'He is Omnipotent. If
He were not, He could not bring things into existence. Everything,
out of powerlessness, would be impossible.' Every single particle,
as well as everything in existence, in a state of ecstasy, says these
four things: '*God* exists; He is One; He is Omniscient; and He is Omnipotent.'" The Revered Master—may *God* extol him[15]—took the
following couplet upon his blessed lips, remarking that it throws
light on what he had said:

> In quest of union with You I came to an idol-temple:
> The worship of idols was a murmuring of love for You.

He said: "No matter what those endowed with mystical knowledge[16] see, they do so in this fashion. Whenever they look at any
particle they see nothing except these four things. This cannot be
contained in books." Afterwards he took this hemistich upon his
blessed lips:

> No matter what I look at, I see You.

He said: "The explanation of this saying is given in these words of
a saintly man:

> 'I don't see anything without seeing God in it.'

That 'seeing' applies here.

A discussion arose about the unity of *God*. Qazi Sharafuddin
Sabuni was present in the gathering. He began to read, from the
Hidaya [Guidance][17] about the proofs for the existence of *God* until

---

15. In future this, and similar expressions, are not included in the
translation, unless there is some specific reason for doing so. Expressions
of respect associated with the name of God, however, are retained, e.g.
"God Most Exalted."

16. This extended phrase is a translation of *arifan*. This is a tone-
setting rendition instead of the normal 'mystics,' which will be used
subsequently.

17. The MSS have *bidaya*—which means 'commencement'—but
the *Hidaya* is a well-known work of Sunni jurisprudence by Sheikh
Burhanuddin Ali, (d. 1197). It is referred to in the sixth and thirty-sixth
assemblies in *Khwan-i Pur Ni'mat*, the second *malfuz* collection of Maneri's

he came to these words: "In the opinion of Sunnis and ordinary believers, in accordance with the Quran,[18] the Traditions,[19] the consensus of the community, rational proofs and accepted arguments, the Creator of the world is One." The Revered Master said: "He is One as far as reality is concerned, not as a number. Thus it is that in the Friday sermon[20] "One without number" is recited in the sense that each created thing comes as one of a series, nothing more. "The Ancient has no end, just as He has no beginning."

Maulana Qamaruddin, son of the Master's sister,[21] opined that, just as an indivisible atom is such because it cannot be divided, it must necessarily follow that it is one in reality. The Revered Master replied: "Since an indivisible atom cannot be divided, it is necessarily one in reality, but since it is capable of contrary qualities, such as movement and rest; locality and form, it is also capable of composition. These are all signs of newness, while our subject

---

sayings. Those familiar with the original alphabet will realize how this confusion could have easily occurred. The above-mentioned work was made available in English translation by Paul Jackson, S.J., with a subtitle *A Table Laden with Good Things,* Idarah-i Adabiyat-i Delli, Delhi, 1986. Currently it is out of print.

18. The text has *kitab.* A literal translation would be, "the book." A Muslim reader would have no difficulty in identifying it, from the context, as referring to the Quran. The identification is made for the sake of readers from different backgrounds. In future it will be rendered as "the Book."

19. The text has *sunnat.* This word is used to denote the customary way of acting. In this context it refers to Muhammad's customary way of acting. The intention of capitalizing the initial letter is to indicate the sum total of Muhammad's way of speaking and acting, as recorded in the *hadith* collections, which are also referred to as 'traditions.' A common translation of *hadith* is 'tradition,' which refers to sayings or accounts of deeds which are "handed on."

20. This is the *khutba* delivered at the noon congregational prayer on Fridays. It precedes the formal prayer.

21. The simple English 'nephew' does not specify whether the parent is the Master's brother or sister. Hence this more accurate, yet elaborated, translation, is given. Based purely on manuscript evidence, it is not clear whether Maneri had only one or more than one sister. Moreover, no sister is named in the manuscripts.

is Ancient.[22] Hence, although the form precludes divisibility, nevertheless, on account of the fact that it is capable of composition, this amounts to being divided, focussing on the capacity thereof. As far as the essence of the Lord Most Exalted is concerned, however, there is no division in reality or in possibility. In reality there is no absolutely one except God—exalted be His glory!"

The *Hidaya* was again taken up till these words were reached. "The Magi[23] say that there are two creators:[24] one creates good, while the other creates evil. They call the creator of good Yazdan, while the creator of evil is called Ahriman." The Revered Master said: "Yazdan is understood to mean God,[25] for good is the work of a good being, while evil is the work of an evil one. This is also why Ahriman is understood to mean Satan.[26] The dualists have been sorely tried by this division. For this reason they gratuitously assert that good is the work of a good being while evil is the work of an evil one. *God* Most Exalted is wise. It is not fitting to add the attribute of evil to a wise person because the creation of evil is foolish. This cannot be the source. It must be from another source, and that is Ahriman. Thus the creator of good cannot be the creator of evil, nor can the creator of evil be the creator of good. May dust be in their mouths on account of this belief!"

Afterwards he said: "The solution to their problem is this. It would be foolish to say that the creator of evil is evil and the creator of bodies is obnoxious because creating them would not show mature wisdom. By creating these things the Lord displays mature wisdom. For example, just as He creates what is useful, He also creates what is obnoxious so that people may ponder the meaning of what augurs good and what augurs evil. This is because anyone who does not experience the enjoyment of blessings and has no

---

22. *Qadim.* This carries the overtones of 'eternal' and, as a consequence, of being unchangeable.

23. The Magi are the Zoroastrians. They believe in a good and an evil spirit as the creators of good and evil.

24. In this theoretical discussion the word for creator is not capitalized.

25. The text has 'Allah.' In this work 'God' is used to translate 'Allah.' Italics are not used. As peviously mentioned, italics are used for the translation of *Haqq*.

26. The original has *shaitan*. In this translation, for the sake of simplicity, it is translated by 'Satan,' while *Iblis* is translated as "the Devil."

knowledge of the pain of torment does not bow in humble submission. The intentions of the commands and prohibitions of the Lord is this. What more can be added to this?"

Afterwards he told this story: "A law-abiding Muslim made his abode in a remote place in the land of the Zoroastrians. He passed his time worshipping *God*. Once a learned Zoroastrian went to that ascetic in order to question him about mystical knowledge and, by this means, confute him. That ascetic was not well versed in mystical knowledge. When that learned man called on him he put questions to the ascetic in order to elicit his responses. In order to convince him he brought forward such things as to confute him. Since that ascetic did not have much knowledge of mysticism, he became silent. He was confuted. In that locality lived a Sunni woman who was a mystic. People informed her that a learned Zoroastrian had called on a certain ascetic. He had put certain questions to him and confused him. He then returned home. When that woman heard all this she was extremely upset. She said: 'This is not good! That ascetic might be diverted from the Way.' Pained at this prospect, she made a scorpion out of wax, wrapped it in a piece of paper and slipped it up her sleeve. She placed a girdle around her neck as a talisman and marched off in the direction of the learned man's house. He was at home. She sent a message to him through someone saying: 'Go and tell him that a woman from your religion has come. She has a difficulty connected with religion. Come out quickly and answer her, otherwise she is going to remove her girdle.'[27] When this message reached that learned Zoroastrian he immediately came outside and said: 'What is this difficulty of yours?' That woman, a mystic, produced the wax scorpion from up her sleeve and said: 'Who created this scorpion?' He replied: 'Ahriman created it.' She put a further question: 'Who put poison in its tail?' He replied: 'Ahriman did.' Thereupon she said: 'Since Ahriman created it and put poison in its tail, was Yazdan aware of this or not? Answer me quickly, otherwise I will remove my girdle!' That man was nonplussed at this, thinking: 'If I say he was aware, then why didn't he make them good? And if I say that

---

27. *Zunnar* means a cord belt or girdle which was used by Christians, Jews and Zoroastrians under the Caliphate. It also refers to the sacred thread worn by Brahmins. The allusion is, of course, to its religious symbolism. The choice of translation obviously depends on the context.

he wasn't aware, then he was ignorant, but ignorance is incompat-
ible with divinity.' He was distressed and confused. He said: 'Wait
a moment! I will first of all remove my girdle, then you can do the
same to yours.' Immediately that learned Zoroastrian removed his
girdle and became a Muslim.'" After this, the Master took this couplet on his blessed lips:

> Yes, when guidance removes a curtain from the eyes,
> An unbeliever, by submission, breaks the girdle's grip.

He said: "Thus it becomes known that a woman, who is a mystic, is
better that a thousand men who are obedient and ascetical, yet are
lacking in learning and mystical knowledge."

A discussion arose about the doubts[28] that arise concerning the
oneness of *God*. The Revered Master said: "Doubts which arise concerning the oneness of *God* are included in the category of those
things men believe in but, because they are invisible, cannot actually be seen. These doubts do not arise or prove harmful unless a
person dwells on them. It is well known, for example, that Aisha,[29]
the mother of the faithful, experienced doubts of this nature. She
communicated her misgivings to the Apostle. The Apostle said:
'You have attained the perfection of faith!'" This Helpless One[30]
put this question: "Since such doubts originate in the heart, if a
person simply ignores them by pushing them aside and doesn't
allow them to disturb his heart, is this a better course of action,
or should proofs for the oneness of *God* be adduced?" The Revered
Master replied: "If by paying no attention to them they are brushed
aside, why should a person get caught up in seeking proofs?" Afterwards he added: "Matters are arranged on one foundation. The
proof for this is that there is one director. Just as day comes and
goes, on that foundation night also comes and goes. Similarly, all
things depend on one foundation. Discord and alteration have no
foundation. Concord has its foundation in the powers of the direc-

---

28. *Waswasa* are suggestions, fears, anxieties or doubts that arise either
spontaneously in a person's mind or at the instigation of Satan.

29. Aisha was the daughter of Abu Bakr, one of Muhammad's leading
followers, who became the first caliph on his death in 632. She was
Muhammad's favourite wife in Medina. From 595 till 619 Khadija had
been Muhammad's sole wife.

30. This is the expression the compiler, Zain Badr Arabi, uses to refer to
himself, as we noticed in his Preface.

tor, for the director is one."

While the assembly was still in progress the time for the noon prayer arrived. A Hindu of about eighty years of age came forward and said he wanted to become a Muslim. The Revered Master instructed him to make the profession of faith.[31] He did so, and became a Muslim. God be praised for this! Afterwards he said: "Bring him something to eat immediately!" They brought sweets and cake and placed them in front of him and those present in the assembly. The Revered Master indicated to those present that they should teach him to say, "In the name of God"[32] before eating. They did so. He then turned towards Maulana Abul Qasim and Abul Hasan and said: "Take him home and have him take a ritual bath today itself. Tomorrow get a pyjama as well as a kurta with long, wide sleeves such as Sufis wear, made for him, and give them to him."[33] Thereupon he exclaimed several times: "Glory be to God! For so many years he was a stranger, and has now become a comrade; he was an enemy, and has now become a friend! The unbelief of so many years has been erased by reciting the profession of faith."

At this stage Qazi Ashrafuddin[34] said: "'Anyone who eats with a forgiven person experiences forgiveness.' Is this a tradition of the Messenger?"[35] The Revered Master replied: "Yes, it is a tradition, but it is expressed thus: 'One who eats with a forgiven person is forgiven.'" Once again he asked: "If this man who has become a Muslim were to die at this very moment, would he have died pure or not?" The Revered Master replied: "He would have departed

31. "There is no god but God: Muhammad is the Apostle of God."

32. *Bismillah* (in the name of God) is the normal prayer before eating. It stands for the full form, "In the name of God, the Merciful, the Compassionate."

33. The lower garment could have been a lungi or a pyjama. The upper garment is clear. Simply put, the instruction is to provide him with suitable clothes. What is of interest is the lack of any reference to circumcision, probably on account of his age.

34. Qazi Ashrafuddin was a senior disciple who featured very prominently in the *malfuz* which follows this present one, i.e. *Khwan-i Pur Ni'mat.* He obviously felt perfectly free to pursue a line of questioning in order to acquire greater clarity for himself and others present in the assembly.

35. Where the Persian has *Paighambar* it is translated literally as 'Messenger.'

pure. He would be included within the ambit of this verse: 'Those who believe and do not taint their faith with wrongdoing shall surely feel secure, for they are guided' (Q6:82). There are many promises concerning such people." Again he asked: "If he were to die at this moment, would there be any apprehension about the end of such a person?" He replied: "That applies to everyone, apart from the prophets, and is hidden. No one has any knowledge of it. A person's end becomes known the moment he gives up his soul." Again he asked: "Does simply saying, 'There is no god but God' fulfil the requirements of Islam, or is knowledge also required as a necessary condition?" The Revered Master replied: "By simply saying the words a person meets the requirements of Islam, whether he knows the meaning of what he says or not, just as if an unbeliever joins in a congregational prayer the Law considers this an expression of his Islam but does not impose knowledge of it as a condition." In connection with this meaning he told the following story.[36]

"Once a band of the companions of the Apostle had sallied forth against a hill on which unbelievers had gathered. They set out to capture that hill. In that day and age it was the custom for an army setting out on an expedition to travel by night in order to reach the place at dawn. The unbelievers were informed that an army had arrived. They all rushed to the top of the hill. Among those unbelievers was a man who had become a believer, but had kept it secret from the others. He rushed to the top of the hill along with the others. After the companions arrived they began to shout out: 'God is Great!'[37] Their cry reached the ears of that

36. *Hikayat* means something related, whether it be historical in nature, or simply imaginary. It is worth noting that Maneri quoted from the Quran; from traditions about the Prophet; from the fund of stories found in Islamic literature; and from his own personal experience. He was a born teacher and knew the value of imagination. His listeners—and readers—loved stories. His whole purpose in narrating all kinds of stories was didactic: he had a point he wanted to make, and it was somehow connected to our relationship to God, or to clarify a disputed point. Hence it is irrelevant to ask if it is a true story or a fable; or to dissect it for internal contradictions or improbabilities—as a discerning reader could do with the story he now narrates!

37. *Allahu Akbar!* This is the cry raised by Muslims as they go into battle.

man. He said: 'This is the war cry of the faithful! They are companions of the Apostle! Since I am a believer, let me go and join them!' He came down from the hill. A horseman, one of the band of companions, had reached the base of the hill. When he saw that the man had come down from the hill, he drew his sword from its scabbard and dashed towards him. When the man saw the horseman galloping towards him with unsheathed sword in order to kill him, he cried aloud: 'There is no god but God. Muhammad is the Apostle of God!' That horseman thought he said this out of fear of the sword. Without hesitating he struck him with his sword. He was killed instantly. When he returned to his companions he told them what had happened. He did not have the least suspicion that he had erred. His companions said: 'Give an account of what has happened to the Apostle and see what he has to say.' When they all returned and presented themselves to the Apostle he was reclining against a cushion. The companions drew near to him and narrated the entire incident to him. When the Apostle heard what had happened he sat bolt upright and exclaimed: 'You killed someone who said, 'There is no god but God!'' He repeated his accusation vehemently: 'You killed someone who said 'There is no god but God!'' He did not say: 'You killed someone who knew, 'There is no god but God!'' Thereupon that companion said: 'I thought he made the profession of faith out of fear of the sword and that's why I smote him.' The Apostle replied: 'Even if he had said these words out of fear of the sword, what of it? I have been ordered to fight against men until they say, 'There is no god but God.''"

When the Revered Master reached these words, he said: "Saying the words suffices to meet the demands of Islam, for the Apostle said, 'I have been ordered to fight against men until they say, 'There is no god but God.'' He did not say, 'Until they know.' This is why many religious scholars say that those who attribute a body to the Lord are not branded as unbelievers. They say that, if mystical knowledge and holiness were conditions for the soundness of faith, it would have been incumbent upon the Apostle not to give simply one order concerning faith, but afterwards he would have prescribed a diligent inquiry as to whether a person has mystical knowledge of the Lord Most Exalted as well as the quality of holiness. Yet, since the order given to people concerned faith without such an investigation, I understand that the latter do not constitute a condition."

CHAPTER 2
A DESCRIPTION OF FAITH AND OF ISLAM, AS WELL AS OF ASSOCIATION, UNBELIEF AND SUCH-LIKE THINGS

Qazi Minhajuddin from the fort[38] said: "There is a tradition which says, 'There is no faith in the person who is not trustworthy.' From this point of view, how can a person who is not trustworthy be said to have faith? How could it be that there is no command about the unbelief of a believer who betrays a trust?" The Revered Master replied: "The point of this tradition is not to deny the essence of faith but to deny qualities and virtues pertaining to faith. There are many such traditions. Their intention is not to deny the essence of faith, but seek to deny qualities and virtues which pertain to faith. For example, 'There is no faith in the person who has no shame.' There are many things resembling this, such as when people say that so and so lacks manliness, he is not a man. By saying this, a person does not want to deny that he is a man, but to deny that he is manly. In other words, he lacks that quality of manliness which he should have. As far as those who follow the Way are concerned, however, from their point of view, it is tantamount to denying the essence of faith. They say that regarding every single thing the intention reaches beyond, not simply to the thing itself.[39] The strength of the intention is what really matters. The essence of faith without qualities and virtues is not faith at all, just as jurisconsults say, 'When anything is emptied of its intention, it dies.'"

A discussion arose about conventional faith and faith supported by proofs. The Revered Master said: "Conventional faith is correct according to the general opinion, but some say that it is not correct." After a while he continued: "There is conventional faith

---

38. The text has Qazi Minhajuddin *darun-i hisari*. Taking into account remarks made about the Qazi in the beginning of the thirty-third assembly in *Khwan,* it seems that he had an official position in the town with a residence inside a specially fortified section.

39. *Goyand dar har chizi maqsud mu'tabar ast na nafs-i an chiz.*

as well as faith supported by proofs. Just as the latter is correct, so too is the former, but both are marked by absence. There is more grace in faith supported by proofs because of further explanations of meaning. This is because these believers understand the proofs adduced." He added: "I have seen it written somewhere that no one actually has purely conventional faith. This is because everyone knows that God[40] created the heavens as well as the earth."[41] Later on he continued: "As far as those who have somehow seen God[42] are concerned, there is no difference between a person who simply believes and one who can adduce proofs. This is in the sense that, just as a simple believer who turns aside from his religious beliefs considers that he had accepted those beliefs without proof and demonstration, in a similar manner, if a person with proofs also turns aside, it could be that in an encounter an adversary presents proofs that are superior to his. Even though his religious beliefs are buttressed by proofs and demonstrations, yet, as far as no actual perception is concerned, both are equal. Just as the simple believer has not seen anything, neither has the person who adduces proofs. For those with personal experience, however, there can be no turning aside. This is because they have progressed beyond proofs and demonstrations and have personally seen and experienced God.[43] There can be no turning back at this stage. Before this their simple faith and religious beliefs were all based on what they had heard. When they attain personal enlightenment, however, they speak about what they have seen and experienced for themselves. At this stage there can be no question of turning aside, even if an adversary presents a thousand proofs and demonstrations in front of them. Since they have seen for themselves, they will not budge an inch. For example, if an adversary says something against their

---

40. The Persian for God, *Khuda*, is used. It, like Allah, is translated as 'God' without italics, which are employed to translate *Haqq*, as previously mentioned.

41. The notion that God is the creator of heaven and earth is so imbedded in the minds of the listeners that they accept it as a known fact rather than as a widely held belief.

42. *Ahl-i mukashafa.* Maneri clearly teaches in the 29th assembly in *Khwan* that there is no question of attaining the vision of God in this life. Hence all references to seeing God in this life are to be understood, in an analogical sense, as referring to some sort of enlightening experience of God.

43. The implied object has been supplied.

beliefs and claims, 'No matter what you say, I shall show you up by miracles and demonstrations' and, for example, if he says, 'I'll turn this wall into gold,' or 'I'll bring this dead man back to life and grant him speech,' and he actually does all this, nevertheless, they would not be turned aside in the slightest.'"[44]

A discussion concerning this verse arose: "One who renounces idols and believes in God" (Q2:256). The Revered Master said: "A person who renounces idols is a believer. This implies that, just because someone calls a believer an unbeliever, no one should immediately brand him as an unbeliever. It could be that, along with renouncing idols, he might have the intention of believing."[45] Later on, he added: "'The person who does not become an unbeliever, does not become a believer.'[46] This appears to be difficult to grasp, but it simply means that renouncing idols is a precondition to becoming a believer in God. In a similar fashion 'unbelief' bears this meaning in some verses. This can be gleaned from the context.'"

At this juncture, the Helpless One recited this hemistich:
"O faithless believer, don't believe, be an unbeliever!"

The Revered Master said: "The import of this is to become a believer in God and not believe in anything other than God." A discussion arose about how some of the close companions of the Apostle became believers. A dear disciple inquired how the Commander of the Faithful, Ali,[47] the son of Abu Talib, accepted the faith while his father did not. The Revered Master said: "The Commander of the Faithful, Ali, had accepted the faith when he was young. It so

---

44. Maneri is speaking from personal experience. The example he uses highlights the depth of his unshakable conviction that the experience is of God.

45. The object is supplied.

46. From the context it is understood that the discussion refers to renouncing idols and believing in God. The reference is to the initial struggle in Mecca which lies imbedded in the first half of the profession of faith, 'There is no god but God.' Its application to the Indian context is clear.

47. Ali's father, Abu Talib, was Muhammad's paternal uncle, guardian and defender. He died in 619 without having become a Muslim. Ali married Muhammad's daughter, Fatima, by whom he had two sons, Hasan and Husain. He became the fourth caliph in 656 and was assassinated in 661. He was given the title, "Commander of the Faithful," partly because he led them into battle with great bravery.

happened that when he was young Abu Talib used to say to him: 'Go to Muhammad and do whatever he tells you.' In accordance with this injunction the Commander of the Faithful, Ali, used to associate with the Apostle. One day he came to be of service to him. The Apostle was performing his ritual prayer. At that time speaking during prayer was allowed. The Commander of the Faithful said: 'What are you doing?' The Apostle relied: 'It is known as ritual prayer. This is the way to worship God. Come and join me!' The Commander of the Faithful, Ali, thought to himself, 'I'll go and ask my father.' With the intention of asking his father he turned and took three steps. As he took the fourth, this thought occurred to him: 'What need is there to seek my father's permission? My father had told me to do whatever Muhammad told me to do. Let me now go and do whatever he tells me!' The fourth rung which came to Ali stems from this. He turned back. The Apostle instructed him in the faith and in ritual prayer. The Commander of the Faithful, Ali, gave his assent and became a Muslim. Abu Bakr, the Righteous, on the very first day, simply on being invited, accepted the faith and became a Muslim. It so happened that he was on a journey to Syria and dreamt that the moon fell from the sky and landed next to him. In the morning he went to a person who interpreted dreams. He told him about the dream. He interpreted it to mean that he would be the first to believe in the final Messenger of all time when he appeared. Afterwards he returned to Mecca where the Apostle had received the command to extend to people an invitation to the faith. He thought to himself: 'Whom should I invite?' The thought occurred to him to go to Abu Bakr and invite him. With this in mind he came out of his house at the very same time that Abu Bakr emerged from his in order to visit Muhammad. They met half way. He said, 'Where are you going?' He replied, 'I am on my way to see you. I am faced with a difficulty which I cannot easily discuss with anybody.' He asked him what it was. The Apostle replied: 'I have been ordered to invite people to embrace Islam.' The esteemed Truthful One said: 'What proof is there?' Gabriel whispered into the Apostle's blessed ear: 'Tell him about the dream he had in Syria!' The esteemed Truthful One immediately said, 'There is no god but God. Muhammad is the Apostle of God.'"[48]

---

48. Some modern readers may find this, and similar stories, uncongenial: God speaking through dreams; giving instructions to the Apostle; and

Thereupon a discussion arose about the virtues of the Commander of the Faithful, Abu Bakr the Righteous. The Revered Master said: "It is related that the Truthful One, in a heightened state as he advanced along the Way, exclaimed, 'What is faith, O Apostle of God?'" Afterwards the Revered Master proceeded with this explanation: "The reason for this is that some people claimed that they had attained perfect knowledge.[49] For this group, however, faith is what is required, so they deepen their faith. It is because the Lord has informed them about His essence and attributes that they have knowledge of them. They do not, however, lay claim to perfect knowledge. They say: 'Our knowledge of the essence and attributes of the Lord is limited to what He has revealed to us. He himself, however, is infinitely greater and more pure than that! How could we have perfect knowledge of Him?' The more intimate their knowledge, the more they themselves realize that they still do not know. Moreover, the more they drink the wine of mystical knowledge, the thirstier they become.[50] That saying of Abu Bakr, the Righteous, is an indication of this thirst. Other companions have related how, when he was quite overcome, he used to come to the doors of his friends and sing out, 'Come, let us believe in God just for now!' This also refers to his thirst. All such expressions should be understood along these lines. Haven't you noticed how the nightingale of the garden of mystical knowledge,[51] in the very stage of nearness to God, expressed his helplessness and said: 'I cannot praise You the way You can praise Yourself!'"

Afterwards he commented that someone had given a hint about this meaning in the following quatrain:

Gabriel whispering into his ear. The reader is invited to remember that such stories are more about God's sovereign activity than lessons in history.

49. *Dar kamal-i ma'rifat.* While *ma'rifat* is normally translated as mystical or intimate knowledge, because of the nature of the phrase and the context, simple 'knowledge' is used here. The object of this knowledge is, of course, God.

50. Maneri is speaking from his own experience of God. The claim to perfect knowledge rings hollow in his ears. It is poles apart from his own experience.

51. Muhammad. The reference is to the *mi'raj*, the ascent to the very proximity of God.

In the eyes of those who have attained perfect love,
Even you, a wise man, are steeped in error.
Inevitably, instead of praising and glorifying You,
The most eloquent of both worlds has been struck dumb!

A discussion arose about some Arab polytheists who did not become believers. Even though they certainly realized that the Messenger was a genuine messenger, still they did not believe. The Revered Master observed: "They were leading men among the Arabs, renowned for their wealth and position. They called the Messenger 'Abu Talib's orphan,'[52] even though they knew for certain that he was a messenger. They did not disclose this, however, because if they had done so, they would have had to believe in him. This would mean abandoning the religion of their ancestors. They thought this would be a shameful thing to do. Their leading position was at stake and they would have had to bear the scorn of the idolaters. They brought Abu Talib along to where the Apostle was standing and praying. He was reciting the Quran in a loud voice. Abu Talib stood behind them, groaning. When some people saw this condition of his they said to him: 'How is it that you know and understand, yet you do not believe?' He replied, 'Fire before dishonour!'" Afterwards the Revered Master recited this couplet:

Do you know what fault the Arabs indulge?
"I'll do this, no matter what anyone says!"

A discussion arose about the religion of Islam. The Revered Master said: "There is one promise of the Messenger which has not yet been fulfilled, but which will be fulfilled. The promise is that all men, from the east to the west, will embrace Islam, and no other religion will remain except that of Islam.[53] Commentators say that, after the descent of Jesus[54] the slaying of the Anti-Christ will take

---

52. Muhammad's father, Abdullah, had died before he was born, and his mother, Amina, died when he was about six years of age. His paternal uncle, Abu Talib, brought him up.

53. In this translation the aim has been to identify and locate all quotations which are from the Quran. The identification and classification of other quotations is beyond the scope of this work. Hence it is not possible to estimate the classification of the quotation in question.

54. The names of persons found in the Bible are given in their customary English form.

place." He added: "Since the religion of Islam will be prevailing, there will be some unbelievers who will retain the religion of their ancestors hidden within their hearts, yet they will profess with their lips that they are believers and will claim that there is now only one religion. In response to all this, commentators have written that, since some are of this persuasion, *God* Most Exalted will make the very clay and rocks cry out, 'O people of Muhammad, this man is a Jew, kill him! This man is a Christian, kill him! This man is a Magian, kill him!' The same applies to others like them. They will be killed and Islam will be the only religion remaining."[55]

As discussion arose about hidden polytheism. Maulana Adam Hafiz[56] was present in the honourable assembly. He recited the final words of the chapter[57] entitled, "The Cow." The Revered Master was reduced to tears when he heard those words. Presently the aforementioned Maulana Adam requested an explanation of the verse,[58] "Let anyone who hopes to meet his Lord do what is right and let him not associate anyone in the worship of his Lord" (Q18:110). The Revered Master said: "The Quraish[59] were worshipping idols and had brought idols into the Ka'ba. They were saying: 'We acknowledge the Lord God and worship Him, but these idols are included in that worship.' Afterwards this verse was revealed.[60] The revelation of the verse was with reference to them. Moreover, men of perception and jurisconsults, since this verse pertains to

---

55. The reader should note that this is what some commentators are said to have written. The sentiments expressed therein are appalling to a modern reader! It serves as an example of where some traditional religious scholars, the commentators in question, caught up in a sea of words and cut off from the very heart of Islamic belief in "God, the Merciful, the Compassionate," let their imaginations run away with them. Perhaps the only reason for this section is to strengthen belief in the ultimate victory of God in the drama being played out in human history, no matter how uncongenial the imaginary depiction of the details.

56. *Hafiz* is a title given to anyone who knows the Quran by heart.

57. *Sura* is the word used for a chapter in the Quran. It literally means "a row of stones in a wall."

58. The word for 'verse' in the Quran is *ayat*, which means 'sign.' Each verse is considered a sign of God.

59. The Quraish were the leading tribe in Mecca. Muhammad belonged to the Hashemite clan of this tribe.

60. Literally, *nazil shud*, "came down."

manifest polytheism from its clear wording, also understand it
to apply to hidden polytheism by way of salutary warning. Thus
it refers to manifest polytheism and hidden polytheism. It is the
former because it was revealed in reference to those people who
were worshipping idols as well as God. 'Have you seen someone
who takes his desire as his god' (Q45:23) is an indication of this
and is hidden polytheism, such as fear of other than God or trust
in other than God. This is hidden polytheism. Dervishes, as a salutary warning, give this explanation. Whenever the members of
this group[61] call to mind this verse they place their hands on their
heads because they seek and yearn to meet *God,* and that depends
on these two conditions: the performance of good works and the
absence of polytheism. They say: 'We do not have either of them. If
we are not free of hidden polytheism, at least the prophets are un-
tainted by it. If there is no good work either, we ourselves spoil the
work by our shameful behaviour and the evils that are perpetrat-
ed.' Have no further thought if a claimant says, 'I do such and such
a good work' and is not aware that it is actually bad, according to
this reading: 'And think they are doing something good' (Q18:104).
That is what is involved. They say, 'We are Muslims and we are believers,' yet they have no idea what this entails! It is nothing more
than a thought when they say, 'We are doing something' and this is
what they are thinking when this cry rings out: 'We have removed
your veil. Today your sight is keen' (Q50:22)." On this occasion he
recited this couplet:

> A man of note imagined he had acquired something:
> What he had acquired was nothing but a thought!

He added: "Who is untouched by this hidden polytheism?" Thereupon the afore-mentioned Hafiz made this remark: "Hidden polytheism is found in everyone except the Revered Master who has
escaped from its clutches." The Revered Master smiled and had
this to say: "O that I had escaped from manifest polytheism, let
alone hidden polytheism! Men have sacrificed body, soul and heart
in order to escape from this polytheism. Some people in this state
have even donned the sacred thread after they had performed

---

61. Primarily the members of the Firdausi regional Sufi brotherhood
founded by Maneri is intended. In a wider sense, however, it refers to
Sufis in general.

whatever ascetical practices and struggle with self they were capable of. Nevertheless, they were not able to escape this form of polytheism. They said: 'Since there is polytheism interiorly, it is no matter for concern if there is a sacred thread exteriorly.' This is the very antithesis of hypocrisy, and hypocrisy is worse than unbelief, for 'hypocrites shall be in the lowest depths of the fire' (Q4:145)." Afterwards he added that those verses which mention idols and sacred threads refer to this polytheism.

A Discussion arose about the generosity of *God* Most Exalted. What does the generosity of *God* mean with regard to Hindus, and what does it mean with regard to Muslims? The Revered Master explained: "Yes, an unbeliever who, on the point of death, recites the profession of faith, dies a Muslim. Everything pertaining to his past life is forgiven. Similarly, if a Muslim who is a sinner repents he dies forgiven." He added: "Ash'ari[62] profited from the thought of his final end and said that it was not proper to observe Islam at one time and commit sins at another time. It is fitting to be concerned about one's end because, if a believer changes at the end of his life, he says it is as though he had always been an unbeliever; but if an unbeliever comes to a good end, he says it is as though he had always been a believer. The Ash'arite school is seriously concerned about a person's end. In the *Tazkirat ul-Auliya* [A Memorial of the Saints][63] it is written that Khwaja Bayazid Bastami[64] used to say, 'Now I rip off my girdle and say that there is no god but God.' A hint about what he meant is that, if an unbeliever in such a state once recites the profession of faith, he dies a Muslim. I also look at myself in this way. This is the context in which I speak. Some advocates of the efficacy of the profession of faith say that, if an

---

62. Abul Hasan al-Ash'ari was born in Basra in 873-4. He followed the Mu'tazilite school of theology but was converted to the traditionist point of view around 912. He used the Mu'tazilite method of argumentation to buttress his new position. He left an abiding stamp on Muslim theology when he died in Baghdad in 935. Maneri followed his line of thought.

63. This work of Sufi hagiography is attributed to the Persian poet Fariduddun Attar, who died in 1220. Maneri was very fond of quoting his poetry.

64. Bayazid Bastami was a famous Sufi from northwest Iran. His utterances proved to be a source of wonder and speculation for Sufis down the centuries. Maneri often refers to him in his teaching and letters. He died in 874.

unbeliever says it once during his life, all his unbelief and sins are forgiven. How can a believer, who ceaselessly repeats these pure words throughout his life, be guilty of sin? All his sins have been forgiven."

A discussion arose about the excellence of a believer. The Revered Master said: "When a believer dies in the present age his angels say: 'O God, we were with him as long as he was alive. Now that his life has come to an end, order us to return to heaven in order to praise and glorify You with the other angels.' The command came: 'There are many angels in heaven to praise and glorify Us.' Again they said: 'O God, what do You command us to do?' The reply came: 'Remain at the head of the grave of that believing servant until the Day of Resurrection and praise and glorify Us and enter it in the register of that believing servant.' There are some who say that the dignity of man is greater than that of the angels. As proof they say that angels are servants of men in this world and in the next. The one served is of greater dignity that the one who serves. Another proof is that when *God* Most Exalted created Adam He ordered all the angels to prostrate themselves before him. All the angels except the Devil did so. The one receiving a prostration is of greater dignity than the one prostrating."

The Helpless One inquired how this could refer to the dignity of all men since they prostrated only before Adam, a unique man, and not before all men. The Revered Master said: "The descendants were in the loins of their father. A holy man said that Munkar and Nakir[65] came to question him. He replied: 'Don't come to me because you prostrated before my father and I was in the loins of my father. I was looking at you. What is this questioning?'"

---

65. Munkar and Nakir are said to be two angels who interrogate the dead about their religious beliefs just after they are buried.

CHAPTER 3
KNOWLEDGE OF THE ESSENCE AND ATTRIBUTES OF THE MOST EXALTED DEITY

The Helpless One asked what the knowledge of the essence and attributes involves. The Revered Master replied: "What is involved in the knowledge of essence and attributes is the being and oneness of *God* and the realization that 'His essence is not like our essences.' In other words, the pure essence of the Lord is neither a substance nor a body. It cannot be contained or limited. It is not in space or time. It is not anything which can come within the ambit of being imagined or thought. On the contrary, He[66] is its Creator. He knows He is endowed with perfect, holy attributes and is free of imperfections or any change for the worse, or anything of this nature.

The purpose of knowing about attributes is to know that His attributes are not like ours. The attributes of the Lord are not identical to the Lord nor are they different from Him. Each quality is not identical to other attributes, nor is it different from them. For example, knowledge is not identical to omnipotence, nor is it different from it. It should also be realized that, just as the essence is eternal, so too are the attributes. They are rooted in the essence of the Lord. They are not incidental, nor are they distinct[67] from the essence. This applies to whatever is fitting in this regard."

Afterwards he said: "This discussion itself is about knowledge which could be called 'rational'. This is the stage of ordinary believers. The members of this group, however, have passed beyond this stage and have attained the stage of certainty. They have even gone beyond this stage. In the shadow of the wealth of their spiritual guides and the eternal favour[68] they have attained knowledge of the essence, and this verse, 'Towards thy Lord is the final goal' (Q53:42), may shed its radiance upon them. May God grant this to

---

66. This switch to the personal pronoun follows the original Persian.
67. *Munfakk.*
68. The reference is to God's eternal favour in their regard.

us and to all the believers through the Prophet and his entire family! The hints contained in the explanation of knowledge, as just described, pertain to a special stage, not to rational knowledge, which is the common stage and is known to everyone. 'Each speaks in his own terminology.'"

A discussion concerning substance[69] arose. The Revered Master said: "The pure essence of the Exalted Creator[70] is not a substance because a substance is said to have two limitations. One is that it is the principle of composition[71] and is called a substance, meaning it is the sole part which is not subject to composition, while the other parts are established upon it and become a compound. Some others say that the limit of a substance is its subsistence in itself.[72] With regard to the first limit, that substance is the principle of composition, *God* Most Exalted is not a principle of composition! Why? Because in appointing this limit, if *God* Most Exalted is called a substance, it is the same as calling Him a principle of composition. On the other hand, it is the consensus of orthodox Sunnis[73] that *God* is not a principle of composition.

Concerning the second limit, that a substance is rooted in itself, *God* is rooted in Himself. In this sense 'substance' can be used. Even though this is a correct limit, yet it is not fitting to use it. Although there is nothing wrong with the meaning, yet it would be a fault to use the word. This is because the names and attributes of the Exalted Creator are agreed upon. No one has the authority, on the basis of personal initiative, to employ a word not found in the Quran or in the Traditions. This would be taking liberties with *God* Most Exalted, even though the meaning is correct. This is because even though, for example, the word 'physician', as far as its meaning goes, is correct, for anyone called a physician is learned in diagnosing diseases and prescribing medicines, and *God* Most Exalted is learned in both of these, yet, because this word has not come down to us, one is not at liberty to use it for the Lord Most Exalted. If someone does so, it would be correct as far as meaning

---

69. *Jauhar.*

70. The original has *Bari'* here and in subsequent usages, not the more common *Khaliq.* Its affinity to the Hebrew verb for the act of creating should be noted.

71. *Asl-i tarkib.*

72. *Qa'im bi-nafsihi.*

73. *Ahl-i sunnat wa jama'at.*

goes, but, as far as words are concerned, it would be a fault."

At this juncture Qazi Sadruddin[74] said: "It is related that Abu Bakr, the Leader of the Faithful, said 'The physician made me sick.' What would you say about him?" The Revered Master replied: "From the point of view that he is not immune from sin, sin can be present. For people who seek meaning, as long as someone is within the limits of knowledge, this word would be sinful. It is not meant to be used. However, if someone were to be overcome by some state, then this word, even though exteriorly it would be sinful, yet, because of his being overcome, he would be forgiven. The words attributed to the Truthful One would be acceptable in this vein."

A discussion arose concerning essence and soul. The Revered Master said: "When 'essence' is used in reference to the Supreme Being something particular is intended. Some words used with regard to that Being are: the very being; entity; existence; essence and self."[75] Afterwards he took as an example a red rose which he was holding in his hand. He said: "Just as people say of this rose, the very being of the rose; the essence of the rose; the rose itself and the existence of the rose, the intention of all of these is to refer to the being of the rose. Similarly those words, which are found in the Traditions and in the Quran, have provided information about the Exalted Creator. Their intention regarding the being of the Creator is apart from the attributes, for they are distinct[76] from the pure essence."

At this point one of those present said: "Can it be said that the attributes of the Creator are distinct from the pure essence?" The Revered Master replied: "Yes! According to orthodox Sunnis all the attributes of *God* are distinct from the essence. This is against the saying of the Mu'tazilites who say that 'the attributes are not really distinct from the essence.'[77] In essence He is knowing and in

74. Letters 8 & 9 in *The Hundred Letters* are both addressed to Qazi Sadruddin. Mention is also made of him in the 4th letter and in the 55th. He was obviously a senior disciple in whom Maneri had great trust.

75. The original words are, respectively: *'ain; shay'; wujud; dhat & nafs.* Other translations are possible.

76. *Wara* meaning "after, behind; beyond; besides, except." The word chosen here, 'distinct', is commonly used in English when describing the Ash'arite position.

77. As Watt remarks in his *Formative Period of Islamic Thought*, where

essence He is powerful. This applies to all the attributes. As proof
of this they say that if the attributes are said to be distinct from
the essence, and both the essence and attributes of *God* are eternal, this necessarily implies plurality from all eternity, because the
pure essence is eternal and so are the attributes. There is necessarily a plurality of eternals. Yet among all beings that exist, apart
from the one pure essence of *God*, nothing else is eternal. This is
why we say in essence He is knowing, without proof of real distinction from the essence, so that it is not necessary to say that there is
plurality from eternity.' This is why they have retreated and fallen
therein. Our position, however, is that plurality from eternity becomes necessary if the attributes are other than the essence.[78] Yet
they are not other than it[79] because the limitation of otherness is
not found. The limit of 'other than' is that one can stand without
another. Yet the attributes of *God* are not such that they could exist without the pure essence of *God*. Moreover they are rooted in
the pure essence of *God*. They do not exist apart from the essence.
The essence is eternal along with the attributes themselves. Consequently plurality from eternity does not arise."

A discussion about the reality of the attributes arose. The Revered Master said: "All the attributes of the Exalted Creator are
real. In this matter also we disagree with what the Mu'tazilites
hold, because they do not ascribe reality to the attributes of *God*
Most Exalted. Moreover, their intention is to deny contraries, not
affirm reality. When you call a person a learned man you thereby
intend to deny ignorance. When you say someone is strong you
intend to deny that he is weak. When you affirm that someone is
powerful you intend to deny that he is helpless. We say that all the
attributes of *God* Most Exalted are real. Knowledge, power and the
rest of the attributes are subsist in Him[80] and their contraries are
not in the pure essence of *God* Most Exalted. The real attributes of
the Lord are no more than this. Any other is a metaphorical attri-

---

he discusses the line of argumentation of both the Mu'tazilites and the
Ash'arites, there are several hypotheses regarding the whole discussion
of the relationship of the divine attributes to the divine essence (p.246).
For our purposes what is of significance is that these questions were
discussed in Bihar Sharif in the 1340's.

78. *Ghayr-i dhat* .
79. *Ghayr-i khud nist.*
80. *Benafs-i u qa'im ast.*

bute, because another, whom we call learned, when compared to Him, would be bereft of knowledge. After *God* Most Exalted imparts knowledge to him, then we can say that so-and-so is a learned person. He would be called a learned man by way of metaphor, because previously he would not have been so. Afterwards he became so. The attributes of *God* Most Exalted, however, without any newness, are other and are all eternal."

A discussion about this tradition arose: "The person who gains intimate knowledge of God becomes tongue-tied." The Revered Master said: "What is revealed to privileged mystics and is made manifest to them is not able to be described by our external tongues. These are the tongues which are intended. It means that our tongues, even if they wanted to describe what had been revealed and made manifest, could not do so. The tradition does not mean to say that anyone who experiences *God* in this fashion becomes dumb and does not utter a single word." Afterwards he said: "A second tradition is this: 'The tongue of the person who gains intimate knowledge of God becomes prolonged.' This pertains to the interior tongue. 'His tongue becomes prolonged' means that his interior tongue keeps on speaking about mystical knowledge. It is fitting that it is also spread abroad by the exterior tongue. It is also fitting that the first refers to the beginning, while the second to the greatest possible reach."

The Helpless One said: "'Whoever gains intimate knowledge of God does not speak about God.' What does this mean?" The Revered Master replied: "It is one of the stages of the sheikhs where two insights are revealed to mystics: one focuses on the glory, greatness and holiness of God, while the other highlights his own calamitous human condition. They find that, compared to the perfection, glory, greatness and holiness of *God,* their human nature is in great peril, nothingness and impurity. At this stage they say: 'In this impurity and unworthiness, it is not at all fitting that we should take the name of the pure essence of *God* upon our tongues!' This explains why they say that they do not want to take the name of God upon their tongues." He then recited this couplet:

If I rinse my mouth with musk and rose water,
I would still not be fit to utter Your name!

He also related this story. "It is related that Imam Shibli[81] initially used to put sugar in the mouth of anyone he heard taking the name of the Lord. When his experience had deepened, he used a stone and some dirt in place of sugar. This has the same meaning."

A discussion arose about the negation of doubt. Qazi Ashrafuddin said: "'There is no doubt about the existence of God.' Doubt about the existence of God Most Exalted is prohibited. Since this is fixed, it necessarily follows that there is no need to prohibit doubting." The Revered Master replied: "Wherever there is something external, there should be no doubt in the mind concerning something which is superior, because the mind needs to satisfy itself about a doubt by having recourse to something external. Comparing anything with something completely beyond experience is impossible. A comparison has to be between two things. Inevitably both things have to be present. No one speaks about comparing something present at hand with something utterly intangible, but God knows best what is correct."

81. Shibli (d. 945) was an eccentric Sufi of Baghdad.

CHAPTER 4

A DESCRIPTION OF THE METAPHORS WHICH ARE APPLIED TO *GOD* MOST EXALTED, SUCH AS 'FACE,' 'HAND' AND SIMILAR THINGS

A discussion arose about words used metaphorically, such as 'hand,' 'face,' 'hearing' and 'seeing,' which are found in the Quran and the Traditions. These words provide a more liberal vocabulary in speaking about *God* Most Exalted. The Revered Master—may God grant Muslims the favour of a long life for him—said: "Externalists are preoccupied with interpreting these words, but seekers after reality are not thus engaged, saying that, if they were to get engrossed in interpreting metaphors, it would be necessary to cease using these words. For example, since the externalists have interpreted 'face' as 'essence,' then 'essence' has been established on the basis of yet another verse or tradition. This means that the word 'face' would be devoid of meaning. They have interpreted 'hand' as 'power.' If we accept this then the word 'hand' would be devoid of meaning, for the meaning of 'power' would have been established. Yet no word pertaining to *God* Most Exalted is devoid of meaning. We hold that 'hand' and 'face' and other metaphors, each and every word, has its own reality, but in a way that befits the Pure Essence. When we say 'hand' it is not like an ordinary hand, and when we say 'face' it is not like an ordinary face. This applies to other metaphors."

Afterwards he added: "This is the path to peace. Both aspects are retained in this way: there is no looseness with words, and the denial of interpretation is respected. Faith in the essence and attributes as revealed, and which befit the pure essence, is maintained." He went on to say: "If metaphors are not discussed in this way, it would not be done by the seekers of reality, because interpretation is done in two ways: one is meritorious, while the other is sinful. How can seekers of reality become engrossed in a particular thing which has two sides to it?" He continued: "What has come down

31

to us concerning noble Adam is, 'I have created [him] with My own hands' (Q38:75). If the meaning of this 'hand' were 'power,' then noble Adam would not have been deserving of praise, because the Devil was also created by power. This would mean that Adam and the Devil were equal. Also, the whole world has been created by power. What benefit would the speciality about 'hand' concerning noble Adam have been? Hence it has become known that this 'hand' refers to a special meaning which befits the Pure Lord. That was the purpose underlying the creation of Adam and he gave praise for it."[82]

Afterwards he said: "If someone interposes at this stage and says that the knowledge of essence and attributes is necessary, then how could this be so without the knowledge of metaphors? Moreover, they are seekers after reality. They follow a superior path, namely, acquiring the knowledge of the essence and attributes as they are. Their reply is like this. 'It is not necessary for us to acquire knowledge of the essence and attributes through analysis. The soundness of faith is not weakened on this account. If we do not know the reality of metaphors, this would not imply a defect in our faith, because there are so many attributes in God Most Exalted that we do not know about. There are also so many books of God Most Exalted of which we are ignorant. There are also so many messengers whom we believe in yet do not know who they are. Nevertheless, there is no harm done to our faith because we do not know these things. This measure is necessary, namely, that we appreciate the beauty of the faith and say: 'I believe in the essence of the Lord and in all His attributes and perfections. I believe in all His books and in all His messengers.' This is rooted in the fact that it is all right if there is something in the Lord's book which is difficult for us to comprehend, with the result that most of the jurists,

---

82. Readers will obviously form their own opinions about the strength or weakness of the various arguments Maneri comes up with in the course of this work. He clearly expresses his own opinion about such discussions in the first paragraph of this chapter. As his assemblies also functioned as 'tutorials' for those present, such discussions could not be avoided. Some of his listeners were undoubtedly interested in discussing theological niceties and Maneri took this aspect of his work as an inescapable duty. In his 100 and 150 letters, however, such points get fleeting treatment at best. The whole thrust of his letters is to help the reader tread the Sufi path towards a loving union with God.

traditionists and Sufis are of the opinion that it is allowable, but the theologians say that it is not allowed. Their firm opinion is that *God* Most Exalted has said: 'Will they not meditate on the Quran? Are there locks on their hearts?' (Q47:24).

Men were ordered to meditate upon the Quran. If there were something in the Quran that was incomprehensible, then the order to meditate on it would not be correct. He also said: 'A guidance for the God-fearing' (Q2:2). How could things which are not known provide guidance? Moreover, the argument of the complainant is that the Glorious, Most Exalted *God* has said concerning metaphors: 'No one knows its interpretation except God' (Q3:7). Here it is necessary to stop. The proofs of the defendant are described in books. Moreover, those who understand this say: 'The actions which we strive to perform are of two kinds. One of these is the kind the wisdom of which we can understand, such as ritual prayer, the poor tax and fasting. Ritual prayer involves humbling and abasing oneself. The poor tax means doing good to those in need. Fasting brings the selfish soul to heel. The second kind is such that the wisdom contained therein is unknown to us, such as all the actions performed during the pilgrimage.' Since there are two kinds of actions, why should there not be two kinds of words?"

A discussion arose about the gracious way *God* deals with His servants. The Revered Master said: "The dictionary meaning of the verb is 'to turn the face towards something' and to make an exaction from it. Concerning *God* Most Exalted, this is not setting at liberty. It has been explained that the turning of *God* towards a servant means that He bestows the blessing of devotion upon the servant and ignores sin. He performs miraculous deeds. The turning of the servant towards *God* means that he turns towards *God* Most Exalted outwardly in service and inwardly in love." Someone asked him to explain what "the Sultan is the shadow of God" means, for *God* Most Exalted is exempted from any shadow. The Revered Master replied: "This 'shadow' has been interpreted as mercy, i.e. the mercy of God. Here the impact of mercy is meant, not mercy itself."

A discussion arose as to whether *God* Most Exalted is a speaker from eternity to eternity.[83] The Revered Master said: "If someone

---

83. The Persian is *dar azal wa abad*. The former word refers to eternity without beginning, while the latter refers to eternity without end.

asserts that what was from eternity would not be for eternity, and what is for eternity was not from eternity, because eternity without beginning is one thing, while eternity without end is something else, then the answer to this question is given in this way. Time is threefold—past, future and present. These times are construed by us according to the movement of the heavenly bodies, whereas time, as it pertains to *God*, is a single point. There is no clubbing together of past, future and present because there are no heavenly bodies or movement in That Place. Thus eternity without beginning or end would be a single point in this context."

CHAPTER 5
A DISCUSSION OF KNOWLEDGE OF THE LAW AND OF THE WAY AND WHAT BEFITS THEM

Qazi Ashrafuddin put this question: "In the books of the sheikhs it is written that whoever enters upon this Way must first of all have knowledge. Without knowledge the work cannot be accomplished. What sort of knowledge is meant?" The Revered Master replied: "This refers to knowledge of the Way. Everyone who enters upon this Way should first of all know about it before he can begin his journey. There are two kinds of people who begin this journey. Either a person should have knowledge of the Way in order to set out and be able to travel along this Way; or he should travel under the protection of someone who is well versed in this Way because he has travelled it himself. Thus a person will walk according to what he sees and hears. His guide's knowledge becomes his own."

Again he inquired: "What should be said if knowledge of the Law is intended?" The Revered Master replied: "The Law pertains to a knowledge of affairs as well as of various aspects of worship. If this latter knowledge is intended then it is itself a preliminary step towards knowledge of the Way. Without it knowledge of affairs is defective. You might say it enters into the knowledge of the Way. If knowledge of affairs is also intended, how would it profit a person? He will derive no profit from reading the chapter on marriage. It will be profitable to read that chapter when he is about to get married. Similarly, buying and selling and other affairs, as well as knowledge of all sorts of things, should be sought when it is needed. What profit is there in seeking knowledge about something which, at the moment, is not needed?" Afterwards he continued: "If someone wants to acquire knowledge of the Law, knowledge of the Way is also needed. If a person has knowledge of the Law but not of the Way, he cannot proceed along this Way, since he has only external knowledge of the Law. If he has knowledge of the Way, however, and knows nothing about the Law except what pertains to worship, then he can make progress along the Way. It is possible for him to attain his aim."

Afterwards he added: "There is a Tradition which says: 'It is obligatory for every Muslim man and woman to seek knowledge.' This has been interpreted in many ways. Some think that this knowledge refers to the knowledge of five things. These are the profession of faith; ritual prayer; the poor tax; fasting during Ramazan and the pilgrimage to Mecca, which are mentioned in many places in the Traditions. Others interpret it to mean that amount of knowledge which we need to have, and the obligation refers to this amount of knowledge. Another interpretation is that knowledge is obligatory in its own proper time. A person seeks knowledge at the particular time it is needed so that he knows what to do in a particular situation."

Shamsuddin Kharizmi[84] paged through *Adab ul-Muridin* [Rules for Sufis Novices][85] until he came to these words: "When the prophet Solomon threatened the hoopoe with a severe punishment, he found deliverance in knowledge."[86] The Revered Master related this story: "When king Solomon went out anywhere all kinds of birds used to provide shade for his head. One day he came outside and all the birds provided shade for him except for the hoopoe which did not show up. Its spot remained empty, leaving a gap. The sun's heat penetrated this gap and reached king Solomon. He looked up and noticed the gap. This was how the sun's heat was reaching him. He inquired about which bird should have been in this place. He was informed that it was the spot of the hoopoe which wasn't to be seen. It had not come. That was when king Solomon threatened to punish the hoopoe severely when it came. After some time the hoopoe turned up. The other birds asked it where it had been, and informed it about what king Solomon had threatened to do to it. 'This time you will have to undergo a severe punishment!' The hoopoe replied: 'At the end of his threat he added something

84. The name indicates a person from what was known as Kharizm, which lay immediately to the south of the Aral Sea—a long way from Bihar Sharif!

85. This work, by Abu al-Najib al-Suhrawardi (d.1168), was Maneri's favourite basic primer for his disciples. His own commentary (*sharh*) on it is extant.

86. This is a reference to the story found in the Quran, 27:21ff. Maneri goes on to relate a popular elaboration of the story.

which affords hope that nothing will happen to me.' They said: 'Yes indeed, after his threat he also added, 'Unless there is an excuse.'[87] The hoopoe replied: 'That is how I shall be saved!' After this he went and presented his excuse to the prophet, king Solomon, saying: 'I went to a certain city which is ruled by Queen Bilqis.' He then proceeded to give a description of the city: 'It is such and such a city, with such and such surroundings, and its inhabitants are such and such like people. This is the information I have brought for you.' Thereupon king Solomon was happy and retracted the threat of punishment he had issued."

When the Revered Master reached these words he continued thus: "The hoopoe bird came fearlessly before the prophet Solomon and presented its excuses in the strength of its knowledge and was saved." After this he went on to say: "In the next world there will be need of liberation and salvation according to the authority of this verse: 'Yet you shall not pass through except by an authority' (Q55:33). This means proof and demonstration. Knowledge is that proof and demonstration."

A discussion arose about knowledge of the unseen and discernment. The Revered Master said: "What becomes known to a believer through discernment is not said to be knowledge of the unseen. This is because there is a difference between knowing what is unseen and knowing through discernment. Knowing what is unseen occurs when something which is hidden is known without any proof or indication. Discernment, however, involves seeing something which provides proof and indication of what is internal and grasping it by means of the proof and indication. It is similar to seeing external things. For example, when we see smoke we conclude that something is on fire."

A discussion arose about the knowledge of the Lord and that of His servants. The Revered Master, with regard to the distinction between these two forms of knowledge, said: "When Moses met Khizr[88] he was sitting on the bank of a river. Suddenly a bird flew down to the river; used its beak to drink a little water; and flew off again. Khizr turned towards Moses and said: 'Do you realize that your knowledge and mine, and that of all creatures, when

---

87. This is found in the Quranic account, 27:22.

88. Khizr is the legendary figure often presumed to be the mysterious person who converses with Moses in the 18th chapter of the Quran.

compared to the pure knowledge of *God*, is like this drop of water compared to this river?'"

A discussion arose about scholars of evil.[89] The Revered Master said: "Scholars of evil are those whose gaze is turned towards this world and their backs towards the life to come. In other words, their efforts are to acquire knowledge but their focus is on this world, not on the world to come. When a person who is in quest of the life to come reads what they write he will say that they themselves and their knowledge are of this world. If a seeker remains content with this knowledge he will never achieve his goal."

A discussion arose about doing things with knowledge. The Revered Master said: "Whoever does anything without knowledge gets entangled with self because that is what the hypocrites teach. It is tantamount to treading the path of Satan. Everything should be undertaken with knowledge and a firm conviction that whatever is in accordance with the Plan of *God* will eventuate." Afterwards he related this story: "When all eleven sons of the prophet[90] Jacob were about to depart for Egypt the prophet Jacob placed this obligation upon them: 'O my sons, do not enter by one gate; enter by separate gates' (Q12:67). What was the wisdom involved in Jacob's charging his sons to enter separately, for they were extremely intelligent men and knew that whatever is ordained by *God* is what comes to pass, so what was the point of the injunction? The answer given is that all Jacob's sons were very handsome. It occurred to Jacob that 'the eye is truthful,' meaning that the impact of the eye is tangible. It should not happen that all of them, by coming in together, should attract an evil eye. He acted with knowledge in order to avoid an evil eye when he told them to enter separately. Later on, when Jacob's sons entered Egypt, they remembered that their father had instructed them to enter separately, so the eleven sons entered by eleven gates. When they returned nine sons came back to Jacob and two remained behind. Afterwards some people wanted to know why it was that, having been enjoined to enter separately in order to avoid an evil eye, nine sons returned but two remained in Egypt. Did they act as instructed? The answer given

---

89. *'Ulama-i su'*. It could equally be, "evil scholars." Whichever genitive—subjective or objective—is chosen, it still seems a very strong term.

90. *Paighambar* literally means 'messenger' and is translated as such when it is used in reference to Muhammad. Otherwise—as in this instance—it is rendered as 'prophet.'

to this is that Jacob acted with knowledge and had a strong belief that, even when we work with knowledge, whatever is ordained by *God* is what will come to pass. Nevertheless if, after acting with knowledge, something contrary to knowledge comes to pass as ordained by *God* Most Exalted, it should not be said: 'If I had acted in such a way, such and such would not have happened!' In this way a person's lips are sealed."

Afterwards the Revered Master said: "Among men it is well known that they say: 'If this had happened, then that would not have happened.' One should not speak in this way, since it is the language of hypocrites." Afterwards he added: "One person is doing something with knowledge while another is acting out of ignorance. As far as each is concerned, what they want is something good and it comes to pass. In this both are equal. The only difference is that the person who works with knowledge does so with lips closed to self, for such is the way the hypocrites speak. Satan appears on such a path. Working with knowledge involves more than this. Whatever has been ordained, however, will be accomplished. On the contrary, the person who acts in ignorance, even though what has been ordained comes to pass, the door of his lips is wide open to self, and Satan is at the door every time someone says, 'If this hadn't been done, that wouldn't have happened.'"

A discussion arose about knowledge and personal effort. The Revered Master said: "Effort is needed until such time as knowledge is attained. When this happens, effort is no longer necessary. A person who strives to understand something does so by thinking and attains knowledge, even its very essence, on account of the command to clarify what is obscure and doubtful and, as yet, has not been clarified. An effort has to be made to attain clarity. Anything which is no longer obscure or doubtful, however, and has been understood and perceived as it is, does not need any further effort. For example, if someone does not know the direction of prayer he will make an effort because it is not known to him. Anyone who knows the direction of prayer, however, has no need for further effort." Afterwards he added: "Effort involves thinking. Those who have attained mystical knowledge, as well as the sheikhs, have passed beyond thinking and striving and have attained knowledge and obtained an insight into each thing as it really is. The stage of knowledge is better than that of striving to attain it. Errors occur while trying to work things out, but not in knowledge. What is knowledge? It is a grasp of something as it is. What error is there in this?" Later on he added: "Ain ul-Quzat has also given priority to intimate knowledge over knowledge[91] and placed it in the fourth stage and given it fourth rank. The first is imitation; the second is effort; the third is knowledge; after knowledge the fourth stage is intimate knowledge. This group has passed beyond imitation and effort and has acquired knowledge. Ain ul-Quzat says that he has gone beyond knowledge and has attained intimate knowledge."

At this point Sheikh Mu'izzuddin[92] put a question: "Linguistically both terms mean the same. What is the difference?" The Revered Master replied: "There is a difference between knowledge and intimate knowledge. Knowledge involves knowing each thing. Knowing something by itself is called 'knowledge.' If that very knowledge becomes a person's habitual state, then it is called 'intimate knowledge.' This is because a person knows something and that has become his habitual state. He is then considered to be a mystic." Afterwards he added: "As far as this group is concerned there is no need to know so many things. What is the profit if you know something but it does not become your habitual state?"

Not everything you see will be granted you, O heart!

This Helpless One said: "According to this group, in this form no word will remain meaningless and obsolete." The Revered Master replied: "Yes, for this reason that they proceed from meaning to a word. Before speaking they experience what is meant. Afterwards they find a suitable word to express it. As for others, however, the word comes first. They proceed from the word to the meaning. Certainly some words will become meaningless."

A discussion arose about some who tread the Sufi Path and have acted contrary to accepted behaviour. Maulana Nizamuddin Mufti, spiritual guide of Maulana Husamuddin of Hisar, said: "If one of the masters of the human heart acts against accepted behaviour, how will externalist scholars react to it? If they raise an objection, what answer should be given?" The Revered Master

---

91. *Ma'rifa* and *'ilm* are the terms respectively translated as "intimate or mystical knowledge," and 'knowledge.'

92. Sheikh Mu'izzuddin was one of Maneri's senior disciples. He features prominently not only in this *malfuz*, but also in the subsequent one, *Khwan-i Pur-Ni'mat*.

replied: "Two types of answer are given. One explains it by saying that this group is permitted to be sinless, but is not necessarily sinless. If something does occur as a rare exception and as a way of testing and proving them, it would be permissible. They should not, however, persist in it, and it should be accompanied by repentance. The second explanation is that anyone who has faith in this group will himself accept it. If we come to someone who does not have faith in this group, however, he will come forward asserting that, as far as the essence of knowledge is concerned, it is all-inclusive. He lays claim to that body of knowledge. He says that knowledge is what has been said by the Apostle and heard by his companions. Apart from this, there is no other kind. It is confined to this. It is all contained therein.

What a difference there is between masters of the heart and other religious scholars! Assuredly if he sees someone from this group behaving in a way that contravenes external norms he will not accept it. The reply to this in *Ihya 'ulum ud-din* [The Revival of the Religious Sciences][93] has been expressed as follows: 'You say that whatever was said by the Apostle and heard by his companions constitutes the sum total of knowledge and, apart from that, there is nothing. This is nothing more than an assertion. There should be some proof, and this is not proof. We seek proof, for knowledge is not confined to what was said by the Apostle and heard by his companions. There is another kind besides this. Consider what has been related about the Commander of the Faithful, Ali, who said that, if he wanted to, he could load seventy camels with interpretations of the opening chapter of the Quran. We know the extent of the interpretations given by Ibn Abbas[94] and other companions. If the interpretation of this chapter was restricted to what Ibn Abbas and other companions had written, then how could the Commander of the Faithful, Ali, have said that he could, if he so desired, load seventy camels with interpretations of the opening chapter? Thus it is known that there is also another kind of knowledge in addition to what was said by the Apostle and heard by his companions. An-

93. This important work was by the famous Al-Ghazali (d.1111). It is interesting to notice that Maneri quotes from this work. He obviously had a copy of it in his library.

94. Ibn Abbas (d.687) was the eldest son of Abbas, Muhammad's paternal uncle, and thus Muhammad's first cousin. He is renowned for the number of traditions attributed to him.

other proof is that, when the Commander of the Faithful, Umar,[95] died, the Commander of the Faithful, Uthman, said: 'Nine tenths of knowledge has disappeared!' If knowledge was confined to what was said and heard, then how could the Commander of the Faithful, Uthman, say that nine tenths of knowledge has disappeared, for knowledge that was spoken and heard remains constant? It has not disappeared with the death of Umar. Another proof comes from what was related by Ibn Abbas: 'Concerning His word, 'God it is who has created seven heavens, and earths similar to them. The divine command is operative among them' (Q65:12). If I explain this fully, you will flog me, and finally you will kill me as an infidel.' If there had been any partnership in knowledge, how could Ibn Abbas have spoken thus? Another proof is that the Apostle said: 'There is some knowledge which is hidden and not known except by religious scholars, by God's grace. If they speak about it, no one contradicts them except deceivers.' Those things are called hidden which are precious, rare and concealed in the treasuries of kings. If knowledge referred only to what was related and heard, then this specialized knowledge 'which no one knows except the religious scholars' would not be valid. That store of knowledge is not part of what was related and heard. It is knowledge of another kind."

Afterwards the Revered Master said: "Thus it has been proved that knowledge is not confined to what has been related and heard.[96] What can be firmly believed about them is that they must have acted out of knowledge. They knew and understood what they were doing. Because of our defects it appears to be against acceptable behaviour. This is an example of inadequate knowledge, and also of our not being aware of that knowledge. It could also be expressed in another way. As long as a person is in the realm of knowledge, it is incumbent upon him to act within the limits of knowledge. He will not be excused if he neglects it. On the other hand, if a spiritual state overcomes knowledge and a person is

---

95. Umar succeeded Abu Bakr as Caliph in 634 and exercised authority until his death in 644. He was succeeded by Uthman, 644-656, and then by Ali, 656-661.

96. A reader who is unfamiliar with Islam might wonder at this process of argumentation. Maneri quotes a Tradition about the Prophet. He then argues that it would not be true if knowledge were confined to what the Prophet said and his companions heard. Since a Tradition cannot be false, the latter assertion must be incorrect.

seized by a mystical state, then he will act according to the imperatives of that state, not those of external knowledge. He would be excused. There is an example of this in the Law. It is binding on a person until he dies. There can be compulsions arising out of different states, however, such as eating carrion in the state of extreme hunger, and similarly for other forbidden things which become lawful in the state of necessity. They are excused by virtue of the state, even though externally they appear to be contrary to knowledge. In this case, even though eating carrion in a state of extreme hunger, or drinking wine in a state of extreme thirst, seems to a beholder to be against the Law, yet between the person and God Most Exalted, since it is done in such a state, it would not be against the Law."

Once again the aforementioned Maulana Nizamuddin objected: "The injunction is found clearly in the Quran and Traditions. If this group does anything contrary to that command, it necessarily goes against the clear injunction of the Quran and Traditions. What answer can be given to this difficulty?" The Revered Master replied: "Two types of answer are given to this difficulty. The first is that it is allowed in extreme hunger, but is not obligatory, as explained above. The second is that this contravening is only apparently against the Law. As far as what the Law is all about, however, it is in conformity to the Quran and Traditions, because the clear injunction established by the Quran and Traditions confirms what is clear in them. By acting in this way people confirm the intrinsic meaning of the Quran and Traditions. Their actions stem from this intrinsic meaning of the Quran and Traditions, but a beholder is not aware of this. They hold fast to the command contained clearly in the Quran and Traditions. They do not deny it. It is not possible to deny it with certainty. I take refuge in God from such a thing! They come up with doubtful opinions. They may even speak or act against the Quran and the Practice of the Prophet. Here no more need be said except that some members of this group have acted against the overt injunctions of the Quran. There should be proof of this. No proof is required for the opposite of this. Anything different is not accepted because it would require an example and respectable men. When there is an example and respectable men advocating something it will be accepted. If there is no example or respectable men found for a particular thing, it will not be accepted."

Afterwards he added: "When an expert in the Law is involved in a particular matter nothing simply happens by itself. This is because an expert comes to a decision through his own effort. Another expert, through his own effort, may issue a different opinion. A person may act upon it. The opinion of one expert about another's opinion does not constitute proof."

The aforementioned Maulana Nizamuddin said: "If a saint does something which is not described in any Tradition or been related by the Prophet, would it be an innovation? What would you say?" The Revered Master replied: "The Prophet was entrusted with the task of inviting the people, and they were obliged to give a response. Whatever the Prophet conveyed to the people was paid heed to by them. We are considering a special situation, however, when a saint does something which is not described in any Tradition or been related by the Prophet. In this situation there are two ways of answering. The first is that, since sinlessness is not necessary here, even though it is legally possible, it would not be impossible for someone to be tested by being caught up in an innovation. Since there is no question of their persisting in sinful behaviour it would be conjoined to repentance. Because of this quality they would not forfeit their state of sainthood. The second explanation is that, since knowledge with regard to this group is not circumscribed by what is said or heard, but is derived from the saints and the masters of the human heart, thus it is fitting that there be matters of the Quran and the practice of the Prophet that have been understood, as well as secrets. This is in conformity with the Law, because 'the Quran contains both clear and hidden matters.' If there existed nothing more than the interpretation of what was said and understood, how could there be both clear and hidden meanings? Moreover, what would be the point of the Apostle's repeating 'In the Name of God, the Merciful, the Compassionate,' twenty times? He was meditating on the hidden meaning. If this were not so, what was the need of repeating the name of God and meditating on it simply to interpret and explain it? It is related that some scholars themselves assert that every verse in the Quran contains sixty thousand meanings, and the meaning that still remains is even more than this. Every well-grounded scholar will find the secrets of the Quran revealed to him, according to the extent of his knowledge; the stage he has attained; his purity of heart and his application to meditation. But this requires renunciation:

'He desires nothing in it.' Also, 'There is no limit to the secrets of the Word of God.' It is for this reason that there is variety in understanding the meaning and secrets of the Quran. If a holy man, a master of the human heart, after discussing the external interpretation and establishing its meaning, acts according to one possible understanding of the Quran which has been revealed to him, then certainly a person who sees it, since he has not attained this stage, will have no other option than to brand it as an innovation, even though he has acted in accordance with the Book and the practice of the Prophet."

The aforementioned Maulana Nizamuddin again said: "It is said about Khwaja Junaid[97] that he was informed about the state of Khwaja Mansur Hallaj. Moreover, he issued a decree authorizing his execution. It seems that he should not have issued such a decree. He should have found out exactly what was happening." The Revered Master replied: "Some mystics say: 'It is better to kill a person who speaks openly about the experience of divine unity than to restore life to another person.' Or again, a decree is issued with respect to something external, not something internal. Moreover, in this instance, what is at stake is something external, not internal. Yet again we have the words of the Apostle: 'Satan is with the person who is alone.' One explanation of this is that, if Muslims reach a consensus concerning a particular command, and one person is in disagreement with it, then Satan is with him. If all this does not suffice, what else can be said?"

Maulana Nizamuddin again asked: "How can you be sure of the correctness of what has been made known to a saint if it is not found in relation to the Prophet or in the writings of reputed scholars and smacks of aberration and deceit?" The Revered Master replied: "He knows its correctness by the light of his sanctity, because there is a consensus that anyone whom *God* Most Exalted has transformed by a special sanctity is beyond the clutches and access of Satan. There is no question of any satanic inspiration behind his actions. Whatever occurs to him has a divine origin."

Qazi Sadruddin spoke up: "Satanic suggestions are dangerous things. Whatever occurs through inspiration is also dangerous.

---

97. Khwaja Junaid (d. 910) was a very famous Sufi of Baghdad noted for his sobriety. He did not approve of the ecstatic utterances of al-Hallaj (d. 922).

Both of these enter a person's heart. How can it be determined that everything that enters a person's heart has a divine origin?" The Revered Master replied: "Satanic suggestions might occur, but they do not gain admission because they don't exceed the limit of ascertaining the true state of affairs. In other words, although for the most part satanic suggestions do not gain admission, nevertheless the possibility of doing so remains for the sake of eternity, as a test and as they are not of necessity sinless." Afterwards he recited this verse: "Surely no authority shall you have over My servants" (Q15:42). It has been interpreted in this way. Since what occurs to his heart is accepted and finds admission, it thus becomes known as not having originated from Satan. This is because if it had been satanic in origin, it would not have been accepted and granted admission, for this does not apply to them, namely, the admission of satanic suggestions."

Qazi Ashrafuddin spoke up: "If something is according to what is enjoined in a written tradition yet a religious person does something which seems to be contrary to that tradition, in such a situation what should someone else, who is his follower, do? Should he follow what is in the tradition or what the religious person has done?" The Revered Master replied: "The first thing to ascertain is whether that religious person is really a master of the human heart, or is an externalist scholar, for such a one is not a master of the human heart. If he is an externalist scholar and has acted against the accepted tradition, then another person should act according to the tradition. On the other hand, if he is a master of the human heart, then another person should not imitate him. Should another person do what he has done or not? If it is beyond his capacity, he should not do it. Even if it isn't, he should not do it, because a master of the human heart, who does something which is against an external tradition, has a reason for doing so, as its meaning is clear to him. On the other hand, if someone else acts in the same way, he would do so without understanding the meaning of his action. What benefit would it be for him unless the master explains it to him by means of signs and instructions? If he is one of his own disciples, it is necessary for him to do so. If he is not, he is free to act according to the instruction of the master or according to the tradition."

A discussion about profound learning arose. The Revered Master said: "It is said that one has to travel far to acquire knowledge.

In other words, those who want to attain the farthest bounds of knowledge penetrate the depths of knowledge. They go very far. They do not stop after one, two or even three introductions. They attain to the extreme limits." Qazi Ashrafuddin said: "What should be said about a person who does not even have as much external knowledge as he should, yet asks questions about states and stages of the Sufi path and Reality?" The Revered Master replied: "He should concentrate on what he should know and is important for him. He should inquire about such things. What is the point of asking questions about matters that are beyond what is necessary and important for him?'

A discussion arose about knowledge which was elucidated in previous times and had an impact on people's hearts. In this connection the Revered Master told an apposite story: "Once a holy man related that a man had said to him: 'Is the knowledge which is being imparted by scholars in this present age the same as that of scholars of previous ages, or is it something else?' The holy man said: 'It is the same knowledge that scholars used to teach previously.' The man asked another question: 'Then how is it that the same knowledge which used to be imparted touched people's hearts and inspired them to act accordingly. Nowadays, however, so much is said, but it has no impact on people's hearts.' The holy man answered the question in this fashion: 'The knowledge is the same, but the mouths are not. They used to be real scholars. It so happened that one of them got sick. A sample of his urine was taken to a physician. The physician looked at it and said: 'This is the urine of a lover of God!' Immediately he discarded his sacred thread and became a Muslim.' This is what scholars used to be like. The very sight of their urine brought about conversions. Their urine was better than our words!"

CHAPTER 6
APPROPRIATE QURANIC
INTERPRETATION AND MEMORIZATION

A discussion about interpreting the Quran arose. Maulana Kar-imuddin[98] said: "There are many commentators who have written commentaries on the Quran. What an abundance they have produced! They are not even satisfied with the commentary of Imam Zahid."[99] The Revered Master replied: "As far as implementation is concerned, this commentary is quite appropriate. If someone is seeking abundant profit, however, he will consult another commentary. As far as the externalist interpretation of the Quran is concerned, the Sufi sheikhs and religious scholars are in agreement. When it comes to benefits, hints, subtle points and secrets, however, they are not all in agreement. This is because the Quran can be understood in a number of ways. It can be understood in one way, or two, three or four—even to more than a hundred ways! Everyone who has written a commentary has done so in accordance with his own understanding, perhaps one, two, three or four levels of doing so. All those who have attained the first level of meaning write from that level of understanding. Anyone who has attained the second level writes from that perspective, and so on. Anyone who studies commentaries does so in order to derive as much profit from them as possible, but it is not correct to interpret the Quran for oneself. The Apostle said: 'Whoever interprets the Quran for himself will find a place in hell.' Imam Sha'bi one day reportedly passed by Abi Salih. He went into retirement saying: 'How can you interpret the Quran when you have not read it?' It is also related that Umar Khattab saw some sheets in the hand of a man with comments written next to each verse. He looked for a pair of scissors, cut off the comments and said: 'It would be proper for

---

98. Like Qazi Ashrafuddin, Maulana Karimuddin was a senior disciple. He also features prominently in *Khwan-i Pur-Ni'mat*.

99. The Quranic commentary, by Imam Zahid, was in Persian and was Maneri's favourite commentary, as is clear from what is recorded in the 39th assembly in *Khwan*.

someone who is acquainted with Arab culture and the occasions of revelation to propose comments!' On the other hand, if someone is a meddler and is not acquainted with Arab culture, then it would not be proper for him to do so, except to repeat what he has heard. This would be considered more of a story than a commentary. Then there would be nothing to fear."

A discussion arose about the recitation of the Quran. The Revered Master said: "It has been said that Gabriel said to the Messenger: 'Recite the Quran in seven letters,[100] all of them clearly and fully.' Scholars disagree about the meaning of 'in seven letters.' Some say this refers to some verses such as *uf likuma,* which is read as seven different words which are not the same in other verses. Some say 'in seven letters' means 'order, negation, history, retaliation, sermon, promise and threat.' These are seven words. Abu Ubaida is reported to have said that 'in seven letters' refers to the seven dialects of the Arabs. It means that in seven letters there are seven forms, yet they are all distinct in the Quran. Some are in the dialect of the Quraish, some in that of Yemen, some in that of Huzail, some in that of a tribe and so on. Some have said that 'in seven letters' refers to the seven ways of reading the Quran which have been accepted by the seven imams."

A discussion arouse about 'the seven oft-repeated verses.' The Revered Master said: "'We have given you the seven oft-repeated verses and the great Quran' (Q15:27). Concerning this verse, Ibn Abbas has said that 'the seven oft-repeated verses' refers to the chapters *The Cow, The Family of Imran, The Women, The Table, Cattle* and *The Ramparts.* He forgot the seventh. Ibn Abbas has another saying attributed to him affirming that 'the seven oft-repeated verses' refers to the opening chapter of the Book, but how can 'the seven oft-repeated verses' refer to the opening chapter of the Book? The reason given is that it consists of seven verses and is recited twice during ritual prayer. Some say that it was revealed twice, once in Mecca and once in Medina, honouring it. That is why it is called 'the seven oft-repeated verses.'"

Qazi Minhajuddin from the fort went through the *Wasiyat* [Testament] of the Sheikh of Sheikhs[101] until he came to these

---

100. 'Letters' is the literal translation of *ahruf.* As the discussion indicates, the real meaning of the word, in this context, is not clear.

101. The reference is to Shihabuddin Abu Hafs 'Umar as-Suhrawardi,

words: 'Don't be satisfied to read the Quran openly, guardedly, privately and publicly, but do so with understanding, comprehension, sorrow and tears.'" The Revered Master explained each term: "'Openly' refers to reciting by heart; 'guardedly' refers to looking and reading; 'privately and publicly' refers to being alone or with others. 'With understanding' means understanding the meaning; 'with comprehension' refers to experiencing relish while reciting a verse of the Quran, such as experiencing consolation while reciting a verse of promise; or fear while reciting one of warning. Such verses should be repeated often. It is related that the Apostle once wanted to recite something. He recited 'In the name of God, the Merciful, the Compassionate' within his blessed heart. He was overcome by a spiritual experience. Time and again he recited 'In the name of God, the Merciful, the Compassionate,' up to twenty times. This is why knowledgeable persons have said that whoever wants to penetrate the divine realm should recite the whole Quran once a month, carefully and perceptively." When the Revered Master reached these words, he recited these two couplets:

> Intelligent people experience delight in their souls:
> Foolish people recite the Quran with their lips.
> Don't think of any abode apart from the Guest!
> Make this your study before reciting the Quran!

Afterwards he said: "It is related that Khwaja Ja'far the Sincere was once so overcome while praying that he fell unconscious. When he recovered consciousness people asked him what had happened. He said: 'I came to a verse of the Quran and repeated it several times until I was listening to the Person uttering the words. This revelation of His power was too much for my body!'"

Afterwards the Revered Master added: "This is what is called progress! It means being lifted up while reciting the Quran to such an extent as to hear the Word of the Lord from the Lord without intermediary. It is also narrated that Ja'far the Sincere said: 'By God Most Exalted! He illumines the Glorious, Exalted Truth for His creatures in His speech, but they do not see it.' The reason for not seeing it has been expressed by the Messenger: 'If devils were not encumbering the hearts of men, they would certainly see the divine realm!' All those things that are hidden from the senses gain

---

the author of '*Awarif ul-Ma'arif*. He died in 1234.

no entry. That is the divine realm, and the meaning of the Quran comes from there. How could they possibly see?"

The aforementioned Qazi Minhajuddin said: "If someone lacks understanding and perception, and does not grieve or lament, should he read it or not?" The Revered Master replied: "Let him read it once aloud. This would be good and not lacking in profit, as the reported words of Ahmad Hanbal[102] indicate: 'I saw the Lord—may He be glorified and exalted—in a dream. I said: 'O mighty Lord God, what is the most excellent thing by which your friends are most intimately united to You?' He said: 'My Word, O Ahmad!' I said: 'O mighty Lord God, both with and without understanding?' He replied: 'Both with understanding and without understanding.' It is also related that Ali, the Commander of the Faithful, said: 'Whoever recites the Quran while standing in prayer is credited with a hundred good works for each word[103] and, if seated, fifty. Whoever recites the Quran outside of prayer has twenty-five good works credited to him for each word, if he has performed the ritual ablution beforehand, and ten if he has not.'"

Afterwards the Revered Master added: "It is said to be desirable for a reader of the Quran to read it completely twice each year if he cannot manage more. Imam Hasan[104] has further related that the Great Imam[105] said: 'Whoever reads the Quran completely twice in a year will have his obligations discharged, because the Messenger recited twice to Gabriel whatever had been relayed to him during that year.'" When the Revered Master reached these words he added: "It is also related that the Apostle, just as he recited to Gabriel, also recited to Abi Ka'b. What does this mean?" He himself replied: "Some say he did so in order to teach his community humility, so that no one should be put out by learning from someone of a lower status in society than he is. Others say that the purpose of the recitation was to enable Abi Ka'b to grasp the words of the Apostle more quickly. The Messenger wanted him to learn the words from him and recite them the way he did. He would learn by listening to him."

102. Ahmad ibn Hanbal was a famous traditionist. He collected and published a volume of Traditions and was also the founder of the Hanbalite school of jurisprudence. He died in 855.
103. The Persian has *harf,* which means 'letter.'
104. Probably Hasan of Basra is meant.
105. The reference seems to be to Ali.

In the meantime, Qazi Ashrafuddin brought his own sister's son to him and pointed out that this was the day fixed for his first lesson. The procedure is to place a writing-tablet in front of the Master. At the top of the tablet the Revered Master writes with his own blessed hand. Thus he wrote these four letters, A, B, C and D,[106] and taught them to him, instructing him to say, "In the Name of God, the Merciful, the Compassionate." The little boy repeated the words fully. He then showed him how to write the four letters. The little fellow repeated the letters after the Revered Master. Afterwards he said: "Praise be to God!" He then made the following petition on his behalf: "May the Glorious and Exalted *God* make you a scholar!" Afterwards he added: "From A, B and C the sky's the limit!" Food was brought and placed before the guests. The Revered Master picked up a cake and some sweets and began to feed the little boy with these words: "Let me perform this service for you!"

Afterwards he added: "It is said that when the first son recites, 'In the name of God,' *God* Most Exalted grants absolution to three people—his mother and father, and also his teacher." He went on to say: "Quranic instruction is of three kinds. One way is to instruct someone without recompense for the sake of the Lord and accepting nothing in return. The second way is to instruct someone for payment. The third way is to instruct someone without any condition regarding recompense. If the person brings him something as a present, he accepts it, but when he teaches out of love he is recompensed and rewarded. He would be doing the work of prophets. When a person gives instruction for recompense, however, religious scholars raise objections against it saying that it is not the proper thing to do because the Messenger was obliged to make known the Quran to the people just as the Lord undertook to make it known to him. So, just as it was not proper for the Messenger, how could it be proper for his community and its present-day members to do so? 'The believers are heirs to it and are obligated to learn it.' The third way—instructing without any stipulation regarding payment—means that if something is given as a present, he accepts it, and this is acceptable to everyone, since the Messen-

---

106. The traditional first instruction took place when the child was 4 years, 4 months and 4 days old. The actual letters written were the first four in the Arabic alphabet.

ger accepted presents when he taught."

A discussion about reading the Quran arose. The Revered Master said: "While reading the Quran it is imperative that the tongue, intellect and heart should all be involved. The task of the tongue is to pronounce the words correctly. The intellect is charged with grasping the meaning and interpreting the Quran. The heart is entrusted with accepting it; not allowing any dissent; and implementing what it ordains. This is what reading involves." A discussion then arose regarding the verse, "Lord, give me respite till the day they are raised" (Q15:36 & 38:79). The Revered Master turned his blessed face towards those present in the assembly and inquired if anyone remembered the chapter in which this verse occurred. Nobody remembered. He went on to say: "I do not remember what I used to. When I was a young boy, I was forced to memorize a number of books such as *Masadir* [Verbal Nouns] and *Miftah ul-Lughat* [A Key to Words]. Sections of books, and even twenty sections of *Miftah ul-Lughat*, to the measure of one volume, had to be learnt by heart. They were checked by having us recite them frequently in full. How I wish they had made me memorize the Quran instead of them!"

Afterwards he related this reminiscence. "In Sonargaon my teacher's brother, Maulana Zainuddin, knew the Quran by heart. If a verse were needed to establish a legal obligation during a lesson, the teacher would need to know the chapter in which it was found. If Maulana Zainuddin were seated there he would ask him to tell him the chapter in which the verse was found. For the sake of a little fun and in order to pass the time, he would remain silent. He wouldn't say anything. He would wink at his friends as though to say, 'Let's see what he says now!' After this the teacher would turn his blessed face towards him and say; 'That's enough! Now tell me the chapter in which it is found!' He would then tell him that it was in such-and-such a chapter."

He also had this to say about Maulana Zainuddin's fine singing voice: "He had such a good voice, sang so well, and knew different melodies.[107] If he sang a verse or a ghazal anywhere, he would cause the door and the walls to shake, so you can imagine the impact that he had on his listeners! He often sang for Maulana Taqiuddin.

---

107. *Az pardha waqif bud.* The reference is to the Indian system of music.

Every time he did so, Maulana Taqiuddin was deeply affected. On such occasions he would gather together a robe, turban, shoes and clogs for him. He would bundle them up and carry them off. He even carried off some of Maulana Taqiuddin's own clothes. Every time he sang, such gifts would be showered upon him. He would gather them up and take them with him. Maulana Taqiuddin uttered this special prayer, 'You will be happy!' As a consequence, in times of distress, Maulana Zainuddin would recite this prayer and say, 'There is no way I can be unhappy, for the Maulana said this with regard to me.'"

He added: "Sultan Shamsuddin[108] was enamoured of his singing. On account of this fondness he had made him his prayer-leader. Sultan Shamsuddin had different prayer-leaders and muezzins appointed for his different dwelling places. For example, there was a prayer-leader as well as a muezzin attached to the royal wardrobe. In a similar fashion, he had them in each palace. Wherever he went the local prayer-leader led the prayers. If Maulana Zainuddin happened to be present, inevitably the local prayer-leader would still step forward and Sultan Shamsuddin would say: 'Zain, you go up front!' Maulana Ziauddin was very close to the Sultan. He was known as the Sheikh of Islam. It so happened that when Maulana Zainuddin arrived from Avadh with three or four friends he came to the hospice and recited something for Maulana Ziauddin. He was smitten by him and became enamoured of him. He couldn't bear it! He gave his friends a message: 'Tell that young man with the mellifluous voice that I won't let him go! I have a daughter and I want him for my son-in-law!' His friends came to him in high good humour. 'Now the door is open. What more do you want?' In short, Maulana Ziauddin gave his daughter to him, along with many goods and possessions." The Revered Master also related many stories about his intelligence, quick-wittedness and remarkable voice, of which as many as possible have been related here.

Maulana Nasiruddin, the prayer-leader of Qazi Safi, was going through a summary of the *Ihya*. He perused the chapter on seclusion until he came to the verse: "And when you withdraw from

---

108. Shamsuddin Firuz Shah was Sultan of Bengal from 1301 to 1322 when Maneri was in Sonargaon, probably from about 1304 to 1323. Maneri's reminiscences indicate clearly that he was often in attendance on the Sultan. It has to be remembered that that these reminiscences date from the second half of the thirteen forties, more than 20 years later.

them and what they worship except God" (Q18:16). The Revered Master said: "Since they had gone to one side, they did not worship anything other than God. This is the story. There was a king called Daqiyanus. He had laid claim to divinity. He set out towards the areas under the control of other kings in order to subjugate them. When this was accomplished, he would demand that a son be handed over to do obeisance to him while the king was allowed to remain in power, but as his vassal. In this way four or five princes remained with him as hostages and did obeisance to him. Each one was carefully instructed how to perform this worship. One day, these princes were standing in the presence of Daqiyanus when, according to the divine decree concerning the happiness of those princes, this thought occurred to one of them: 'He is a man and I am also a man. He is just the same as I am. Why am I worshipping him?' By divine decree at the very time that this was passing through the mind of one prince, the very same thought was occurring to the others. Not one of them remained unaffected. The first and seemingly the only one to have thought thus left the presence of Daqiyanus and went home. He then came outside and said: 'I must exert myself and go to some place where I can worship my Protector.'

Thus he went outside the city and stood at the top of the road. At the very same time, each of the others left their homes and, in the same way, came outside individually to the road. According to the divine decree all of them took the same road where the first prince was standing. When the young man saw them, he grew fearful that they had set out in order to capture him. All of them had the same thought about the others and were seized with fear. Thereupon they asked him what was happening, and why he had run away. He came up to them and said: 'This is the reason why I ran away' and went on to explain what he meant: 'I pulled myself together and came out in order to worship my Protector.' All of them said: 'This is exactly what happened to us! The reason and the road are the same. We should all come together.' They did so. 'Where shall we go? At this very moment soldiers must be getting ready to come and capture us.'

A hill was visible close by. They said: 'Let's go at once to that hill!' They set out towards it. When they reached the foot of the hill they saw a shepherd grazing his flock. There was a dog at his heels. This would become the dog of the Companions of the Cave.[109] When the shepherd saw them looking handsome and well dressed, he realized that they must be princes. He inquired: 'Where have you come from? And what's going on?' Once again they explained to him what had happened. The shepherd exclaimed: 'This exactly applies to me!' He became their friend. They all gathered together. After this the shepherd said that there was a cave in the hill. 'We should go to the cave.' When they entered the cave, God Most Exalted blessed them by casting them into a deep sleep. Each one of them fell asleep. Gabriel was instructed to turn them from one side to the other otherwise, if they all remained sleeping on the same side, there would be continuous pressure on their flesh and it would get bruised. The dog crouched at the door. It became the dog of the Companions of the Cave. It is said that, on the Day of Resurrection, that dog will be honoured by being raised up in human form and among the ranks of men."

The Revered Master then recited this couplet:

The dog of the Companions of the Cave for some time
Remained close to pious men and became a man.[110]

Qazi Minhajuddin from the fort went through the *Wasiyat* of the Sheikh of Sheikhs until he reached these words: "In all commands refer to the Quran!" The Revered Master said: "Have recourse to the Quran with regard to all commands! If you don't find the solution in the Quran, examine the practice of the Prophet. If you do not find it there, have recourse to consensus. If you do not find it there either, then you will have to form your own opinion. This presupposes you are competent to do so.[111] In a similar way a disciple should first approach his spiritual guide about his own affairs and explain the situation to him. If his guide is not available he

---

109. The story of these Companions of the Cave is found in the eighteenth chapter of the Quran. Some readers may recall the story of the seven noble youths of Ephesus who were miraculously cast into a deep sleep during the persecution of Christians by the Emperor Decius.

110. The whole point of the story is that by associating with good people we ourselves can become transformed into better people.

111. These steps are well known to those involved in interpreting Islamic Law. The consensus referred to is that of religious scholars. A qualified person may ultimately have to employ analogical reasoning—*qiyas*—to arrive at a conclusion.

should explain his situation to someone who has taken the place of his guide. He should not speak about it to a stranger, for it ill befits a disciple to do so. On the other hand, it would be perfectly correct to approach someone taking the place of his guide whenever he might be away. If there is no one in his place then the disciple should look into the Quran. For example, if something crops up and he does not know whether it is of satanic or divine origin, he should consult the Quran. It might so happen that he discovers in the Quran that it is divine in origin. If he does not, he will have to study the practice of the Prophet. If he does not find it there either, he will realize that it is satanic."

A discussion about the following verse arose: "When they listen to that which was sent down to the Apostle, you will see their eyes fill with tears" (Q5:83). The Revered Master said: "The descent of this verse was connected to the Negus. After the Apostle migrated from Mecca he sent his friends in twos and threes in all directions. He sent some of them to the Negus. He was the king of Abyssinia. When he had previously heard about the virtues of the Apostle he had become obedient to him. While the friends of the Apostle were on their way to the Negus, news of their approach reached him. He received them. They then entered the city. The Negus then began to ask them about the virtues of the Apostle and they gave him a full account of them. He then inquired about the descent of the Quran, saying: 'If you remember some of it, recite something for me.' They began to recite verses they knew. The Negus and his friends took their seats and listened to the recitation of the Quran. They were all reduced to tears. Finally, all became Muslims. Thereupon this verse descended with regard to them: 'When they listen to that which was sent down to the Apostle, you will see their eyes fill with tears' (Q5:83)."[112]

---

112. In the translation of Ishaq's *Sirat Rasul Allah* by A. Guillaume, OUP, Karachi, 1970, p.152, the Negus and his bishops are reported to have wept when they heard some verses from the Quran recited by Muslim emigrants in 615. On p.657 the same work speaks of a letter sent by the Negus via Muhammad's emissaries in which the Negus thanks God "who has guided me to Islam." In *The Bounteous Koran*, edited by M. M. Khatib, Macmillan Press, London, 1984, footnote 35 on p.153, we read that the verse refers to "Christian priests and monks of Najran (north of the Yemen) who wept when they heard the Koran." It is important to reflect on the underlying reasons for such differences.

A discussion arose about the descent of "Say: 'I take refuge with the Lord of creation'" (Q113:1) and "Say: 'I take refuge with the Lord of men'" (Q114:1).[113] The Revered Master said: "It refers to when a spell was cast upon the Apostle. It happened like this. People had made an image on which they tied seven knots and inserted a needle in each of them. The effect of this sorcery was felt in the blessed body of the Apostle. He was lying awake when two angels appeared and he heard what they said. One asked the other: 'What's the matter with this man?' The second angel replied: 'This is the result of a spell that has been cast upon him.' The first one said: 'What is the cure for it?' The second one replied: 'People made an image and tied seven knots on it.[114] In each a needle was inserted. They put it in such and such a well and put a stone on top of it. If it is brought out of the well and "Say: 'I take refuge in the Lord of creation'" and "Say: 'I take refuge in the Lord of men'" are recited over each knot, healing will occur.' This was how the two angels talked to each other. The Apostle immediately got up, stood and sat down. He ordered Ali, the Commander of the Faithful, to be sent for. He narrated to him how two angels had come to him and told him about the remedy. 'Go and remove it from that well!' Ali set off and removed the image from the well. He saw that seven knots had been tied upon it and a needle had been inserted into each knot. It was in that situation that the last two chapters of the Quran descended.[115] Thereupon he recited both chapters over each of the knots and blew on them. The knots were untied and, with each release, his blessed body experienced relief until finally, when all seven were untied, he was completely cured." The Revered Master commented thus: "Magic is confirmed to have an effect. It is not true to say the opposite."[116]

A discussion arose about prophetic miracles[117] and magic.[118]

---

113. The wording is from the text. It is obvious that the full chapters are meant. Both are extremely brief.

114. The normal practice was to tie knots in a piece of string or twine and blow on each knot. Presumably a garland of knotted string or twine was placed around the neck of the image.

115. Chapters 113 and 114.

116. The unmarked text has: *As-sihr haqq ya'ni sabit asaruhu wa in na an (az) haqq ast ki zidd batil ast.*

117. *Mu'jiza.*

118. *Sihr.*

The Revered Master said: "A prophetic miracle is something contrary to nature which is wrought by a prophet and the like of which nobody else would be capable of effecting. By acting thus prophets bring about something contrary to nature. Magicians also, by means of their magic, bring about things which are contrary to nature. The answer to this difficulty is given in this fashion, namely, that magic does not contravene nature, but is in accord with it. Moreover, since its means and tools are subtle and difficult, not everyone does it. Nevertheless, if someone utilizes those means and tools according to the requisite conditions, it is because a magician who practises magic has learnt it from somebody who has also learnt it from someone else. This is consonant with nature, not contrary to it, even though it might appear to be."

Maulana Qamaruddin, the son of the Master's sister,[119] put a question: "Suppose at a particular time there are two people, one a liar and the other a truthful person, who lay claim to be prophets and both bring about something which is contrary to nature. The truthful person performs a miracle while the liar does something magical. How can they be distinguished?" The Revered Master replied thus: "Circumstances, states and deeds bear witness to a person regarding his truthfulness or mendacity. Pharaoh, for example, along with his claim to divinity, did something contrary to nature, namely, he caused the Nile to flow and then to stop at his command. Although this would be contrary to nature and would constitute a proof of his claim, nevertheless thousands of his circumstances, states and deeds would proclaim that he is a liar. In the same way, if a magician does something contrary to nature by means of his magic, a hundred things—circumstances or states—bear witness to his deceitfulness. This is the basis for discernment. There is a second answer as well. It is not admissible for *God* Most Exalted to enable a false claimant to prophethood to do anything contrary to nature, which is what He would do for a genuine prophet. When an impostor lays claim to prophethood it would not be admissible for *God* Most Exalted to effect something contrary to nature, even if the person is a magician. If it were not so, it would mean that the work would be hidden from people. *God* is not discovered in something absurd!"

At this point a discussion arose about spells. The Revered mas-

---

119. We do not know which sister this refers to.

ter said: "Religious scholars have various opinions about spells and medication. Some disapprove of them. Their argument is that the Messenger said: 'In the next world there will be 70,000 members of my communities without reckoning.'[120] They said: 'O Apostle of God, who will they be?' He replied: 'Those who do not cauterise a wound, nor apply anything as a medicine, nor utter spells, nor use something to evoke an evil omen, but have firm faith in their Lord.' Yet the common opinion of scholars is that spells and medication are allowed. One of the proofs they adduce is that the Messenger used spells in the last two chapters of the Quran. Another proof comes from Ibn Masud who is reported to have said that *God* Most Exalted has not sent any disease without, at the same time, sending its remedy as well, with the exception of death and old age. With regard to the prohibition which has been discussed in this chapter, it has to be said that it applies to those who attribute a return to health to spells and medication. Anyone who attributes this restoration to health to God, however, has nothing to fear if he considers medication as the occasion[121] of this restoration. With regard to the tradition held fast by the first group, God knows best, because the intention of that obligation applies to people of resolve, but it is permitted for ordinary people."

A discussion about the following verse arose: "And the day We will cause the mountains to move away and you will see the earth emerging" (Q18:47). The Revered Master said: "The mountains will move and you will see the earth emerging and it will be level. This will be before the Day of Resurrection. In the Quran you will find in many places something about mountains in relation to the Apostle, such as: 'And the mountains shall be as carded wool' (Q101:4).[122] It is clear that they exhibit different forms so that they oppose one another. In other words, if someone says that since the mountains have all become like carded wool, in another way which has come in this chapter, it should not be so that there may not be any opposition. The answer to this has been given by asserting that there is no opposition, but rather that the mountains will assume states, one of which could be like carded wool. They are agreed about

---

120. The Persian has: *Az ummatan-i man haftad hazar beghair-i hisab.*

121. *Sabab* can be translated as 'cause' or 'occasion'. Granted the Asharite position, with its exclusive acknowledgement of divine causality, 'occasion' seems to be what is meant.

122. In the original text the first verse quoted is repeated.

that and about a state of another kind. Whenever mention is made of mountains in the Quran their states refer to what they will be like on the Day of Resurrection." Thereupon he turned his blessed face towards those who were present in the assembly and added: "Be aware of all that has been said and keep in mind that there is no contradiction but rather a description of states, namely, that mountains change from one state to another in this fashion."

Afterwards he said: "The last quarter of the Quran mainly describes the Day of Resurrection. The Apostle is reported to have said: 'The chapter entitled *Hud* has made an old man of me!'" He then added: "This is the verse which descended in relation to the Apostle: 'Go straight as you have been commanded' (Q11:112)!" Afterwards he added: "Many threats are contained in this chapter."

Khwaja Jalaluddin Hafiz Multani recited this verse: "Today I have perfected your religion for you, and have completed My favour towards you, and I have approved for you Islam as religion" (Q5:3) and asked whether that verse, or some other, was the last to descend. The Revered Master replied: "In the commentaries we find that it was the last of all to descend, so much so that, after its revelation, the Apostle did not survive many days afterwards." Again he asked: "Since it was the last to descend, why isn't it written at the end of the Quran?" The Revered Master replied: "The compilation of the Quran was done according to the order found in the Protected Tablet,[123] not according to the order in which it was revealed. Whenever some event occurred, however, a verse would come down in accordance with that event."

Qazi Ashrafuddin asked: "Was this arranging the order of the Quran done during the lifetime of the Apostle or afterwards?" The Revered Master replied: "It was done during his lifetime. The Commander of the Faithful, Uthman, did the arranging and used to ask the Apostle. When he, through the revelation of Gabriel, found out, he would say that this particular verse descended in relation to this verse and it goes here. The Commander of the Faithful, Uthman, would write it down as indicated by the Apostle. With regard to 'In the Name of God,' which is not written at the beginning of 'An Acquittal,'[124] the reason given is that when the Commander of the

---

123. *Lauh-i Mahfuz,* the heavenly prototype of the Quran.

124. All 114 chapters or *suras* of the Quran begin with the invocation, "In the Name of God, the Merciful, the Compassionate," with the sole

Faithful reached this chapter, which the Apostle related, yet the first line of this chapter is very much like the previous chapter and is in conformity with the contents of this one. When the Apostle was relating all this, his attention was on the Preserved Tablet, not on inquiring if he had omitted 'In the Name of God.' Some others say that this chapter, 'An Acquittal,' descended to cancel the agreement between the Muslims and the unbelievers.[125] 'In the Name of God, the Merciful, the Compassionate' was not written because writing 'In the Name of God, the Merciful, the Compassionate' augurs safety. This invocation was not written in order to indicate the absence of safety."

The aforementioned Khwaja Jalaluddin said: "The companions were saints and in a state of perfection,[126] yet they were not granted awareness of the Preserved Tablet."[127] The Revered Master replied: "Being aware of the Preserved Tablet is not a condition for the quality of sainthood, nor is it necessary that wherever sainthood is found, this should also be found, even though it is possible. It is fitting for everyone to whom it is granted, and to the extent that it is granted."

The Helpless One thumbed through a compendium of *'Aqidah-i Nafasi*, [Nafasi's *Articles of Belief*][128] until he came to the words, "God leads astray the one He wants to and guides the one He wants to" (Q35:8). The Revered Master adduced arguments and went on to add: "One must be careful in this matter. In the Quran 'leading astray'[129] occurs in many places. In some of them it is in reference to *God*; in others to *Satan*; and in some places it is in reference to

---

exception of the ninth, normally named 'Repentance' from this word found in verse 112. Some commentators, however, refer to it—as does Maneri in this instance—by the first word which is variously translated as 'an acquittal,' 'immunity' or 'dispensation.'

125. Treaties were an important aspect of Arab life. Muhammad was careful to observe any treaties he made. Apparently four months' notice was required if either party wished to withdraw from the treaty.

126. *Ahl-i wilayat wa kamil ul-hal.*

127. This is another name for the heavenly prototype of the Quran.

128. This refers to a compendium of the work by the Maturidite, Najmuddin Abu Hafs al-Nafasi (d. 1142), usually called *'Aqa'id*, in the plural, hence the translation. Along with a commentary, this work is still widely studied.

129. *Izlal.*

idols. In all of these 'leading astray' refers to divine activity.[130] It operates in this way. When it is used in reference to *God*, it refers to a completing activity, whereas when it is in reference to Satan or idols, it has a metaphorical significance."

Khwaja Hamiduddin, a merchant, said: "When a copy of the Quran or a book of prayers has become so old as to be unusable, what should be done?" The Revered Master replied: "They should be buried in some suitable place."

A discussion arose about the sayings[131] of *God* Most Exalted. An esteemed person present said: "There is a story in *Rauh ul-Arwah* [The Refreshment of Souls] about an ascetic who fasted by day and kept vigil by night. He performed many acts of worship and devotion and lived in seclusion. A command was given to the messenger of that age to ask the ascetic why he was engaged in so much worship and devotion as he had been destined for hell from birth. The messenger passed this message on to the ascetic. He simply increased his acts of devotion and worship. People asked him why he was increasing these acts since he was destined for hell. He replied: 'I do not see myself as capable of being weighed on the wings of a fly! Now that I am fit for hell, which is an effect of the quality of His wrath, I have learnt that I count for something!' Afterwards this command was given: 'We have accepted you with love.' How could this be, since any alteration in what *God* Most Exalted has said is not fitting? The first command was, 'We have created you for hell,' and finally, 'We have accepted you.' What do you have to say about this?"

The Revered Master replied: "This story, as well as others in like vein that are found in various books, does not seem to be in accordance with the Law and first principles, because a divine saying cannot be altered. This presupposes that the story is correct. A correct interpretation of this should be sought according to the first principles of the Law. This is accomplished by studying commentaries on the Quran or by listening to songs,[132] but as for what a person experiences in this state, God knows best! It is clear that, even though this appears to be a saying, as far as we are concerned

130. *Taufiq.*
131. *Akhbar.*
132. *Besama'* means "by listening" and probably refers to listening to religious songs in a gathering held precisely for this purpose. Maneri has written about this practice in letter 93 in his *Hundred Letters.*

its real meaning is that it is a trial and a test for a person so that what is known to the Lord about him might become known, not for the sake of investigating what was said, for this comes from God Most Exalted. After entering paradise there is no exit from it. With regard to Adam, however, after going in, he came out again. In spite of this, there is no alteration in what was said. In this instance I say that this particular entering was a trial and a test, not a recompense. In a similar fashion, bringing back to life someone who has died, as is said about the messenger Esdras,[133] by God Most Exalted, for in death there is no precedence or delay regarding its appointed hour. In spite of this the messenger Esdras, after dying, was brought back to life in this world. In this instance I say there was no alteration in what was said, for the death which was experienced by Esdras was a trial and a test, not the termination of death. It is possible that this applies in this instance also."

---

133. *Uzair* is in the original. There are many stories about him and many names, e.g. Idris and Enoch, in addition to Esdras.

CHAPTER 7

TRADITIONS OF THE APOSTLE:
A DESCRIPTION OF SOME OF THEM
AS VERIFIERS OF THE TRUTH;
AND COMMENTING ON SOME OF
THE SAYINGS OF THE SHEIKHS

A discussion arose concerning the traditions of the Apostle. The Revered Master said: "The traditions of the Apostle are of three kinds: undoubted, widely-known and rare.[134] An undoubted tradition is related by the Apostle; passes from group to group, and is found in different cities and provinces. Such traditions are equivalent to the Book of the Lord. In collections of commands their acceptance is an article of faith. Their rejection is tantamount to unbelief. Widely-known traditions are similar to undoubted ones, but nothing further can be said about them except that, in the first period, it was a single tradition, but in the second, third, fourth and fifth periods it has gained the status of an undoubted tradition. The difference is that the rejection of an undoubted tradition amounts to unbelief, while the rejection of a widely known one does not. It is an innovation.[135] This is on account of its single origin. This fact leaves room for doubt. A rare saying[136] does not approach either an undoubted or a widely known tradition. Where a rare saying is concerned, there is doubt with regard to its trans-

---

134. *Mutawatir, mashhur* and *ahad.* The first term strictly means "in an uninterrupted order," while the last term is the plural form of 'one.' The translation—following Hughes—gives the intended meaning.

135. *Bid'at.* The word has occurred previously, and will occur further. The whole idea behind this watchfulness against innovation is based on the firm conviction that the example of the Prophet is by far the safest path to tread. If something is added, there is the danger of extremism. If something is subtracted, there is the danger of gradually whittling down religious practices.

136. *Khabar-i ahad.*

mission, not with what is said in it. The command with regard to a rare saying is that it should not be rejected or accepted until the condition of its genuineness is fulfilled by a saying, i.e. by its conformity to the Book or to a widely-known tradition."

Afterwards he continued: "In Arab lands there are many who employ extremely eloquent language. Many sects developed. It was possible for someone, for the sake of vindicating his own sectarian belief, and in order to have his opinion accepted, to adorn something by asserting that 'The Apostle spoke thus.' Some respected scholars have themselves collected weak traditions.[137] It is asserted that Imam Abu Yusuf Qazi[138] had learnt several thousand weak traditions by heart. It should be realized that it is not permitted to hold fast to a rare saying concerning knowledge of the essence and attributes of the Lord Most Glorious and Exalted. According to orthodox scholars, this applies: 'Surely conjecture is no substitute for truth' (Q10:36). Moreover, a rare saying is a conjecture in the sense that its relators are not preserved from sin. Nevertheless, if religious leaders hold fast to a rare saying, it is permitted because they have mature minds. A definitive proof is not a condition here, since its foundation depends on something external. Another way of answering those who hold fast to a rare saying to corroborate eyes, image and suchlike things concerning the Lord, is to compare them to an idolater, who, in order to confirm a body and image, holds fast to this tradition: 'God created Adam in His own image.'"

A discussion arose about relating traditions. The Revered Master said: "There is a difference of opinion among scholars concerning the relating of traditions. If you say 'it was said'[139] instead of 'it was narrated,'[140] or vice versa, would it be admissible or not? Some traditionists have said that, if you recite a tradition to a traditionist, your intention is to have him recite it so that you can say, 'so-and-so said.' On the other hand, if a traditionist has recited it to you, you can actually say that you are relating what he said. In this instance you should say, 'it was narrated by so-and-so.' Yet most

---

137. Ahadith-I muftariyat.

138. Abu Yusuf was a disciple of the great Imam Abu Hanifa. He is also accorded the status of 'Imam' and was made legal consultant and chief Qazi by the Caliph, Harun Rashid. He died in 798.

139. Akhbarana.

140. Haddathana.

scholars hold that both are the same.[141] This opinion is authentic, for it is related that Imam Abu Yusuf Qazi said: 'When you recite a tradition to a jurist-consult,[142] or if he recites one to you, your intention is to relate something, whether you say 'it was narrated' or 'it was said,' or you could say, 'I heard from so-and-so.' There is also a difference of opinion with regard to relating a tradition with the meaning. Some say it is not permissible unless the actual words are used, while others say it is permissible. This is more correct. To prove their position the first group assert that the Apostle said: 'May God help the person who relates to another a tradition he has heard from me, just as he heard it.' Since he said, 'just as he heard it,' it should be in the actual words.[143] The proof of the second group is that the Messenger said that the conveying of a tradition should be in a general manner.[144] This conveying can be done by using the actual words or by giving the meaning. It has been related that Wasil bin Asqi', one of the companions, said: 'I related to you the meaning and your accepted it,' and Imam Wasi' Waki' said: 'If the field of meaning had not been broad, many people would have perished!' Imam Sufyan Thauri[145] said: 'If I say to you that I have related to you exactly what I heard, don't believe me!' Thus it is proved that the meaning has credibility, as opposed to accepting solely verbal exactitude.'[146]

---

141. This is the common opinion of scholars in Bihar. In the early period of Islam students would go to a scholar reputed to know many traditions and would listen to him recite the chain of transmitters (*isnad*) and then the contents (*matn*) of the tradition. On the other hand, the student might have heard a tradition and he recited it in order to have it checked by the scholar. Once the authoritative collections of *hadith*, such as the *As-Sahih* of Bukhari (d. 870), were made, the common practice was for the student to read out the contents. The master would correct any pronunciation mistakes and clarify the meaning of the tradition. This is the procedure still followed in Bihar.

142. *Faqihi.*

143. The printed text has an addition here. It is omitted in the translation.

144. *Bar sabil-i 'umum.*

145. Sufyan Thauri, from Kufa, was a prolific and independent-minded religious scholar, noted particularly for his contribution to *hadith* studies. He died in 778.

146. This illustrates clearly how Maneri uses *hadith* in his process of

The Helpless One thumbed through the *Lawami'* [Flashes] of Qazi Hamiduddin Nagauri[147] until he reached this tradition: "God created my light from His light." The Revered Master said: "In this tradition there are two difficulties. One is that the light of God is eternal. It is not capable of being divided and apportioned. Yet this is what the words, 'from His light' imply, for the preposition has a partitive sense. What form is lost? The second difficulty is this. It would imply that the light of Muhammad is eternal, because the light of *God* is. Since it comes from this light, it should be eternal also."

After a while he continued: "My reply to both of these goes like this—but God knows best! The light of the Apostle is like a grace, not like a division and apportioning, since it is not necessary that everything pertaining to something should be susceptible of division and apportioning. This is similar to a person who looks at his image. There is no division or apportioning between them. It is not necessary that when something originates from something else there is necessarily a division and apportioning between them. As for the argument that it should be eternal, I would say that the creation of the Apostle from the light of *God* indicated the reality of his humanity. This has been explained in two ways. One refers to something new, while the second is other than created.[148] Something new refers to something that did not exist, and then came to be. This is the realm of newness. The thing is new. Something other than created refers to something that has no quality. It is neither contiguous nor separated; nor is it outside or inside; qualified or circumscribed."

Afterwards he said: "The created world belongs to *God* Most Exalted, the created world and the world of command. Whatever is found in the created world is limited and accepts qualities. Whatever pertains to the world of command has nothing to do with qualities or with being susceptible to change, such as the soul. If you read somewhere in the writings of the members of this group that the soul has been attributed created qualities or, for some oth-

---

argumentation.

147. Hamiduddin settled in Nagaur in Rajasthan. He was the most prolific writer of the early Sufis in India, though only portions of his writings are extant. He died in 1274.

148. *Ghair-i makhluq.* This is not a felicitous expression, for anything at all, apart from God, is created, according to Islam.

er reason, the soul has been qualified so that, on this account, it is necessarily not created, then its interpretation is that it does not come under the listing of something new or as a quality, not that it isn't something new or created."[149]

Afterwards he said: "Ain ul-Quzat wrote that *God* Most Exalted has made many kinds of creatures yet none of them was chosen to receive the homage of angels. Among so many creatures it was Adam who was selected for their homage. Since he had been granted the status of receiving the homage of angels, it can be understood how great his dignity is, and who and what he is." Afterwards he recited this couplet:

> All religious leaders and unfettered angels
> Prostrating, seek mercy from God's beloved.

Mubarak Qusuri[150] was present in the assembly. He produced a copy of the letters of Ain ul-Quzat and began to read out one of the letters to the Master until he came to these words: "O God, feed me with both hands like a child!" He asked what the words meant. The Revered Master replied: "This is a tradition of the Messenger. It means, ' O God, take care of me and look after me, just as a mother takes care of her son and looks after him. A small child in front of his mother is devoid of qualities. He has none of his own. He knows nothing about integrity or corruption. He sees with his mother's eyes; hears with her ears; speaks with her tongue; and walks with her feet. This applies to all qualities. If someone says something to a small boy his mother will answer on his behalf, for a mother or father speaks in this way on behalf of their son. In this sense the mother's tongue becomes his own. If someone gives something to her small son she holds out her hand and accepts it on his behalf. In this sense his mother's hand is his hand. If a snake approaches him his mother sees it, runs up and snatches him out of harm's way and flees. In this sense the mother's feet are his feet."

When the Revered Master reached these words he added: "When a traveller belonging to this group writes about the disappearance of qualities he intends this type of disappearance, and by the perduring of the traveller in the qualities of *God* he means this

---

149. The thrust of the argument is that the soul is immaterial yet nevertheless created.

150. His name indicates that he was from Qusur in Punjab.

perduring. Amir Hasan[151] has a couplet in this sense:

> Since it is through Your perduring that I perdure,
> You exist forever for Yourself, no matter what I want."

He also said: "'By means of me He holds, speaks, sees, hears and moves' sums up this meaning. Also 'perduring in oneness' can be understood in this sense. Wherever words similar to these are found, this is what they mean."

A discussion arose about this tradition: "Poverty is black-faced in both abodes." The Revered Master explained: "Externally this applies to a poverty of baseness and necessity. Poverty is of two kinds. One is precious, while the other is abject. It is also said that one is embraced, while the other is imposed. Abject poverty is the condition of a person who complains about it and is not content with it. Out of distress with regard to bread and water, he is known for disregarding divine precepts and necessary duties. He passes his days in questioning people and being involved in what is not lawful. He becomes a spectacle in mosque and bazaar. I take refuge in God from all this! This form of abject poverty is quite prevalent in our world. It enmeshes the heart in darkness, so to say. Moreover, since in this life he gave himself over to sin and inviolable things, in the next life he will be black-faced on account of sin and being bereft of acts of devotion. 'Poverty is close to unbelief' also bears this meaning. In other words, since someone was poor out of compulsion, sin would be involved as well as the abandonment of devotion. It could also become the cause of his not believing, because it is very easy to fall from serious sin into unbelief. Wherever we come across the prayer, 'O God, preserve me from the affliction of poverty,' this is what is meant. On the other hand, poverty which is precious and embraced is that with which a person is content. No shortcoming is found in his devotion or worship. No complaint escapes his lips. This is what saints seek and is beloved of prophets—the mercy of God be upon them as well as a domain in both worlds! Khwaja Khaqani[152] has expressed it thus:

---

151. Amir Hasan Sijzi (d. 1328) is well known as the compiler of *Fawa'id ul-Fu'ad* (Benefits for the Heart), an account of the discourses of Nizamuddin Auliya (d. 1325) covering the years 1307-22. He was also a gifted poet.

152. Afzaluddin Badil Khaqani (d. 1199) was a famous Persian poet who was greatly devoted to Muhammad and to the Sufis.

After thirty years this insight dawned upon Khaqani:
Reigning implies poverty, while being poor is to reign.

Nevertheless, those who delve into reality associate poverty with blackness. The reason for this is that black is the one colour which cannot be changed into any other colour. It does not become red, or gold, or white. This is in contrast to other colours. If red is mixed with black, it turns black. It can also be mixed to form gold, and so on with other colours, but black cannot be changed into any other colour. It does not become red, or gold, or white. If gold is desired, mix it with gold. If you desire another colour you can make it, but black cannot be changed into any other colour. In a similar way, poverty demands singularity. Singularity in no way permits of duality. Whoever has attained poverty has attained singularity because there is no way that duality can enter therein." At this stage he recited the following:

The road is not long, yet you cause a delay:
Unbelief and faith are like your different coloured feet.
All these colours filled with colourlessness
Twist singularity, making all a single colour.
Remain with black, since you do not flee,
For black accepts no other colour.

"The tradition, 'poverty is close to unbelief' draws attention to the fact that poverty has a subtle meaning which is beyond the comprehension of ordinary people. Since its comprehension requires subtlety, they do not grasp its meaning. If its meaning is explained, they totally reject it and compare it to unbelief. For this reason poverty is said to be close to unbelief. It is related that Ibn Abbas said: 'If I give an explanation of this hadith, you will consider me an unbeliever.' This is also why the people do not understand their refined and subtle explanations. If this were not so, no matter how Ibn Abbas explained the meaning—I take refuge in God from all this—it would lead to unbelief."

Qazi Sadruddin said: "The meaning of 'poverty is black-faced in both abodes' and 'poverty is close to unbelief' has been satisfactorily explained by this group, but what is the meaning of this prayerful appeal on the lips of the Apostle, 'O God, preserve me from the affliction of poverty,' as well as of 'precious poverty.'" The Revered Master said: "Since we said that poverty is of one colour, there is no entry for duality. The entrance of duality into poverty would be an affliction. This would be an addition to the meaning of 'in:' 'The affliction of poverty' would mean 'afflicted in poverty.' Duality would result from two things. One would be manifest polytheism, while the other would be hidden polytheism. In manifest polytheism, duality would be in the very root of belief in One God, while in hidden polytheism, it would be in the perfection of belief in One God. In as much as fleeing from manifest polytheism would be involved, so too would fleeing from hidden polytheism."

When the Revered Master reached these words he himself went on to say: "This is a prayer of the Apostle and the perfection of prophethood. Just as he is unstained by clear polytheism, so also he is unstained by hidden polytheism. What meaning could therefore be ascribed to 'fleeing?'" He himself proffered an answer: "No matter how much this may be so, he nevertheless sees himself in the light of 'because he is a man,' and also 'to instruct the people.' There are many other things similar to this." Afterwards he added: "In the very *Letters* of Ain ul-Quzat in which, here and there, he has praised unbelief, he is referring to this unbelief. He also said: 'If this is unbelief, how good it is!' In some verses where the word 'unbelief' occurs and is praised, it bears this meaning." In this connection he recited the following couplets:

> Unbelief in its innermost self is the foundation of faith:
> Easy, is it? It is not possible to live as an unbeliever!
> O unbelief, how is it that fire-worshippers boast about you?
> They worship your name, but do not grasp your essence!

The Helpless One was going through some holy sayings until he came to these words: "O Ahmad, whoever incites his fellow-Muslims against the Sultan will find all his actions profitless." The Revered Master said: "This is why it so happens that the dark side of religion is not beautiful, and accusing someone falsely is a crime. How is it possible to render actions void of such things? God knows best! This can be answered in one of these two ways. The mention of frustrating a work was made either for the sake of the affliction of a threat, or because the accusation became the reason for unbelief by way of considering something lawful, and unbelief being the reason for frustrating a work. All of that would be the cause of frustrating a work, for a reason is a reason for a reason, even if it is varied, such as this tradition: 'Whoever abandons prayer is close to unbelief."

A discussion arose about collating traditions. The Revered Master said: "There is a tradition that the Apostle said: 'After two hundred years it would be better for a mother to give birth to a pup than to a son.' That is called a tradition concerning generations."[153] Afterwards he continued: "In this age we have gone beyond a pup. There is another tradition which says: 'My community is like rain. It is not known whether there is benefit at the beginning or the end.' This indicates that they are the special people of the community; or are among the leaders; or among the last. There is also another tradition which says: 'Mine is the best generation. Then comes the second generation, and then the next. After that, falsehood will spread.' In other words, after the second generation of followers and the subsequent one comes the fourth one, when falsehood will become clearly visible. This tradition proves that goodness prevailed until the third generation of followers, while the above tradition highlights the goodness of the first generation, not regarding the followers." Afterwards he added: "God knows best! The supposition for this rests on the intention of the word, 'my community.' Was it after three generations or itself from the word 'good,' because 'it is not known whether there is benefit at the beginning or the end.' The meaning and attribute have a common intent. It could have been at the beginning or at the end. In all of this consulting the Book and the traditions is required in order to ascertain now what interpretation is found in the traditions for the words 'my community' and 'good.'"

Qazi Sadruddin and Ashrafuddin mentioned that Sheikh Ladhu, one of the disciples of Sheikh Ruknuddin,[154] had arrived at this time. On the day of Ashura[155] they had gone to greet him. He was

---

153. *Tabaqat.* The contemporaries of Muhammad—the first generation—were called 'companions.' Then came the second generation of people who had actually seen companions, the *tabi'in.* Then came the followers of this generation.

154. It is most likely that Sheikh Ruknuddin, the half-brother of Sheikh Najibuddin, Maneri's spiritual guide, is the person in question. This information is supplied in the fortieth assembly in *Khwan.* The invocation of mercy upon him, after his name, indicates that he is deceased.

155. The feast of Ashura occurs on the 10th of Muharram, the first month of the Islamic calendar. It is of particular significance to Shi'a Muslims who commemorate the martyrdom of Husain on that day.

saying that he had sent an inquiry to Maulana Husamuddin Mufti about these words. He wanted to know what they meant. One possibility found in '*Awarif*[156] is: 'What seems good to pious people seems sinful to those near God." The Revered Master said: "The sins of the near ones and of the mystics are both the same." Afterwards he added: "What is the difficulty in this? What needs to be asked? What else is there? This also has to be considered: 'If those involved in remembering God realized what they have omitted they would wail more and laugh less.'" He went on to say: "This has been written because persisting in remembering God is a veil to nearness. Persisting in nearness is a veil to intimacy. Persisting in intimacy delays the blessing of union." The Revered Master added: "The meaning of 'What seems good to pious people seems sinful to those near God' should now be clear. It refers to getting stuck in a station.[157] For example, consider someone who imparts knowledge. This teaching of his, granted his station, is good for him. A person in the station of nearness is on the brink of union. If he neglects this state and becomes engrossed in knowledge then this situation, considering his actual station, would be sinful, because it would be a falling away from what is higher to something lower. As far as they are concerned, such a thing would be sinful. There are many people who are like this. It is related that Malik Dinar[158] once came out of his house weeping. People asked him what had happened. That master of the Way replied: 'I committed a sin last night.' One bold fellow said: 'What was it?' He replied that he had prayed: 'O God, forgive me!' As far as you and I are concerned, this would be something good, but in their blessed state, it is considered sinful. In a similar fashion, a dervish prayed thus: 'Praise be to God for the way He makes events turn out happily!' and 'I seek refuge in God for my faults.' A mystic cried out to him and said: 'I thought you were a Unitarian, but you still associate things with God.' He asked him why he said this. He replied: 'Because your prayer is a

---

156. '*Awarif ul-Ma'arif* [Known Aspects of the Mystical Sciences], by Abu Hafs Suhrawardi (d. 1234), was a very popular basic Sufi text in Mediaeval India. The title has been translated in various ways. Another suggested translation is *Insights from Intimate Experiences*.

157. Sufis visualize progress from one station—*maqam*—to a higher one on the Path to God.

158. Malik Dinar (d. 748) was a disciple of Hasan of Basra and a well-known traditionist.

quality of yours. If you had not seen your own quality, you would not have seen your fault. Because your service is something other, your fault is also something other, and affirming something other implies associating something with God.' What for you and me is good and accounted as worship, is sinful for them on account of their station." At this juncture he recited the following:

> While you are alive religion makes no appearance:
> The night you die will give birth to the day of religion.
> Try hard to become something, although you are nothing,
> For thus you will become intoxicated by divine wine.

"With regard to what has been said, namely, that 'persisting in remembering veils nearness,' the meaning would be that remembering is a quality of the person remembering, because what is sought by remembering is whatever is remembered. As long as someone is actually remembering, he is firmly established in his own quality. He is still caught up with himself. This means he is preoccupied with another, and any 'other' is a veil. As long as he is preoccupied with any other, he is far from nearness. In this sense persisting in remembering would constitute a veil." Afterwards he recited these lines:

> Remembering is simply being at the threshold of struggle:
> Remembering in an assembly is not beholding.
> What the foolish do is imprudent:
> They simply call to mind someone who is a dervish.

"When they say, 'persisting in nearness veils intimacy,' they mean that their attention is on 'I am near.' For this reason, it veils intimacy, because a person's attention gets stuck there and no further progress occurs. It is only through intimacy and abandoning this fixation that one experiences Him." At this stage he recited this couplet:

> If you seek the Hidden, abandon the mail of self:
> What interest does the Hidden take in a place to stay?

Qazi Ashrafuddin commented that it also happens that a person could be close to someone else yet not be on intimate terms with him. The Revered Master explained: "If a person's form is very close to another's, nearness is implied, because intimacy is required for love. It can also happen that, while there is nearness, there is no intimacy. This would be on account of self-seeking in nearness. Moreover, there would not be any intimacy, which is necessary for love. In this situation it can also happen that nearness could be on account of the fear of hell or the desire of paradise, and yet there is no intimacy, for intimacy pertains especially to love, as does a heartfelt longing. As for the other point that he made, namely, that by persisting in intimacy the blessing of union is found, if a person gets stuck there, it would mean the same as if a person's attention were on 'I am experiencing intimacy.' That becomes his stage of 'being seen.' As long as this persists, he makes no progress. The blessing of union occurs by forsaking looking at Him. This is the meaning of the saying, 'Whoever pays attention to his spiritual standing casts a veil over his Leader.'"

Maulana Karimuddin observed: "Ain ul-Quzat wrote in a letter that 'On the Day of Resurrection people will be able to see the tents of the prophets but not the prophets themselves.' What does this mean?" The Revered Master replied: "God knows best, but it could be that 'tent' refers to a person's shape and form. At the time of the Resurrection everyone who sees them actually sees their shape and form, but does not see their reality, eminence and high spiritual standing, just as in the world people see the shape and form of prophets, but do not see their actual reality, eminence and high standing. The prophets, however, can recognize one another. Something similar can be said about saints. People in the world see their shape and form, but who sees or even can see their sanctity, high standing, reality, eminence and miracles?" Afterwards he added: "After the Day of Resurrection, if but a particle of their radiance should shine forth in paradise, the inhabitants thereof would cry out, 'The Almighty has shone upon us!' This is because it is said that there will be such a flash of lightning in paradise that it will be completely illuminated and all its inhabitants will cry out together, 'The Almighty has shone upon us!' The angels will reply: 'It is not what you imagine! The leader of the faithful, Uthman, changed his abode. It was the light of this movement of his that shone forth. Hence if a particle of that light could not be seen, how could something far superior to it be seen?"

The aforementioned Maulana Karimuddin said: "It is also written in the letters of Ain ul-Quzat that paradise is the pasture of Adam's cattle. What does he mean?" The Revered Master replied: "God knows best, but it could mean that Adam's cattle refer to

Adam's shape and form, for eating and drinking, and the famous decrees are related to his appearance, and that cannot but be a portion and pleasure experienced by his outer self. The reality of Adam, however, is something else. It is beyond paradise. It is a completely different stage. People in this stage, however, look for no other abode or dwelling than paradise. Moreover, the reality of paradise for them means being occupied with eating and drinking, because they have no contact with paradise and its blessings. This is because in this world prophets and saints have to eat, drink and sleep. In addition to this, however, they are preoccupied with *God*. That has no contact with this. Similarly, in that place there will be no relationship with this eating, drinking and the blessings of paradise. Understood in this way, paradise is certainly the pasture of Adam's cattle."

He put this further question: "In one place in the letters it is also written that, when a mystic reaches this stage, if some sign is asked of him, he says, 'A crocodile has swallowed it.' What does he mean to say?" The Revered Master replied: "This is a hint about the all-encompassing world of Oneness. Anyone who passes through the world of all-encompassing Oneness is like a drop of water falling into the ocean. When this happens, who can speak about even a sign of it any more? Thus it can easily be compared to a crocodile swallowing something. This explanation is even found is some places, namely: 'Say, The truth has come and falsehood has perished' (Q17:81). In some places this explanation is given: 'When the light shines, falsehood disappears.'" He then recited this couplet:

> The shining light is beneficent:
> Exposing lies is body and soul.

CHAPTER 8

THE PROPHETHOOD[159] OF THE APOS-TLE: HIS ASCENSION AND MIGRATION; VISITING HIS BLESSED TOMB; THE EFFECT OF A PARTICLE OF THE GRACE OF THE COMPANIONS ON ALL THE BELIEVERS; THE EFFECT OF THE GRACE OF THE COMMUNITY ON ALL COMMUNITIES; AND A DESCRIPTION OF WHAT IS FITTING

A discussion arose about prophethood. The Revered Master—may God bless Muslims by granting him a long life[160]—said: "Prophethood does not depend on being acquired or chosen by a human being. It comes from a very special grace." He related the following story to explain his meaning: "Concerning this very matter, when Luqman[161] was given the choice between prophecy or wisdom, he was told: 'Think it over! Do you want to be a prophet or a wise man? You have to choose one of the two.' He thought about it and then chose wisdom, not prophecy. People asked him why he had passed over prophecy and chosen wisdom. He replied: 'O foolish ones, so many people had prophethood bestowed upon them! Did they choose it or ask for it? It was bestowed upon them! That's why I chose wisdom.'"

---

159. The word *nabuwat* can mean either 'prophethood' or 'prophecy.' Both words are used according to the context.

160. The reader is reminded that "The Revered Master" often has expressions of praise or petition—as in this instance—attached to it. These are normally omitted.

161. Luqman is a wisdom figure in Islamic literature.

A discussion arose as to whether messengers were[162] messengers in both situations, i.e. before the manifestation of revelation[163] as well as after its manifestation. The Revered Master replied: "Yes, in both situations messengers were prophets. Before revelation the manifestation of the signs of prophethood used to appear in them. They were all indications of prophethood. When our Messenger was small, for example, and was still feeding at the breast, so many signs and indications appeared in him that they knew no limit." Afterwards he narrated this story: "There was a custom among the Arabs that wet nurses from each tribe would come to Mecca each year in order to suckle a baby girl or boy for a fixed amount. They would take them from their parents for a period of one or two years. They would take the children, each one of them, from Mecca to their own tribe. Once it happened that the wet nurses gathered together from their respective tribes and came to Mecca to children with their parents. They took a child each so that the parents would give them a generous wage and returns for their trouble. They were not accepting any child that did not have parents, for no one would give anything on behalf of such a child. In short, all the wet nurses in this manner acquired a child. One of these women, however, did not find a child to accept on wages. The Messenger at that time was a child at the breast. Since he had no mother or father,[164] no one accepted him.

When it was time to return that woman thought to herself that everyone had secured a child for wages, but she would be returning empty-handed. She then decided to take the child without parents in order not to return empty-handed. The woman took charge of the Apostle. This woman had a donkey. It was lean and weak. While they were coming it lagged behind all the other donkeys. All the other women who were seated on their donkeys had gone on ahead. When this woman picked up the Apostle, placed him on her hip and mounted her donkey, it headed off as swiftly as a horse and outstripped all the other donkeys. The other women began to say: 'When we were coming, your donkey was behind everyone

162. The tense was chosen in view of the Islamic belief that Muhammad was the "Seal of the Prophets."

163. *Wahy.*

164. It is normally believed that Muhammad's father died before Muhammad was born but that his mother died when he was about six years of age.

else's. Now that we are returning, it's ahead of all of us. Is it the same donkey, or did you buy another one?' She replied: 'It's the same donkey I had when I came.' Afterwards they all said: 'There is something special in this child on account of which this is happening.' When she brought him home, good things and blessings began to increase daily within her house. The woman and her husband began to love him and their affection for him increased daily. When a woman's affection for her child increases so too does the quantity of her milk. Thus she had an abundance of milk. She wanted to suckle the child. She attended with such great care to his upbringing that everyone in the tribe was convinced that the light that was poured forth on her house was on account of the child in whom there was an abundance of goodness and blessings. The child was certainly someone so important that these blessings knew no limit. For example, the woman kept some sheep which produced twice the number of lambs as the sheep which belonged to other members of the tribe. Thus her house became the biggest one in the tribe. When the Messenger grew big enough to play games that were allowed, such as shooting arrows and so forth, he used to go outside with other boys in order to play. It so happened that the Messenger had gone out to play with the other boys one day when two angels in human form appeared in the midst of the boys. They picked the Apostle up from among the boys and carried him away out of their sight. They then cut open the blessed belly of the Apostle. They removed something from his belly which then reverted to its original state."

At this point Maulana Karimuddin inquired: "What was it that they removed?" He replied: "It was something that belonged to Satan that they removed, or it could have been something else. At any rate, when the children saw that Muhammad had disappeared from their midst, they were bewildered. They informed his foster parents about what had happened. Thereupon they ran around in search of him. Finally they found the Apostle. He was pale and it looked as though he had been frightened. They asked him what had happened. The Apostle replied: 'I was playing as usual. Two men came and took hold of me. They took me away and opened up my belly and took something out of it. They then made my belly like it was before and disappeared.' They took fright and said: 'Before another calamity strikes, let us take him to his paternal uncle. We shall entrust him to him in order to avoid further criticisms.'

With this in mind they took the Apostle to Abu Talib and entrusted him to his care."

Afterwards the Revered Master said; "The Messenger was still but a child when all those signs and indication appeared in him. And besides that, so many other signs and indications occurred that the Quraysh[165] were all astounded." Afterwards he added: "Of necessity, when someone has a special gift, even before it becomes manifest, some signs and indications of it will appear in him which are not found in other people."

A discussion arose about the ascension of the Apostle. The Revered Master said: "The ascension of the Apostle occurred while he was awake and in a bodily manner. The Mu'tazilites deny this. They assert that it occurred during sleep, not while he was awake, nor was he borne bodily aloft, for it goes against right reason that a human being, in a single night, should traverse the seven heavens and come back again. Those who follow the prophetic path, however, say: 'If it occurred during sleep, it would not be a grace peculiar to the chosen One, for Jews and Christians see heaven and hell in dreams. Something which is found among unbelievers can scarcely be called a grace peculiar to the Messenger!'"

Afterwards he continued: "What God Most Exalted granted as a special gift to the Chosen One was not given to other messengers. One was the ascension while still in this world, and the other was intercession in the world to come. The reason was that prophethood belonged to him, but it was also found in others. If a law was granted to him, the same applied to others also. If a book was granted to him, the same applied to others as well. His excellence over others consisted in what was peculiar to him and not shared with others. One was the ascension while still here, and the other was intercession in the world to come. The Mu'tazilites deny both. Some who deny the ascension are unbelievers. Others who deny it are inventors of new opinions, but not unbelievers. It is an act of infidelity to deny the ascension to the Holy House,[166] for

---

165. The Quraysh was the leading tribe in Mecca.

166. *Bait ul-muqaddas.* This is the site of the temple in Jerusalem where the Al-Aqsa Mosque and the Dome of the Rock now stand. The Quranic reference is Q17:1. The *mi'raj* (ascension) of Muhammad has many scholarly interpretations and popular expressions in a wealth of literature. For Sufis like Maneri it is a kind of prototype of the ascent of the soul to God.

this is proved by the Book. Those who deny the ascension from the Holy House to the heavens are not called unbelievers because this is based on traditions, and anyone who denies a tradition is not an unbeliever but a light-minded person."[167]

Concerning the wisdom of the ascension he had this to say: "People have asked what wisdom is contained in the ascension. One group has said that a divine favour lies at the heart of the ascension. The Lord—may He be honoured and glorified—wanted to bestow the treasures of His own kingdom upon him, just as kings, when they want to honour one of their servants in a special way, show greater favour to him than to others. He reveals the secrets of his treasures to him, something he does not do to anyone else in the kingdom. He shows him his treasures. This revealing of the secrets of the kingdom is what is meant by the saying of the Messenger: 'A land was shown to me that stretched from east to west, and what was shown to me will be granted to my community.'

Another group has said that the wisdom contained in the ascension is to liberate the Chosen One from preoccupation with self on the Day of Resurrection so that he can be totally occupied with his community. If he had not experienced the ascension then, on the Day of Resurrection, he would see things he had never before seen, just like everyone else. He would be afraid and would cry out, 'My soul! My soul!' By showing him beforehand the Day of Resurrection, heaven, hell and other things, it means that on the Day itself everyone else will be seeing things they had never seen before. In the hope of blessings and out of fear of punishment all will cry out, 'My soul! My soul!' He will be seeing things he has already seen and will not be caught up by them. 'My community! My community!' will be his cry. Another group says that the wisdom contained therein is to make known the high-mindedness of Muhammad, for the earth was rolled up, brought forward and presented to him. It was on account of him that 'I am your highest lord' (Q79:24)[168] was said, and also on account of him that the mantle of the heavens was bestowed. A group of friends desired this in prayer, 'My Lord,

---

167. *Hawadar.* Maneri's distinction is significant, granted the fact that he was an acknowledged scholar of traditions in his day and age.

168. While the Quran is full of expressions containing the word *rabb* (lord), meaning God, these exact words are found only once. They are the supreme expression of human pride and are uttered by Pharaoh. Perhaps they serve as a warning in this context.

grant me a kingdom' (Q38:35)! What is this worth? On account of his singular steadfastness, he diverted his gaze from the creatures of the seven heavens and the earth. Astonishment reigned because something that Solomon had prayed for was granted unsolicited to him! He turned away his face. This is why holy men have said that, when the world was presented to the Chosen One, if he had taken hold of it, he could never have acquired the world to come. Moreover, when the world to come was presented to him, if he had taken hold of it, he would never have attained the Lord. 'The world to come will elude anyone who lays hold of this world; and the Lord will elude anyone who seeks the world to come. Whoever seeks the Lord, however, will also be given this world and the next.'"

Afterwards he related this story: "On the night of the ascension Gabriel was ordered to speak to Paradise[169] in this fashion: 'So many years have passed since We created you. We did so on account of Our friend. Tonight is the ascension of that friend of Ours. Spruce yourself up and present yourself to that friend.' Gabriel conveyed this order to Paradise who donned her jewellery and finest garments. Was there anything lacking in Paradise's beauty? Now she was all prepared. When the ascension of the Apostle occurred she came and stood to the right of him. As soon as she stood to his right, he turned his blessed face to the left. Paradise then came and stood to the left of the Apostle, who then turned his face again to the right. Thereupon Paradise exclaimed: 'O Apostle of God, what is lacking in me that you are turning your blessed face away from me? If a bride is beautiful, so am I. If there is a wine that purifies, it is in me.[170] If there is a heavenly wine, it is in me.' In this fashion she described all her qualities to him. The Apostle replied: 'This is all true, but until I see the beauty of *God*, I won't look at you.' The high-mindedness of Muhammad regarding these things does not stem from his averting his gaze from them. What is special is that his gaze is fixed on *God*. 'Although you are very beautiful, your value is not more than a word. If my community desires you, its members can purchase you at the price of that word.' Thereupon Paradise inquired: 'O Apostle, what is that word?' The Apostle replied: 'Your price is the recitation of, There is no god but God. You

---

169. For the sake of the imagery employed paradise has been personified in this story.

170. *Agar sharab tuhur ast dar man ast.*

are worth no more than this expression. What's the point of all your coquetry?'"

The Helpless One inquired whether the Apostle had seen the Lord on the night of the ascension. He wanted to know what could be said about this matter. The Revered Master replied: "All the members of this group and saintly men affirm that he did not see the Glorious Lord[171] with his eyes. Nor does anyone see Him in this world according to the tradition from the mother of the faithful, A'isha, who said: 'Whoever says that Muhammad saw his Lord lies.' Most of mainstream Sunni opinion agrees with what the mother of the faithful said. There is a group, however, which asserts that the Messenger saw the Glorious Lord on the night of the ascension. He was made special among the people by this vision, as Moses was made special by conversing with God without intermediary or proof. Besides this, Ibn Abbas, Asma and Anas, three of the Companions, assert that the Apostle saw the Glorious Lord on the night of the ascension. The group that accepts this position says that three of the messengers are special on three accounts: Abraham for friendship, for no one else has obtained the title of 'friend' except him; Moses, for conversing, for no one else spoke with the Lord except him; and Muhammad, for seeing, for no one saw the Lord except him. Most mainstream Sunni scholars, however, do not agree with this assertion. They call anyone who says this an unbeliever, innovator and one who has strayed. They also say it is a fault, because it is not proper to add to the words of the Companions of the Apostle, nor would it be proper to attribute unbelief or innovation to them. On the other hand, they are not preserved from faults."

Zakaria commented: "People say that Khwaja Bayazid experienced an ascension." The Revered Master replied: "They all experience an ascension. It is a metaphor for nearness. For the Apostle, it was a bodily experience, but it was something mysterious for saints. The ascension of each individual depends upon the stage he has attained." To illustrate his meaning he told this story: "In the Discourses of Sheikh Nizamuddin[172] it is related that Maulana

171. Maneri treats this subject in *Khwan*, cf. English edition, p.105.

172. The most famous *malfuz* (discourses) relating to Nizamuddin Auliya is *Fawa'id ul-Fu'ad,* translated as *Morals for the Heart*, by Bruce Lawrence, Paulist Press, New York, 1992. In the earliest biography of Maneri, *Manaqib ul-Asfiya* [The Glorious Deeds of the Saints], however, we read:

Fariduddin[173] sat down and all his disciples sat down behind him. Suddenly one of his disciples uttered a loud cry and slumped unconscious. There was a commotion in the mosque. The Qazi and his son were present at the time. They were not happy at what had happened. They ordered an attendant to grab hold of his leg and drag him outside. When the Sheikh saw this, his anger was apparent but, like a mendicant, he said nothing.

After a while, the disciple came to his senses. Maulana Fariduddin turned his blessed gaze in his direction and said: 'Praise be to God! You experienced a portion of my ascension. At the very moment you cried out, I experienced an ascension, but you received a portion. Just as the Qazi and his son did their work, so too should you do your work.' A few days later the Qazi's son fell ill. The Qazi felt certain that this misfortune had occurred on account of what had happened to the Sheikh's disciple. It stemmed from the Sheikh's anger. 'To prevent things from getting worse, I'll go to the Sheikh and appease him.' Through an intermediary, he arranged to meet Sheikh Fariduddin. He confessed that he was guilty of a sin, saying: 'Revered Master, grant me forgiveness and purify me!' He pleaded for healing. The Sheikh did not acquiesce to his requests. He said: 'Just as you did your work, so also has he done his.' Again he began to plead and others interceded on his behalf. The Sheikh said: 'Let us now clarify the matter, but on condition that the Book acts as an arbitrator between you and me. Let the Book be opened and see what sort of verse appears. If it is a verse about mercy, he will be cured. If a contrary verse appears, he won't be cured.' The Qazi and the others agreed to this. The Book was opened. As it had been ordained, a verse about enmity happened to appear. The Sheikh said: 'Now there is no room for reconciliation.' The Qazi returned home. Afterwards his son died. He himself and all that he owned fell to pieces." When the Revered Master reached these words, he commented: "The whole point of this story is that

"It is related in the eighth chapter of *Siraj ul-'Arifin* [A Lamp for Mystics], a collection of the discourses of Sheikh Nizamuddin...", p. 127 of the version printed from Nur ul-Afaq Press, Calcutta, 1895. No extant copy of *Siraj* is available, but it seems to have been the *malfuz* in question.

173. The reference is undoubtedly to the famous Chishti Sufi, Sheikh Fariduddin Ganj-i Shakar (1173-1265), referred to as "Sheikh ul-Islam Fariduddin." Although he is referred to as 'Maulana' here, the title quickly changes to 'Sheikh' as the narrative continues.

everyone experiences an ascension according to his state. On account of this it is said that 'prayer is the ascension of the believer.'"
Qazi Khan spoke up: "Since this group is noted for grace and generosity, and is famous for wholeheartedly forgiving faults, how can this be?" The Revered Master replied: "Seeking justice with regard to an oppressor is what justice is all about, whereas forgiveness pertains to grace. Here the work pertained to justice. Here such a thing is not necessary. Perhaps there was no misapplication on his part, and it came from God as a command meant to be a warning. There are many such instances—but God knows best!

CHAPTER 9

THE MIGRATION: PATERNAL UNCLES: AND THE APOSTLE'S COMPANIONS OF THE BENCH

A discussion arose about the migration.[174] The Revered Master said: "When the Apostle received the command to migrate, Abu Bakr the Righteous approached the Apostle who said: 'I have been commanded to emigrate. I shall be migrating.' Thereupon Abu Bakr said: 'Me too, O Apostle of God!' The Apostle replied: 'Indeed, you too!' He then wept. Abu Bakr wept. These tears of Abu Bakr flowed from joy, for just as tears can flow from grief, so too can they flow from joy. This is why when two friends, if they meet after a long interval, weep, their tears would not be of sorrow but of joy. If anyone wants to discover if they flow from joy or sorrow he should taste the teardrops. If they taste sweet, they flow out of joy; if they are bitter, they indicate sorrow, for catching sight of a friends brings joy, not sorrow." At this juncture he recited the following couplet:

> Do you know what delight the sight of an absent friend entails?
> It is like a cloud bursting upon thirsty people in a desert.

After this he told the story of the migration: "After the command to migrate was given, the Apostle slipped out alone by night and Abu Bakr went with him. His enemies had posted men around Mecca to prevent the Apostle from escaping. When they discovered that he had escaped they set out in pursuit. After escaping, the Apostle took shelter in a cave. Abu Bakr sat at the entrance of the cave. A snake had hidden itself in a hole in the cave. When Abu Bakr saw the snake's hole he placed his blessed foot over the

---

174. The reference is to the *hijra*, the migration of the nascent Muslim community from Mecca to Medina in 622. The Muslim calendar begins from the 1st Muharram of this year. The reader will note that this, as well as some other topics, was announced in the heading of the previous chapter but not actually discussed.

entrance to the hole so that the snake could not come out. Time and again the snake bit his blessed foot. One of Abu Bakr's slaves was grazing his camels near the cave. News reached him. He came to the cave. Every day, as long as they were in the cave, he brought them milk. According to one tradition they spent three days in the cave. Abu Bakr had a camel. He had it brought from those his slave was grazing. The Apostle mounted that camel and set out from there in the direction of Medina. When the inhabitants of Medina learned of this they sent people to say: 'Come! We are ready to devote ourselves and all that we have to your service! We give you our friendship.' When the Apostle reached Medina all the inhabitants of Medina earnestly wanted him to grant them the favour of staying with them. The Apostle, however, had been given this command: 'You are to settle down and get buried at the very spot where this camel crouches down.' Everyone was flaunting his house and wealth in an attempt to entice the Apostle to lodge with him. Finally the camel stopped at a place where there was no building at all. The Apostle alighted at that spot and constructed his dwelling there. And that was also where he was buried." Afterwards he added: "Since it was obligatory for everyone to migrate, people began to come one or two at a time.[175] In Mecca there were some sons who had accepted the faith but whose parents had not, while other parents had become believers, but their sons remained unbelievers. Thus, when someone wanted to come to Medina, some people who had not become believers were not allowing them to go. Without saying a word to anyone people would slip out and come. If they were found, they were killed so that they could not come to the sanctuary of the Apostle." At this point someone put this query: "Didn't they say anything to anyone about their coming?" The Revered Master replied: "There was no scope for them to say anything. They were leaders and kings."

A discussion arose about the Apostle's paternal uncles. The Revered Master said: "There were ten brothers. The eldest was Abu Talib. Then came Hamza. The tenth brother was the father of the Apostle." Khwaja Jalaluddin Hafiz Multani asked how many years the Apostle lived after the battle of Badr. The Revered Master replied: "He lived at least ten years after the migration. This is what

---

175. The standard account of the migration depicts the migration of the Muslim converts before that of Muhammad.

is recorded." He then asked about Abbas, the paternal uncle of the Apostle: "He was in Mecca, and the Apostle was in Medina. How did he become a believer?" The Revered Maser replied: "There was a meeting held in Mecca between the Quraysh and others, and the inhabitants of Mecca. They said: 'Let us all go to Medina and put them to the sword so that this religion of Muhammad may be totally destroyed! May they all perish!' There were three hundred companions—God knows best—with the Apostle. No one had a horse or arms. They had only three camels and three or four swords. Their opponents had thousands of armed horsemen. After a while news reached the Apostle that the Meccans were coming to do battle. In the meantime, a promise of victory had been revealed to him: 'We have ordained that victory will be yours on this occasion.' The Apostle shared this good news with his companions. They rejoiced and were filled with courage. When the Meccan army arrived in Medina they captured the well at Badr because it supplied water for the inhabitants of Medina. Their aim was to destroy them. Thereupon the Apostle and his companions went out to engage them in battle. Although there were only three hundred men with the Apostle, nevertheless, because they had been assured of victory, they advanced unhesitatingly. When the army of the Apostle confronted the army of infidels with drawn swords they joined battle and routed them. The Apostle's army emerged victorious. They killed seventy of the leading men of the Quraysh and captured another seventy. One of them was Abbas. That was when he became a Muslim."[176]

Afterwards the Revered Master went on to say: "Those companions who participated in this battle along with the Apostle had the title 'Badri' added to their names after this victory. They were held in the highest esteem by the other companions. This was because there were few companions alongside the Apostle during the battle, while the Meccans numbered thousands. This is also why they were called companions and were held in the high-

---

176. Accounts of the battle of Badr differ in some details. For example, in other accounts the Muslims were better armed than is here depicted, and the Meccans numbered close to a thousand, but the number of Muslim fighters, Meccans slain or captured, are standard. Moreover, it was the Muslims who held the wells of Badr. The wells were an important watering spot on the caravan route from Mecca to Damascus, which ran close to the coast. Badr is situated about 50 kilometres from Medina.

est esteem among all the companions. As a consequence of this, if one of them approached a group of companions he was given a seat higher than anyone else as a way of showing respect for him." One of the friends asked: "Where did the well of Badr get its name from?" The Revered Master replied: "There was a man by the name of Badr. He had the well dug. It was called after him." Someone else said that Khwaja Hasan Basri[177] had made the acquaintance of seventy of those who had fought at Badr. All of them wore woollen garments. The Revered Master added: "This is why in the *Tazkirat ul-Auliya* it is mentioned that Khwaja Hasan Basri told his companions: 'I have made the acquaintance of a group of the companions. If you were to see them you would say they were mad, and if they were to see you, they would say you were devils.'"

A discussion arose about the Companions of the Bench.[178] Even if they were weak from hunger, they would not beg from people. The Revered Master commented: "Not only did they not beg from people, they did not beg from *God* either! The reason for this was that if they were to beg from people it would reveal their hunger. This would be an implicit criticism of the Friend in front of others. This is not fitting. They do not ask from *God* either because the selfish soul is the enemy. Asking from the Friend something that pertains to the enemy is not proper. Moreover, they are well grounded in trust. They would have known that the Lord was well aware of their situation, as has been narrated about Abraham, the Friend of God. When the accursed Nimrod[179] had him placed in a catapult and flung him in the direction of the fire, while he was still in the air Gabriel arrived and said: 'Is there anything I can do for you?' He replied: 'You cannot meet my need.' Gabriel said: 'Then ask God!' The Friend replied: 'My request is fixed. He knows my situation.'" The Revered Master recited this couplet at this point:

It matters naught if people are ignorant of my state:

---

177. Khwaja Hasan Basri (d. 728) is an extremely important figure of early Sufism.

178. This group of special Companions who are reputed to have shunned all form of livelihood and spent their time in devotion in the Prophet's mosque is important in Sufi lore but of doubtful historical reality.

179. The biblical reference to Nimrod is found in Genesis 10:8. He is mentioned several times in the Quran. He persecuted Abraham and is often associated with Pharaoh as typifying human pride.

My condition would be better if You knew my state.

He explained: "The same thing would apply to hunger. If someone is meant to die, let him die. If our lives depend on God's good pleasure, and it is time for us to die, that is also according to His good pleasure." In connection with this he narrated the following: "It is related that someone asked Khwaja Ibrahim Adham[180] this question: 'What should a dervish do who goes hungry for a day?' He replied: 'Let him practise patience!' A further question was put to him: 'If he goes hungry for two days, what should he do?' Again came the reply: 'Let him practise patience!' He was then asked: 'If he goes hungry for three days, what should he do?' The reply was the same: 'Let him practise patience!' His interlocutor exclaimed: 'Going hungry for three days would kill him.' To which he replied: 'His aim would be to kill him.' In other words, if He had not wanted to kill him, He would have provided him with bread and water. These would have been found in His treasury as destined for him. Since He did not provide them, it is clear that He wanted to kill him. It is understood that anyone He kills would receive his recompense." In this context he recited this couplet:

> The recompense for anyone killed by man is a gold coin:
> The recompense for anyone killed by the Friend is vision.

The Helpless One said: "It is related as a basic principle that the selfish soul has to be kept in check. Abandoning asking as something in which we experience the checkmating of our selfish soul means that we will perish, and this is not correct according to the Law which allows, for example, eating carrion or drinking wine in case of extreme necessity. If a person waits quietly in this situation, it would make him a sinner. If he keeps quiet in order to die, then he should be considered a sinner." The Revered Master replied: "This is a matter which is disputed. According to Imam Shafi'i and the majority of religious scholars, with regard to refraining from eating carrion or drinking wine in a situation of extreme necessity, they said that, if the person does die, he would not be a sinner. On the contrary, he will be recompensed. There is also a saying from Abu Yusuf. He used the analogy of someone who is being forced to renounce his faith or eat something forbidden. If he is patient in

---

180. This Sufi was from Balkh. His conversion story is reminiscent of that of the Buddha. He died around 782.

such a situation and consequently dies, he will be recompensed. The same thing applies here—but God knows best!"

CHAPTER 10

THE EXCELLENCE OF THE COMPANIONS COMPARED TO OTHER BELIEVERS, AND OF THIS COMMUNITY COMPARED TO OTHERS; THE QUALITIES OF A'ISHA, THE MOTHER OF THE BELIEVERS; AND THE STRUCTURE OF THE BLESSED TOMB

A discussion arose about the excellence of the companions of the Apostle. The Helpless One asked: "Does the excellence of the companions compared to other believers depend solely on association or on other qualities as well, such as knowledge, worship, asceticism, piety, trust and so on?" The Revered Master replied: "With regard to this whole matter, the most excellent of the entire creation in an absolute sense is Muhammad, the Apostle of God. The next in excellence are the prophets and apostles. After them come the members of the community of Muhammad. The most excellent of his community is Abu Bakr the Righteous. After him comes Umar Khattab, then Uthman Affan, and then Ali the Approved. Furthermore, it should be known that the most excellent of the sons of Adam, namely, the prophets and apostles, are more excellent than the most distinguished angels, such as Gabriel, Michael, Israfil and Azra'il. These are more excellent than the ordinary sons of Adam. Finally, the sons of Adam who are pious and God-fearing are more excellent than ordinary angels. This is the hierarchy of mainstream Sunni opinion. Now we are in a position to take up the question you raised, namely, whether the excellence of the companions compared to other believers depends solely on association or also on other qualities, such as knowledge, worship, asceticism and so on, according to the saying of the Apostle: 'My companions are like stars. No matter which one you follow, you will find guidance.' This applies in general terms. In other words, just as following the four caliphs[181] provides guidance, so too does following all the companions. Guiding others is laudable, especially by way of good example. It stands to reason that the person who is providing the good example is more excellent than the person who is following it. This holds good in all senses. Because they excelled others in companionship, they excelled in all other qualities as well. Moreover, they were endowed with all qualities, such as knowledge, piety, scrupulosity, asceticism, trust and others similar to these. Nevertheless, because the effect of companionship and its benefits far outweigh all other qualities, the net result is that the companions, even though endowed with all these qualities, derive their excellence from companionship alone, not from these qualities. Moreover, it is possible and even allowable to say that some of the saints were endowed with higher qualities—other than companionship—than they were, but where else can be found the riches and blessings that are contained in companionship, especially those associated with it?" At this point the Revered Master recited this couplet:

> My Beloved, if You don't think I'm someone, then who am I?
> A stone cannot become a ruby unless it has been polished!

Qazi Ashrafuddin inquired if the result was solely due to the companionship and gaze of the Apostle. The Revered Master replied: "With regard to the companions, the effect was solely on account of their glance and companionship. Whatever glance of theirs fell on a believer was one of compassion. This glance of theirs towards a believer was definitely effective. The glance of the Apostle was all compassion. On each person that it shone it communicated this compassion. Whoever was honoured by being the object of his gaze, or by experiencing his companionship, was ennobled. Even if it was only his companionship or gaze, that was sufficient to have an effect on a person's behaviour, speech and deeds. Thus the blameless and edifying words and deeds of the companions stemmed entirely from the measure of their association with the Apostle. What they possessed to a limited degree was greatly increased. Whatever deeds or actions those who were not companions would perform would not be devoid of blame or harmful ef-

---

181. The reference is to the first four caliphs—Abu Bakr, Umar, Uthman and Ali. They are collectively known as "the rightly guided caliphs."

fects, no matter how many they were."

A discussion arose concerning some of the companions who used to disclose their sins to the Apostle. Qazi Ashrafuddin spoke up and said: "Even though they knew about the disclosing of sins, namely, that in principle they should be concealed, nevertheless, if someone did commit a sin, he disclosed it to the Revered Apostle, as mentioned in the story of Ma'iz." The Revered Master replied: "Although they knew that, in principle, they should be concealed, nevertheless, overcome by an abundance of religious sentiments, they did not think it was fitting to keep anything hidden that pertained to themselves. They would disclose immediately what they had done. This is allowed because a person who discloses his sins to the leader or his deputy thereby establishes where the boundaries of the Law lay. The disclosure of their sins by the companions could also mean that they did so in order that the Apostle might indicate their due atonement. It also needs to be considered that, if one of the companions committed a sin and disclosed it to the Apostle, and a command was issued in relation to the matter, then the wisdom contained therein would be that a command of the Law was the result, as is found in the story of Ma'iz. He disclosed his sin to the Apostle, and the expiation imposed upon him became a clear statement of the Law."

Qazi Ashrafuddin had another question: "Nowadays the expiation for each sin is known, so why should a disciple disclose his sin to his spiritual guide? It has been said that a disciple is obliged to disclose any sin that he commits to his guide. Why? It is as though the expiation for a particular sin was not known! Why should he disclose it to his spiritual guide?" The Revered Master replied: "In the present age sin has taken a very strong hold on people's hearts. On account of the widespread nature of this disease it could happen that, if someone commits a sin[182] and performs the prescribed expiation, full atonement may not take place. For example, fasting has been prescribed as the expiation for some sins. Imagine a disciple has sinned and it seems easy for him to observe a fast for two or three days. Without any struggle on the part of his selfish soul,

---

182. *Ma'siyat az murid dar wujud amad* literally means "sin has come into existence through a disciple." This kind of expression is also common in Hindi and Urdu. A difference in perspective is reflected in the translation.

he observes a fast for two or three days. His guide notices that this seems effortless for him and involves no struggle with his selfish soul. He then takes note of his love for possessions. Any expiation involving possessions is difficult for him. This is what his guide imposes. This is the real reason for disclosing one's sins to one's spiritual guide. It ensures that expiation takes place together with the subjection of one's selfish soul. That is what was enjoined." At this point the Revered Master recited this couplet:

> Insight more luminous than the sun's light is needed
> To discern the inner reality of each possessed one.

A discussion arose about the excellence of the Apostle's community. The Helpless One inquired if there was a great difference between the Apostle's community and other communities. The Revered Master replied: "Just as the Messenger of this community is the most excellent of all the messengers, in the same way, this community is more excellent than those of the other messengers." He then recited this verse: "You are the best community" (Q3:110). He continued: "The Messenger said: 'How could that community be destroyed of which I am the leader and Jesus the precursor?' In other words, 'I draw them from the front and Jesus keeps them moving from behind. I am their head and Jesus is their heel.'"[183]

A discussion arose about the wives of the Apostle. Maulana Najmuddin the poet said: "The Apostle had nine wives. Were there any others as well?" The Revered Master replied: "These nine wives are mentioned in books. No more than these have come to my notice." He again inquired: "I've seen it somewhere written that there were six more wives in addition to the nine, but the Apostle divorced them before consummating their marriages." The Revered Master replied: "It would have been unlikely, because he had been forbidden to seek more.[184] They would have been divorced wives of the Apostle. Traditions concerning them would certainly be rare." Qazi Sadruddin inquired: "Would they be forbidden to others simply after a marriage was contracted, or would its consummation also be

---

183. The original quotation is in Arabic: *wa Isa sabiquha*. Maneri then gives a translation which is an adapted interpretation completely unfamiliar to the present writer. There can be no question of doubting the temporal precedence of Jesus—as the Arabic indicates—but the role attributed to Jesus is most unusual.

184. Q33:52.

required?" He replied: "Marriage alone was sufficient, because 'his wives are their mothers' (Q33:6)[185] is unconditional. Clearly divorce after marriage alone makes them forbidden to others." Afterwards he related this story: "I have read in the commentary of Imam Za-hid that one of the nine wives was advanced in years. The Apostle wanted to divorce her. She found out about this and came to the Apostle and said: 'O Apostle of God, I have given what is due to me to my sister, A'isha. Don't cast me out from among your wives! In this way I won't be deprived of the honour of being one of your wives, and this honour would be mine in this world and in the next.' The Apostle did as requested. He did not divorce her."

A discussion arose about the praiseworthy deeds of A'isha, the mother of the believers. The Revered Master said: "She is known as the community's expert in the Law. Half of the Law originates from her,[186] for the Apostle said: 'Accept half your religion from this ruddy-complexioned one!'"[187] Afterwards he added: "After the death of the Apostle there was a difference of opinion among the companions concerning an unconsummated sexual approach,[188] namely, whether a full bath was needed or not. Abu Bakr the Righteous and the commander of the faithful, Umar, as well as all the leading companions, were present. They agreed among themselves to compose a query about this matter and request an answer from the mother of the faithful. This is what they did. They wrote their query and took it to A'isha, the mother of the faithful. In reply she wrote an official opinion which stated that a full bath was necessary. She immediately recited a tradition of the Apostle in this regard." When the Revered Master reached these words he added: "Abu Bakr the Righteous and the leading companions were present. Even though they were present, a disagreement had arisen among the companions. When the ruling in favour of a full bath was written and sent to them, the commander of the faithful, Umar, said: 'If anyone after this says that a full bath is not needed, I'll whip him!'"

185. Any normal Muslim woman is legally free to marry again after the death of her husband, or after being divorced. The sole exception to this was the wives of the Apostle, Q33:53.

186. The reference is to the large number of traditions which originate from A'isha. The figure of 1,210 is sometimes given, but Bukhari and Muslim cite only some 300 traditions.

187. The reference is to A'isha, known for her beauty.

188. *Iksal.*

Qazi Badruddin Zafarabadi entered the distinguished assembly. He was disgusted with someone. At this juncture the Revered Master asked him what he was upset about. He began by saying: "I had gone to him and said such and such to him. He replied at length in such and such a fashion." These words gave the Revered Master much pleasure. He turned aside and repeated them several times to himself. He then turned his blessed gaze towards Qazi Badruddin and said: "These words remind me of a story concerning the mother of the faithful, A'isha. It is quite well known. The point is that when the mother of the faithful, A'isha, was suspected of impropriety,[189] one of the companions of the Apostle, when he heard the allegation, was extremely upset. He came home. The wives of the companions used to be waiting for their husbands to return from the honoured assembly of the Apostle. They would question them about what had happened and what instructions the Apostle had issued. The companions would then relate to their wives all that had taken place. Well then, when that companion came home, his wife saw that her husband was upset and ran towards him and exclaimed: 'What's the matter? Has something terrible happened?' Her husband related to her what had happened. She exclaimed: 'Why are you all upset by this? If someone were to make a similar accusation against me, your wife, and were to tell it to your face, would you believe him or not?' 'No,' he replied. She said to him: 'Just as you wouldn't believe it with regard to me, then don't believe it at all with regard to the mother of the faithful, A'isha! Know for certain that it is a lie, for she is more pure than I am.' Her husband replied: 'Now I don't believe it and consider the allegation to be false.'" At this point the Revered Master recited this couplet:

Whether I see the face of my friend or not,
The sun dips beneath the horizon each night.

A discussion arose about the holy tomb of the Apostle. The Revered Master said: "In the beginning there were no four walls or dome enclosing the tomb of the Apostle. After Arabs began coming on

189. The incident in question refers to the time A'isha was accidentally left behind in the desert and a young man found her and brought her to the camp. This occasioned the suspicion of sexual misconduct.

pilgrimage[190] and flinging themselves on top of the blessed tomb, weeping and wailing, as well as performing similar unseemly actions, some of the inhabitants of Medina objected that this was not the proper way to behave. How could such unseemly behaviour be tolerated? 'Why don't we build an enclosure around the tomb to prevent such behaviour? People could pay their respects from a distance.' An enclosure was built. The height of the four walls was such that the blessed grave was visible to anyone standing outside. People paid their respects from outside the enclosure. In spite of this some people, out of ignorance and arrogance, would jump over the wall and enter the enclosure and, as previously, would fling themselves upon the blessed tomb of the Apostle. After some time Bibi Zubaida, the wife of Harun Rashid,[191] had a dome erected. She left an opening at the top of the dome. Later on, the Caliph of the period came on pilgrimage. He said: 'If it is possible, I'll go inside the dome to see the blessed tomb for myself and acquire many blessings.' No matter how much people tried to dissuade him, he ignored them. He climbed up to the dome; made his way inside through the opening in the dome; and came down inside it. After getting inside his eyes were dazzled by the light of the pure tomb of the Apostle. He paid his respects and came outside. He had the opening in the dome covered up."

Qazi Sadruddin inquired: "Is there any other companion buried in the pure enclosure of the Apostle?" The Revered Master replied: "Two companions are buried inside the enclosure, a little apart from his tomb. One is the commander of the faithful, Abu Bakr the Righteous, and the other is the commander of the faithful, Umar Khattab. Outside the enclosure a written sign indicates which is the blessed tomb of the Apostle and which are the tombs of the two companions. Thus all those who come on pilgrimage can stand in front of what is written and pay their respects to the Apostle and his two companions."

Afterwards the Revered Master narrated this story: "There was a holy man who helped keep the enclosure clean. The idea occurred to him that it would be his great good fortune to be buried in front of the enclosure after he died. His fellow attendants agreed

---

190. The term used is *ziyarat*, which indicates visiting the tomb of a holy person. The pilgrimage proper (*hajj*) is to the Ka'ba in Mecca.

191. Harun Rashid was the Caliph from 786 till 809.

to carry out his wish. When he died he was buried in front of the
enclosure. He had made a will which stipulated that, if he were
to be buried in front of the enclosure, a plaque should be erected
which read: 'Their fourth 'their dog lay at the entrance with fore-
paws outstretched' (Q18:18).'" The question about reciting two cycles of prayer for the pure soul of the Apostle arose. Qazi Badruddin Zafarabadi said: "If someone asks why the prayer should be
said twice, for the Apostle stands in no need of a double amount of
merit, what answer should be given?" The Revered Master replied:
"Foolish people speak like this, not good people! Even though the
wealth and station of the Apostle are perfect, and of this there is
no doubt at all, nevertheless, the mercy and blessings of *God* are
limitless. No matter how many blessings and wealth a person acquires, he always needs more. From the point of view that the mercy and blessings of that Threshold are limitless, there is always a
need for more, and it is obligatory to say 'God bless Muhammad!'
This means, 'God be merciful to Muhammad!' If there was no need
to seek mercy and the bestowal of blessings, there would be no
such obligation on the community to do so."

Zakaria Gharib[192] inquired: "Where does the saying come from
that there is a flower which people praise?"[193] The Revered Master
replied: "I have not come across this in any book, yet it is a common
saying. Nevertheless, there are reliable stories in favour of seeking
blessings." In this connection he related this story about when Khwaja Muzaffar Dariya was in the company of Khwaja Khizr: "When
Khwaja Khizr was sailing across the sea and Khwaja Muzaffar was
with him, they reached an island where they found a rose.[194] Khwaja Khizr plucked it; pronounced a blessing; and placed it over each
of his eyes. Afterwards he said to Khwaja Muzaffar Dariya: 'Make
it your practice whenever you see a rose to pronounce a blessing
and rub it on your eyes.'" The Revered Master explained: "Thus it
was that, on the night of the ascension of the Apostle, when the
Apostle was borne aloft, he went to a place where, by means of his

192. The original meaning of *gharib* was 'stranger.' In the Indian context
it took on the meaning of 'poor.'

193. The Persian has a negative statement: *bar na durud namiguyand*.
The negative *na* could be a scribal error, for the context suggests the
given translation.

194. *Gul* could mean a rose or a flower. The former seems more
appropriate in the context.

---

blessed perspiration, he produced a rose. Thus it is that, whenever someone sees a rose, the story comes to mind about how it was produced by the perspiration of the Apostle. Its recital is a reminder of the Apostle and, in memory of the Apostle, a blessing is pronounced. This meaning is found in all flowers. Moreover, perfume was very pleasing to the Apostle. Whenever a believer smells any perfume he thinks of the Apostle. When he does so, he pronounces a blessing. In this sense all are equal. What basis is there for any distinction?[195] It is related that Maulana Taqiudddin used to say that roses should not be discarded as they stimulate the utterance of blessings."

Afterwards he added: "This is also the reason why roses are placed in the shrouds of the dead. Since roses come from the blessed perspiration of the Apostle, therefore, as long as they are on the dead person, the fires of hell can do nothing. That is why plenty of roses should be placed inside the shroud. In vessels meant for holding drinking water, there should be some rose petals. This perfume itself is pleasing to the Apostle. The perfume would be like the fragrance emanating from the Apostle who said, 'God made three things pleasing to me: perfume, women, and being lost in prayer.'"

---

195. The reference is to the equality of all perfume-bearing flowers.

CHAPTER 11
PURITY

A discussion arose about purity. The Revered Master said: "In *Ihya' 'ulum ud-din* [The Revival of the Religious Sciences] purity has four stages attributed to it. The first is external purity from impurities and novelties. The second is purity of bodily members from sin and opposition. The third is internal purity from base qualities. The fourth is purity from anything that is not God. This is the territory of the mystics and the stage of the proficient. They call it 'a holy secret' and 'genuine purity.' It is something great. Masters of perception and those proficient in travelling the Sufi Path anxiously shake their heads over this verse, 'None may touch except the purified' (Q56:79.'[196] They know the import of this verse!" Afterwards he added: "There is no access to the Pure One except for the pure." When the Revered Master reached these words he recited this couplet:

> How could I describe Your purity,
> I who am polluted by selling wine?

He explained: "The purity of the body with regard to the heart is just like the purity of clothes with regard to the body. Even if the clothes are pure but the body is not pure, then, according to the external Law, ritual prayer would not be correct. If the body is pure but the heart is not, then, according to the opinion of the followers of the Way, ritual prayer would not be correct." At this juncture the Helpless One said: "This could be the reason for some people to abandon prayer when they find their hearts are not pure and, according to the followers of the Way, without a pure heart, prayer would not be correct. Surely they would abandon prayer?" The Revered Master replied: "In this way some do abandon it here and there, but it has never been said that they should do so. None of the sheikhs has said that a person should abandon prayer in this situation. On the contrary, prayers should be offered, but a person should be aware that, according to the men of the Path, his prayer

---

196. The reference is to the Quran.

is defective. Foolish people abandon prayer. They know nothing beyond the fact that, as far as Sufis are concerned, without purity of heart prayer is defective, so they abandon prayer. They have not progressed enough to know that they should not abandon prayer. Further progress would mean that they would learn that the demands of the Law depend on a person's particular situation. For example, if someone does not have the strength to stand, the Law obliges him to pray while remaining seated. If a person cannot even sit and pray, the Law obliges him to pray by using signs while remaining prone. In this way he should understand that, as long as it remains difficult for him to pray with a pure heart, then he is obliged to ensure that his body is pure when he prays, but not to abandon prayer. Thus, there is no excuse for abandoning prayer. Later on, when purity of heart is obtained, in that situation the obligation arises for him to pray with purity of heart. This is because the cycle of the demands of the Law depends on a person's situation. The mistake occurs when a person tries to travel the Path by himself. If he seeks the protection of an experienced guide, however, this mistake would never occur."

He went through the *Maktubat* [Letters] of Ain ul-Quzat[197] until he reached the words where he divided purity into: 1) external purity pertaining to the body; 2) purity of the senses; 3) purity of the mind from imaginations; and 4) purity of heart. The Helpless One inquired: "Is this modified classification given by Ain ul-Quzat the most accurate one, or some other way?" The Revered Master replied: "This is the correct order. Unless it is done in this way, it is not correct. First attend to purity of the body, and then become engrossed with the heart." The Helpless One again inquired: "Does is take long to purify the body?" The Revered Master replied: "How much time is needed to keep the body pure? When clothes and the body are washed they become pure. Prolongation involves purification of the senses. This demands a great deal of effort. The tongue has to turn aside from lying. The eyes have to be diverted from prohibited things. The ears have to be closed to the sound of such things. The stomach has to refrain from forbidden food. The same applies to all the bodily members. Then purity of the senses is achieved. This process takes time."

---

197. Ain ul-Quzat Hamadani was a Sufi who was executed in Baghdad in 1132. His *Letters* were well known in India.

An esteemed person asked: "If someone begins with the purification of the heart and, since the other members follow the heart, when the heart is purified and sanctified, the other members, following the heart, would of necessity become pure. So the order mentioned is not necessary." The Revered Master replied: "Here two ways of looking at the matter are involved. One says that, since the heart is the place of origin, and the members follow it, if the heart becomes purified the members, of necessity, will follow suit. On the other hand, since each of the five senses is a doorway leading to the heart, everything that is acquired by means of the five senses will inevitably have an impact on the heart, rendering it dark and impure. The net result is that, although the first way is possible yet, on account of the second explanation, it is not correct. The sequence mentioned is needed for orderly progress. Sheikhs normally proceed in this fashion, yet there are some whose custom it is to begin with the heart. They nevertheless acknowledge that it is exceedingly difficult and also very dangerous."

The Helpless One inquired: "If a person sits in a place of retirement then all his senses are cut off as long as he remains there. At such a time should he become preoccupied with his heart, or what should he do?"[198] The Revered Master replied: "But of course at such a time he should be preoccupied with striving for inner purity, but together with external protection. He should be engaged in protecting himself from what is external and become fully occupied in internal matters, i.e. externally in protecting and internally in concentrated striving. This should not take place except under the watchful care of an experienced guide, a person who has travelled this Path and experienced things for himself, a person who has become a proficient physician in treating inner defects and ailments." Once again the Helpless One inquired: "Just as there is an order to be followed in achieving external purity, does the same apply with regard to inner purity, beginning with one thing and moving on to another?" The Revered Master replied: "There is

198. Maneri himself almost certainly performed the *chilla*, a forty-day retreat, in a hujra or prayer-cell close to the tomb in Delhi of his own guide, Najibuddin Firdausi. He also lived in a cave in Rajgir for some time. Even in his *khanqah* in Bihar town there was a cell, used by him and still in existence, about 100 metres from the *khanqah* buildings. A person has to bend low to enter it through a single, narrow entrance. The discussion is about a secluded retreat in such a prayer-cell.

an order applicable to interior matters also. There are reprehensible and praiseworthy qualities. What is reprehensible has to be taken note of. Its extirpation is a person's first task. After this, let him attend to other matters."

At this juncture Maulana Mu'izzuddin inquired: "What comes next after getting rid of reprehensible qualities?" He replied: "Just as a disciple should be purified of reprehensible qualities, so also should he be purified of praiseworthy qualities." The Helpless One inquired: "A person is purified of reprehensible qualities by abandoning them, so how is a person purified of praiseworthy qualities?" The Revered Master replied: "The purification of these qualities is achieved by not paying attention to them. Just as reprehensible qualities constitute a veil for a disciple, so also taking notice of praiseworthy qualities acts as a veil. Hence it is said: 'Scholars are veiled by their knowledge, i.e. by taking note of it; ascetics are veiled by their asceticism, i.e. by making much of it; and devotees are veiled by their devotion, i.e. by paying heed to it.' For a mystic, paying attention to anything except God is polytheism. This applies to them."

The Helpless One again inquired: "Does any order exist with regard to reprehensible qualities which indicates where a person should begin, e.g. with anger, or with hatred, or with some other reprehensible quality?" The Revered Master replied: "Begin with what is easiest and then move on to what is more difficult. If you attempt what is difficult first, you will not succeed." The Helpless One again asked: "How could a novice know the remedy or the method of eradication?" The Revered Master replied: "How could he possibly know unless his guide tells him, or he reads about it in the book of some saintly person? He could read his advice and try to follow it all by himself, but this is not the correct way to go about it. This is because he will not be able to get a correct perspective and grasp of his situation, just as a sick person, all by himself, cannot prescribe the remedy for his sickness. The same applies, without any difference, to someone with a sickness of the soul." The Helpless One continued: "Wherever a guide is available for a novice, why should he consult books? He is in a position to seek a remedy for every pain and thus act in an appropriate manner." The Revered Master replied: "Wherever there is a guide, he is his book. What need does he have to consult books?"

A discussion about perfect purity arose. Someone said that he had read somewhere that a servant could not attain perfect purity. The Revered Master commented: "Perfect purity here refers to absolute purity, meaning utterly without fault and completely pure, and that refers to *God*—exalted be His glory! On the other hand, if it is a question of purity, but not of absolute purity, it does not apply. The reason is that a servant, when he emerges from reprehensible qualities to praiseworthy ones, becomes pure as a result. This is because it behoves a disciple, by pursuing the Sufi Path, to emerge from all that is harmful and defective to a state where perfections become possible. Nevertheless, it is not possible to emerge completely from manifestations of the self, which is the source of all faults. No creature has emerged entirely from this. Another fact is that we subsist through Him." He added: "'Our subsistence is through Him and our existence is from Him'[199] are two things from which escape is impossible. On the other hand, people do break free from what is harmful and defective and acquire perfections. It is said of some people, 'I am less than my Lord in things regarding different interpretations, but—and God knows best—these two things are certain: 'Our subsistence is through Him, and our existence is from Him.'"

Afterwards he added: "It was the practice of our predecessors to give themselves over wholly to the purification of their hearts, in whatever way possible. They used to push themselves to the limit. Acquiring external purity was easy for them. They also used to fix the bounds of knowledge. It is related of the commander of the faithful, Umar, who, in spite of his exalted position, performed his ablutions from a pitcher belonging to Christians. He did so, even though it was known that it might not be without a trace of wine, for they consider wine to be pure and lawful, just as water is for us. The noble companions used to pray on the ground, without a prayer rug, walk around bare-footed, and wash themselves perfunctorily after urinating. Their preoccupation with external purity stems from this situation. Sufis are similarly concerned about external purity. Nowadays, however, you will see someone who, in his ignorance, is so preoccupied with talking about external purity that he exceeds the bounds of knowledge. In his ignorance he calls this 'being cautious.' If his clothes become polluted he instantly changes them. With that he thinks he is pure, yet he

---

199. *Qiyamuna bihi wa wujuduna minhu.*

is not at all pure. This is because his inner being is full of envy, hatred, haughtiness, dissimulation and hypocrisy. If he sees anyone going bare-footed he immediately shows his disapproval, even though it is permitted by the Law. On the other hand, there is no sign of disapproval of the envy, hatred, haughtiness, dissimulation and hypocrisy that have corrupted his religion. All this is the result of his paucity of knowledge and his failure to acquire correct behaviour by associating with sincere men and solid scholars—but God knows best!

A discussion arose about performing ablutions and benefiting from doing so. The Revered Master said: "Abu Huraira[200] related that the Messenger said to Bilal just before the morning prayer: 'O Bilal, tell me what is the most acceptable task in Islam that you have performed so that, on the night of ascent, I heard the sound of your clogs ahead of me in heaven?' He replied: 'O Apostle of God, I do not hold any work in Islam as being more acceptable than others, yet every time I become defiled, whether by day or by night, I perform my ablutions and two cycles of prayer.'" When the Revered Master reached these words he commented: "This is why one of the practices of the Sufis is diligence in performing ablutions, for ablutions are weapons in the hands of a believer. When his bodily members are protected by ablutions, one result of this, according to the Law, is that Satan's machinations in his regard are rendered ineffective. Anas Malik[201] related that the Messenger, on his arrival in Medina, when he was eight years of age, said to him: 'My lad, if you can, always be diligent in ablutions. Whoever is diligent in ablutions and dies in this frame of mind will be granted witnessing, i.e. he will die as a martyr.' He should be careful not to waste water while performing his ablutions. He should also remain within the limits of what is prescribed, according to what Abi Ka'b related about the Messenger's having said, 'There is something sa-

---

200. He is known as "The father of the kitten" (Abu Huraira), but his real name is not known. He became a Muslim in the year 629 and, on account of his close association with the Prophet, is the origin of more traditions than any other person. This has led many to doubt his reliability. On the other hand, it is possible that others falsely attributed a number of traditions to him.

201. Anas ibn Malik was a young boy in Medina at the time of the Prophet's arrival in 622. He was also a prolific traditionist and founder of the Malikite School. He died around 711.

tanic associated with ablutions—distractions!' A person should be careful not to waste water. Abu Abdullah Roodbari said: 'Satan always tries to extract his own portion from all the works of men. He has no fear of doing so by getting people to do more than what has been commanded. Experience has taught people that safety for a believer lies in knowing the limits prescribed by the Law, not in going a hair's breadth ahead or behind what was prescribed.'

After a while he continued: "Some people talk while performing their ablutions. They should not do so, for it is forbidden to speak while performing one's ablutions. A person should first be recollected during his ablutions in order to pray in a recollected manner.[202] It is said that a person will be as recollected during prayer as he is during his ablutions. Recollection during ablutions leads to recollection during prayer. It is said: 'Ablution means separation, while prayer means being united: without separation there is no union.' A person should seek to be recollected during ablutions and not be preoccupied with anything else in order to be recollected during prayer. The saying, 'ablutions means separation' means separation from everything else, while 'prayer means being united' points to 'there was a time when I was with God.'"[203] He went on to add: "Nowadays people perform their ablutions while chatting to all and sundry. They pay no attention to what has been explained above. I have been astonished at some of the things I have seen people doing during their ablutions.[204] The way to perform ablutions is to ensure, while pouring water over the hands, that the water is poured over the tips of one's fingers and then to the elbows." The Revered Master then demonstrated how it was done, making use of his own blessed arms, saying: "This is the way to wash. Nowadays I see people pouring water on their elbows and letting it run down to the tips of their fingers. This is forbidden. There are also some who ask others to pour water for them. This should not happen, for it is asking assistance, but if someone spontaneously steps forward with the good intention of being of assistance, it is not forbidden, because of the person's good intention."

---

202. The soundness of this advice is clear to anyone who is serious about regular prayer.

203. The speaker in this tradition is the Prophet.

204. This is one of the rare occasions on which Maneri uses the first person singular, apart from the conventional phrase, "the likes of you and me." He was obviously upset by what he saw.

Several times he said: "Recollection in prayer follows upon being recollected during ablutions."

CHAPTER 12
RITUAL PRAYER
AND ITS CORRECT PROCEDURE[205]

A discussion arose about the two cycles of prayer. The Revered Master said: "*God* Most Exalted knows how many thousands of angels there are in heaven and on earth. Each angel has an assigned form of worship. Some angels bow; some prostrate; and while one praises Him, another glorifies Him. This they have been doing from the moment of their creation. As long as they exist, this will be their perpetual form of worship. In other words, whichever angel is standing will remain standing; those bowing will remain bowing; those reciting the Quran will continue to do so; those sitting will remain seated; those prostrating will remain prostrated; those glorifying God will continue to do so. From the day of their creation until the Day of Resurrection they will continue to display their particular mode of worship. All of these are contained in two cycles of prayer performed by a believer. This is in accordance with what the Apostle wanted. When he was borne aloft on the night of ascent he saw each angel engrossed in a particular form of worship. Seeing each special form of worship of the angels he thought it would be wonderful if the members of his community could do the same. *God* Most Exalted answered his prayer by ordaining all these different forms of worship in two cycles of prayer. Thus anyone who prays in this way with heartfelt devotion could be said to have included all the forms of worship of the angels, and thus to be worshipping the Lord just as the angels did. There is so much honour in two cycles of prayer that its value cannot be estimated."

The Helpless One asked: "If during the recital of 'God is Great' the prayer-leader and the members of the congregation do not

---

205. This chapter contains instructions with regard to various aspects of the daily ritual prayer. It will be particularly meaningful for people who actually pray in this specifically Islamic form of prayer. On the other hand, the whole tone of meticulous respect due to God at the time of prayer is both instructive and inspiring for people who use other forms of prayer.

pray in a synchronized manner, what should be done?" The Revered Master replied: "This lack of synchronization occurs either at the first recital of "God is Great' or during subsequent recitals. With regard to the first recitation, the follower does not go ahead and there should not be any delay either. A person becomes a follower. With regard to subsequent recitations, it should not happen. There should be no racing ahead or lagging behind during the recitation. The follower should synchronize all his actions with those of the leader for the sake of uniformity. When the leader says, 'God is Great,' the members of the congregation should repeat it immediately. For the sake of uniformity, there should be no conflict at all with the prayer-leader."

Sheikh Mu'izzuddin inquired: "If the prayer-leader raises his head after bowing and prostrating and a follower is still engaged in reciting the praises that accompany these actions, what should he do? Should he synchronize his actions with those of the leader, or complete his prayers?" The Revered master replied: "In such a situation he should synchronize his actions with those of the leader, for that is necessary while reciting praises and bowing and prostrating. On the contrary, when seated and reciting 'There is no god but God: Muhammad is the Apostle of God,' if the leader rises and the follower has not finished his recital, in this situation he should complete his prayer. Just as it is necessary to follow the leader, so too is it necessary to profess one's faith in God and His Apostle, as is found in many traditions. In this way both are necessary."

Sheikh Karimuddin inquired: "Should a person spend a lot of time ensuring his intention is sincere?" The Revered Master replied: "Several things are involved in a sincere intention. A person is required to be aware that he is about to perform a particular prayer. This much is required for validity. Anything beyond that is additional. A person who is caught in a hurry should at least know that this is the noon prayer or the afternoon prayer." Afterwards he said to those present in the assembly: "These prayers which you perform are the products of words, not deeds. First of all, your words should be correct, then your deeds will be correct. There are some things which are omitted in prayer and, according to some scholars, render it defective. The correct procedure in prayer is like this. While a person is in the bowing position, after reciting 'I extol the holiness of my Lord, the Great,' while still bowed down he should begin to recite 'God helps him who praises Him,' and complete it when he stands upright. While standing upright he should compose his whole body and become tranquil. After reciting 'God hears him who praises Him,' while still standing, he should begin with the first syllable of *Allah* and hold it for some time, and then complete *akbar* as he prostrates.[206] While engaged in prostrating, after reciting 'I extol the holiness of my Lord, the most High,' in the same position a person continues with the first syllable of *Allah* until he has finished with that posture. His posture should be such that his whole body is tranquil. When he proceeds to the second prostration he again begins with *Allah* and completes his praise in the same position. While still in it, after reciting 'I extol the holiness of my Lord, the most High,' he again begins with the drawn-out first syllable of *Allah* and completes *akbar* as he stands up. The other cycles of prayer should be performed in this same manner so that, during prayer, there should not be any time during which the person is not remembering God. If any of this is omitted and a person does not recite 'God is Great' at the right time, the prayer would be defective.

Imam Zafar says that, if 'God is Great' is not recited at the proper time, the prayer becomes defective. Imam Yusuf says that it is a duty to ensure that bodily movements are performed correctly and scholars are in agreement about this. Thus it is necessary that all the conditions of prayer and correct bodily movements be properly observed so that no one can say that the prayer is defective and, according to the general consensus, beyond what one is obliged to do. This is because, if a person has an argument for something and, on the Day of Resurrection, someone speaks out in its favour, God Most Exalted would be his proof. The opinion of some others says nothing about what is permitted. This is the basis for accepting it."

Sheikh Mu'izzuddin at this stage proposed a difficulty: "What everyone is obliged to do depends upon the school he belongs to. What hold can the opinion of anyone else, which is not obligatory for him, have on him?" The Revered Master replied: "The governing principle of a school is that, with regard to anything that is

---

206. The phrase is, *Allahu akbar,* which means "God is Great." The word 'great' is spelt stylistically with a capital 'G' in order to indicate that the Arabic adjective is in the elative degree, meaning 'greater' or 'greatest' according to the context. The word in the positive degree for 'great' is *kabir.*

disputed by scholars, it is considered better to perform such an action rather than abandon it. If there is something which it is not necessary to abandon according to one's school, yet doing so, on the basis of a majority opinion and as an act of prudence, is a good thing. This forms a basis for setting something aside."

Afterwards he added: "What is of prime importance is that there should be no time during prayer when a person is not remembering God. If something is omitted, either by going ahead or delaying in reciting 'God is Great,' then that period would pass without the remembrance of God. There are many innovations in prayer. A person should be very careful about such things. It is necessary to recite each prayer at its allotted time. For example, 'I extol the holiness of my Lord, the Great' should be completed while bowing, and 'I extol the holiness of my Lord, the most High' while prostrating. If part of it is recited after the head is raised, then this would be an innovation, because it has been recited outside its proper place. Although this innovation would not vitiate the prayer, nevertheless, in this matter one should imitate the correct example given by men of repute. It is said of prayer that, even if ten aspects are correct and one is faulty, that one aspect leads to faulty prayer. Be careful!"

The Helpless One inquired: "In *Targhib us-Salat* [Evoking the Desire to Pray][207] it is mentioned that, if in prayer, nine aspects are faulty and one is lawful, the judgement is in favour of what is lawful. What should be said about this saying?" The Revered Master replied: "This concerns someone else. If a believer has performed his prayer in such a way that he does not notice anything defective about it but sees it as lawful, yet is only minimally lawful, then in this situation 'having a good opinion of a Muslim' comes into play and inclines a person towards that aspect. I have been speaking about a person with regard to himself." Afterwards he added: "Nowadays people justify themselves by words rather than by deeds. A person should justify himself by his deeds. The first place they should do so is in prayer. There are some disciples who are so completely correct in what they do that they don't feel the need for any further study."

Again the Helpless One inquired: "If a prayer leader is such that

---

207. *Targhib us-salat* deals with ritual prayer, ablutions and purification. It was written, in Persian, by Muhammad bin Ahmad uz- Zahid.

he hastens from bowing to prostrating, and from prostrating to standing in such a way that it is not possible to complete the intervening movements, in such a situation, how can a follower keep up with the leader? Also, how can the correct movements, conditions and procedures be observed?" The Revered Master replied: "You should not perform your prayers behind such a leader, because his recitation is defective. On account of his defect, his prayer is defective. If you perform your prayer behind such a man, then you will have to repeat it. For the sake of the dignity of the congregation, let people imitate him only if no other leader is available."

The Helpless One continued: "If the leader in the nearby mosque is such that he does not observe the required movements and conditions, while there is another mosque some distance away where the leader performs his office properly, and is pious and firm in his religion, in such a situation what should a person do?" The Revered Master replied: "In this situation he should go to that mosque unless he is a person whose departure would mean that the quorum required for the congregation in his neighbourhood mosque would suffer. In this situation he should not go." Afterwards he added: "Nowadays prayer leaders perform their duties for a fixed stipend. Acting as prayer leader for a fixed stipend is not proper.[208] Scholars themselves have done nothing about this or about praying in the prescribed manner. They do not adhere to the practice of holy men." Several times the Revered Master exclaimed with great feeling: "Begin by making yourself holy by what you do, and the first thing you have to do is pray correctly![209] Nowadays nobody can pray with full observance of the conditions of prayer, unless God wants it. For example, it is clearly written in books that the hands should not be placed on the ground when people are getting up, but foolish people do so, even though it is forbidden. In such a situation what can be said about reciting 'God is Great,' standing, sitting or performing actions correctly?"

Once again the Helpless One put a question: "If after the first

---

208. *Makruh* is the technical term for something which is disapproved of but not invalid.

209. This is one of the rare occasions in the source material when Maneri's normally serene tone becomes charged with emotion. His emphasis on prayer is because of the influence attentiveness in prayer exerts on a believer's other activities.

two cycles of prayer the blessing and prayer of petition[210] are recited, what should be done?" The Revered Master replied: "If a
person does so intentionally, it would be lawful, yet defective. If it
is done inadvertently, then a compensatory prostration is necessary. This is when a person would recite the blessing, namely, 'God
bless Muhammad and the descendants of Muhammad!' And if a
person says, 'God bless' but does not add 'Muhammad,' and then
remembers that he is seated for the first time,[211] in such a situation a compensatory prostration is not required. And if a person
recites the prayer of petition, then it would be better to perform a
compensatory prostration."

Maulana Lutfuddin inquired: "How did the Apostle handle
inadvertency in prayer? And a holy man expressed this desire:
'Would that the inadvertence in question were mine!' Who was
the holy man who expressed this desire?" The Revered Master replied: "For him it was a matter of compensating something lower
by something more exalted. For us it is a question of compensating
something more exalted by something lower. It is related that, on
the night of ascent, when the Apostle reached two bows' length,[212]
he was delighted with the stage he had attained. He expressed the
desire to remain there and not return to the world. An order came:
'O Muhammad, We have sent you to invite the people so that, by
means of you, We might grant them salvation. We are able to bestow this stage upon you in that very place. However, you are not
able to invite them from this place. After you return to the world,
whenever the desire of experiencing this stage occurs, enter into
prayer so that We may bestow this stage upon you there.' Whenever the Apostle began his prayer, he would see and experience that
stage, which is more exalted than prayer. As he was caught up in
contemplating this stage while at prayer, his attention lapsed. This
is why the Apostle used to say, 'Show me the way, O Bilal!' With
regard to who had desired that inadvertence, there is a difference
of opinion. Some say it was Abu Bakr the Righteous, while others say it was Khwaja Junaid. Having this desire is in conflict with
right order, for included in that desire is the stage of relationship

210. These should be recited when all the cycles of prayer have been
completed.

211. This means after having performed only two cycles of prayer, with
more to follow.

212. This expression indicates very close proximity to God.

to prophethood. That involves setting aside right order. Attributing this to Khwaja Junaid is preferable to doing so to the eminent Truthful One."[213]

Qazi Ashrafuddin inquired: "Nowadays people pray in mosques but they are unable to do so according to the demands and conditions of prayer. As for the prayer leaders of our day, we know what they are like! Would it be all right for people to pray at home with their friends?" The Revered Master replied: "If prayer conducted at home in this fashion is common, namely, if both important people and ordinary people are present,[214] then it would be better to pray in such a place, since no loss of the excellence of congregational prayer would occur. If these prayers are not open to all, however, as I have explained, then some people do not agree that the merit of congregational prayer is obtained. If someone wants to obtain the merit of congregational prayer he should do as I have said, namely, he should perform his prayers according to the common opinion in order to obtain the merit of congregational prayer. In order to make sure, he should repeat his prayer. Moreover, there are many promises attached to going to a mosque in order to pray."

Afterwards he added: "Nowadays people acquire knowledge but nothing comes of it. The saying is correct: 'They acquire knowledge, but what use is it put to? What profit is it to anyone?' Some people come and say: 'Why is a sense of presence not experienced during prayer?'[215] The answer is: 'Because the various prayers are not recited at the proper place, and standing and sitting are omitted, so how could it be experienced?'" At this point he added these words about a sense of presence: "It is said that prayer should be on a prayer-carpet, for a sense of presence would be experienced to the degree that is mentioned. Do you know what is said about what *God* Most Exalted said? 'Do not try to pray when you are drunk until you know what you are saying' (Q4:43). In other words, do not come for prayer while you are intoxicated until you are ca-

---

213. Because Abu Bakr has a higher rank than Junaid it is better to attribute a fault—a desire for the stage of prophethood—to the latter.

214. *Khass o 'am.* Just as anyone can pray in a mosque, where the worshippers are all equal before God, so too this condition should apply in a private house.

215. *Huzur dar salat chun na hasil ayad?* A little ahead the expression is expanded to *huzur-i dil.* The proffered translation takes this into consideration.

pable of understanding what you are saying. How can anyone pray if he does not know what he is saying? *God* Most Exalted has forbidden that! Whatever a person says while intoxicated is not said with an attentive heart. The same comment applies to any thoughtless utterance. It is equivalent to being intoxicated. In *Ghar'ib-i Tafsir* [Ambiguous Interpretations] it is said of this verse uttered by God Most Exalted: 'Remove your sandals, for you are in the sacred valley of Tuwa' (Q20:12). 'Your sandals' refers to your wife and sheep. In other words, thoughts about wife and sheep should be expelled from your heart. Thinking about anything except God would be tantamount to being intoxicated during prayer. This is why it is said that it is like the intoxication produced by drinking wine, as it indicates preoccupation with the world. Concerning intoxication we have, 'Don't pray when you are drunk' (Q4:43)." At this juncture the Revered Master recited the following couplet:

> Floods and winds rage and you are heedless of your house:
> Sometimes you lie drunk therein, and sometimes asleep.

Thereupon Sheikh Mu'izzuddin recited these two couplets:

> You are at prayer but your heart is elsewhere:
> Distractions are like guests you are entertaining.
> Such a situation should be cause for concern,
> Yet shamelessly you go on reciting prayers.

The Revered Master said: "In *Kashf ul-Mahjub* [Revealing What Lies Hidden],[216] in the chapter devoted to the benefits of being present for the first recital of 'God is Great,' it is mentioned that some people say that an effort should be made to be present by the time the prayer leader begins to recite the introductory chapter of the Quran. Others say a person should be present during its recital, but a holy man has said; 'According to me, being present for 'God is Great' means that I see that a person who misses being present for it experiences grief and regret. This would indicate being present, even though ostensibly he has missed the leader's recital of 'God is Great.' If this is not experienced, a person would not really be present for 'God is Great.'"

---

216. Hujwiri's *Kashf ul-Mahjub* set the trend of producing works of Sufism in Persian. It has been translated by Nicholson. Hujwiri died in Lahore c. 1071.

In connection with this meaning the Revered Master said: "Khwaja Hasan Basri was sleeping at the time for morning prayer. Satan came and woke him up, saying: 'Get up and pray!' Khwaja Hasan Basri replied: 'O Accursed One, your work is the very opposite of this!' He replied: 'True, but I was afraid that, if you kept on sleeping and missed out on the first recital of 'God is Great' then, when you got up, you would express much grief and regret. As a result, the merit of being present a thousand times for this initial recital of 'God is Great' would be inscribed in your account book. It would be just like the time when you were absent for the first recital and you expressed so much grief, regret, pain and sorrow, that the merit of being present a thousand times was ascribed in your account book. I was afraid you might be absent today and the same story would be repeated. This is why I woke you up. The merit of being present on only one occasion will be inscribed.' It is also related that the custom of our ancestors with regard to failing to be present for the first recital of 'God is Great' was to mourn for three days. From this you can realize what Islam used to be, and what has become of it today!"

At this point, the Revered Master had this to say: "We are entangled in the deceits of Satan and are not even aware of it, and no trace of Islam remains!" He then recited the following:

> Shops abound with fraud and deceit:
> The gleefully snatching hand is the Devil.
> No bribe has produced light from religion:
> People have sold themselves to the Devil.

He added: "A hint about this is contained in the words of the Lord of the Law:[217] 'A time will come when men will gather in mosques and pray, but there will not be a single Muslim among them.' This applies to people who pray like us." Afterwards he continued: "The initial 'God is Great' indicates that a person is leaving this world and journeying into another world, even though apparently there is no departure involved. In reality, however, he abandons the world because his aim is to depart from the world of his possessions. Reciting 'God is Great' makes those possessions unlawful. When it is recited, a person has left the world in reality. This is what 'leaving' means. Externally, what lesson can be learnt? The

---

217. *Sahib-i Shari'at* refers to the Prophet Muhammad.

greeting of peace at the end of prayer helps us understand this, because anyone who returns to his own country after being on a journey certainly greets people with 'peace!'"

A discussion arose about habit and worship. The Revered Master said: "Nowadays people pray as a matter of habit. They pray in the same way their parents taught them to when they were children. What they learnt as children is what they continue to do as adults. Who can escape from the clutches of habit? Doing so is a great work. A worshipper is a person who has emerged from habit. In many places in the writings of Ain ul-Quzat one comes across these words: 'The worship of habit is idol-worship.'"

A discussion arose about performing supererogatory prayers at the wrong time.[218] Nasrullah, the son of Maulana Alam, inquired: "Has anything been recorded about performing supererogatory prayers at the forbidden time?"[219] The Revered Master replied: "There are some accounts of disapproval, as described in the books of scholars of the Law, but Sufis perform them at any time and teach this to their disciples. They consider this to be perfectly all right." He told a story about this: "The disciples of Sheikh Ruknuddin of Multan used to perform two cycles of supererogatory prayer before the obligatory dawn prayer. Once a scholar came to the mosque. He saw that the disciples had come before the obligatory payer and had performed supererogatory prayers. One day that scholar attended the assembly of Sheikh Ruknuddin when his disciples were also present. The scholar addressed the Sheikh thus: 'Your disciples perform supererogatory prayers before the obligatory dawn prayers. This is forbidden, and you are unaware of it.' Sheikh Ruknuddin replied: 'Not at all! I myself do the same. Don't say it is not allowed!'" He related another story: "It is likewise narrated that, in the time of Sheikh Baha'uddin Zakariya,[220] there was a disciple who was rather ignorant. He was instructed to perform

---

218. The word *makruh* means 'disapproved of, but not invalidated by, according to the Law.'

219. It is forbidden to perform the obligatory prayers at the actual time of sunrise, noon or sunset. These are meant as markers of time. Moreover, the danger of worshipping the sun must be obviated. From the examples given, however, this does not seem to be the point at issue.

220. Baha'uddin Zakariya (d. ca. 1262) was the leading Suhrawardi Sufi of Multan. This order, in contrast to the Chishtis, believed in associating closely with rulers in order to influence them for the common good.

these prayers. One day he came up to the Sheikh and said: 'Some scholars are annoying me. They ask me to explain the basis for these two cycles of voluntary prayer before the obligatory dawn prayer. What answer should I give them?' The Sheikh replied: 'Tell them that this is the prayer of lovers.'"

Qazi Ashrafuddin asked: "If Friday prayer is missed, yet the required conditions for a congregation are present, as happens nowadays in some places, namely, that there is a delay in the Friday prayer, even to the point of approaching the limit of the stipulated time frame, and only then performing the prayer, in such a situation should the noon prayer be recited or not?" The Revered Master replied: "It is safer to recite the Friday prayer.[221] O brother, who experiences this sadness nowadays? Who goes in order to pray? People go in order not to miss the message of the ruler.[222] If only people knew of someone who experiences this sadness they should speak to him! People experience another sort of sadness, such as stemming from what has befallen them. This is not really the sadness of religion. It doesn't even resemble it.[223] In fact, when I go for Friday prayer I do so with this in mind that real men existed in previous ages who used to go to the mosque each Friday in order to pray. Nowadays only their resemblance remains. Oh that even once I could have their dedication!"

Ahmad Sa'id Baf asked: "Was there any sermon before the time of the Apostle?" The Revered Master replied: "Before the time of our Apostle there was no Friday gathering! Sermons are specific to this community. No previous messenger had established the fast of the month of Ramazan. This is also specific to this community. There are some other things as well that are specific to this community." Qazi Ashrafuddin commented: "At today's congregational prayer the leader incorrectly recited 'and some day We shall cause the earth and the mountains to move away,' instead of 'and some day We shall cause the mountains to move away and you will see the earth exposed' (Q18:47). What should be done about this?" The Revered Master replied: "It is an alteration, but not a serious one. For this reason it should be condoned. Nevertheless, in order to

---

221. This involves two extra cycles after the normal noon prayer.

222. The prayer leader is the person who actually delivers such a message, not the ruler in person.

223. It is one thing to be sad about a personal misfortune, but quite another thing to be sad because God is not honoured as He should be.

prevent scandal, if a person recites the noon prayer there would be no harm in doing so."[224]

Sadruddin, the son of Sheikh Ahmad, was reading an abridged version of *Ihya 'ulum*. He came to the place where the 'sanctified hour' is described. The Revered Master said: "Every Friday there is a particular hour during which whatever a person desires is granted. It is an important time. Some say it refers to the morning prior to the rising of the sun. Some say it refers to the time when the preacher descends from the pulpit until he begins the Friday prayer. Some others say it refers to the period between the afternoon prayer and sunset." The Helpless One inquired: "What is the wisdom of the uncertainty about the particular hour of Friday?" The Revered Master replied: "In the *Rauzat ul-'Ulama* [The Garden of Scholars],[225] concerning the uncertainty about the Night of Power[226] in the whole month of Ramazan, it is stated that the wisdom of this uncertainty lies in the fact that, if the actual night were determined, everyone would celebrate that night only. The other nights would all be neglected. The Master of the Law kept it uncertain so that people would celebrate all the nights of Ramazan in expectation of the arrival of that particular night. Our predecessors, who used to go to the mosque in the early morning and spend the entire day there until sunset, could have done so with this in mind that, for the sake of that particular hour, they occupied themselves in the mosque for the whole day."

The Helpless One inquired: "If during Friday prayer there is a period of time before the sermon begins, how should a worshipper spend that time?" He replied: "With regard to Friday, various prayers have been described, including the recitation of chapters of the Quran, such as *The Cave* [no.18] and *Ta Ha* [no.20], and other than these, whatever takes a person's fancy. He should occupy himself in reciting them. The performance of four cycles of prayer has also been described. During each cycle, after the Opening Chapter of the Quran, he should recite *Unity* [no.112][227] 50 times. This

---

224. As already noted, the noon prayer is shorter than the Friday congregational prayer.

225. This is a less well-known work on Sufism written in Persian.

226. Nowadays this Night of Power, *Lailat ul-Qadr,* is celebrated on 27th Ramazan. It commemorates the initial revelation of the Quran.

227. *Al-Ikhlas* consists of some fifteen words in Arabic. It is a succinct statement of God's incomparable uniqueness.

means that it would have been recited 200 times." Afterwards the Revered Master added: "Many promises are attached to prayers for the Apostle on Thursday night and Friday. Some of them are called 'prayers of benediction'[228] which should be recited eighty times, according to what is said of the Apostle: 'God will forgive the sins of eighty years of anyone who recites a blessing upon me eighty times on Friday.' People inquired: 'O Apostle of God, how should we pray for you?' He replied: 'Say: O God, bless Muhammad Your servant, Your prophet, Your apostle and unlettered prophet!'"

A discussion arose about the excellence of Friday. The Revered Master said: "It is related that 'every Friday the Lord sets free 600,000 from the fire of hell which each one of them had deserved.' Ka'b Ahbar has related that *God* Most Exalted has bestowed a special excellence on some of the things He has created. Thus Mecca was the most excellent of all cities; Ramazan of all the months; and Friday of all the days in the week." Qazi Ashrafuddin asked: "After finishing their prayer, most people perform a prostration. Where does this practice come from?" The Revered Master replied: "After prayer they prostrate because they make prayers of petition. They pray while prostrating. It is voluntary prayer." Again he asked: "There are some people who do not say traditional prayers. They pray in Persian." He replied: "There are also prayers in Persian." Again he asked: "There are some people who bow their heads in prostration and then rise up again, but do not actually pray. What do you have to say about this?" He replied: "If it is said with the intention of giving thanks then, according to the teaching of the companions, it is correct, event though a fixed prayer is not recited. People also say these prayers after the dawn and mid-afternoon prayers. If a person wants to perform a prostration as a form of prayer he should recite a verse of the Quran and then prostrate. His wish will be granted." Again he asked: "What about kissing the place of prostration?" He replied: "I have not seen this mentioned, neither have I heard of it."[229] Afterwards he told this story: "On the Night of Immunity[230] the Apostle came out of his blessed cham-

---

228. *Durud.*

229. This simple statement highlights the fact that Maneri had an extraordinarily retentive memory, as any perusal of his writings will confirm.

230. *Shab-i barat* is the night on which it is believed God ordains events for the coming year. Hence prayers are recited for a favourable decree. It

ber and A'isha, acting on womanly intuition, followed him outside and saw the Apostle had prostrated himself. According to her, the Apostle of God had prostrated like an old, crumbled garment on a heap of cotton. In that position he displayed his weakness and helplessness."

A discussion arose about performing two cycles of prayer after meals. The Revered Master said: "It should be done. These two cycles become a thanksgiving for the meal. Previously thanksgiving after meals used to be associated with words. It was sufficient to say, 'Praise be to God,' because there was no defect in what people did. It is evident that their saying 'Praise be to God' constituted complete prayers. In our days, however, words do not suffice. They have to be joined to actions to render complete praise." Afterwards he added: "How can the performance of these two cycles become easy? If a person performs them he acquires less rectitude, because if he wanted to do so in somebody's house, could the performance of these two cycles be his aim, or could he want to acquire the habit of eating and drinking there? For this reason the meal time should be fixed in such a way that the two cycles are performed afterwards."

A discussion arose about two cycles of prayer in gratitude for performing the ritual ablution and the salutation of the mosque. The Helpless One asked this question: "If the ritual ablution has been completed but a person goes to the mosque without having performed the two cycles in gratitude, should he perform two in salutation of the mosque or in gratitude for the ritual ablution?" The Revered Master replied: "He should greet the mosque, for this is the more important of the two."

Qazi Ashrafuddin inquired: "Some people sit down when they enter the mosque and perform the salutation later on." The Revered Master commented: "A person should salute the mosque on entering it before sitting down. This is because the two cycles of prayer in salutation of the mosque can be compared to an ordinary greeting of peace, and people do not sit down first and then greet people. As soon as they enter, they greet people. Similarly, the salutation of the mosque should be performed immediately on entering it. If a person sits down and later on performs the salutation,

---

is also an occasion to visit the tombs of one's relatives and pray for them. It falls between the 14th and 15th of the month of Sha'ban.

he will not receive its due merit. It would simply be a voluntary act. This is according to what the majority of religious scholars affirm. Some of them, however, say you can first sit and then get up and perform your salutation."

The Revered Master's son[231]—may God increase his knowledge—went through *Siraj ul-'Arifin* [A Lamp for Mystics] until he came to these words: "One day the son of a holy man, a traveller who had seen Damascus and Constantinople,[232] visited the Revered Master, Sheikh Nizamuddin.[233] At that very moment someone came and prostrated, placing his head upon the ground. The traveller raised an objection: 'Prostration should be reserved for God alone!' He spoke a great deal in this vein. Finally, the Sheikh spoke: 'It is quite likely to be lawful, because people used to prostrate as a form of salutation to the reigning monarch. Our forefathers also prostrated as a form of salutation. It is fitting that its usage should continue.'"

At this juncture Qazi Ashrafuddin interjected: "Since this has been abrogated, how could it be lawful?" The Revered Master replied: "It is not necessary from the point of view of abrogation that its legality should not perdure. It could happen that something is abrogated and some sort of legality remains in it. For example, think about fasting on the 10th Muharram or on the brightest days of the moon, the obligatory nature of which has been abrogated, but which nevertheless remain lawful." Again he spoke up: "In *Kanz ul-Masa'il* [A Treasure Trove of Sayings] it is related that any form of prostration, except before God, is infidelity. How can this objection be answered?" The Revered Master replied: "If the person prostrating intends to perform an act of worship, then it would be infidelity. On the other hand, if the intention is simply to salute or greet someone, it should be considered as allowable, as I have said."

---

231. Maneri's son, Zakiuddin, had come along with Maneri's own widowed mother to stay in his *khanqah*. This is the first time he is mentioned in this work. The impression one gets is that he was undoubtedly respected as Maneri's son, but no special treatment was meted out to him.

232. *Sham wa Rum* would normally refer to Syria and the Eastern Roman Empire, or possibly to their capitals. Obviously a traveller would have seen more than the capitals. These are mentioned to highlight his experience as a traveller.

233. Nizamuddin Auliya.

Maulana Nizamuddin, the Revered Master's sister's son,[234] quoted this verse: "He helped his parents to a raised platform and they prostrated before him" (Q12:100) and inquired what exactly was meant. If they prostrated before Joseph, then how could a father prostrate before his son?[235] If the worthy Jacob is involved, then it is clear." The Revered Master replied: "If this reflection refers to the messenger Joseph, then it is because of the established custom that the more eminent person greets the less important one. On the night of ascent the Exalted and Glorious Lord greeted the Messenger. He said, 'Peace be to you, O Prophet!' In their law, prostration was like wishing someone peace in our Law. Hence no necessary conclusion can be drawn from this example."

Qazi Ashrafuddin said: "In a discourse of Sheikh Nizamuddin it is related that a holy man used to leave his home five times a day in order to recite the daily five prayers behind a scholar of the Law. One day the holy man came for the morning prayer. He found the scholar performing the second cycle of prayer. The holy man joined in the prayer and imitated his actions. When the prayer-leader sat to recite the profession of faith, the holy man, before the leader recited the greeting of peace, stood up to perform the first cycle of prayer which he had missed. When the prayer was over the leader turned to him and said: 'Why did you stand up before the leader's greeting of peace? It could have happened that the leader had omitted something and then performed the omitted prostration and you would have missed out on it!' The holy man replied: 'If someone, by an inner illumination, knows that the leader has not omitted anything, it would be all right for him to stand up before the greeting of peace.' The scholar retorted: 'Any light that is not in accordance with the Law is darkness.' After this incident the holy man never returned. It is not known what meaning is contained in his not returning, but what did the scholar mean by saying that 'any light that is not in accordance with the Law is darkness?'"

The Revered Master replied: "That scholar spoke as an externalist, because anyone who has missed out on some part of the

234. As previously mentioned, we do not know the name, or names, of Maneri's sister, or sisters.

235. In *The Holy Qur'an* printed at the King Fahd Holy Qur'an Printing Complex, p.664, footnote 1779-A states: "with the advent of the complete and final revelation prostration before anyone other than Allah is a grave sin strictly prohibited."

prayer stands up after the greeting of peace and completes what he had missed. That holy man, who stood up before the greeting of peace, was externally in contravention of the Law. There is an acceptable interpretation, however, since he knew, by an inner illumination, that the leader had not forgotten anything. That is why he stood up. An ordinary person stands up after the greeting of peace because of his ignorance, for he does not know if the leader has omitted anything or not, whereas the holy man, by an inner illumination, knew the situation. What actually happened, therefore, was in conformity with the Law, although it did not seem to be so. What harm is there in this, except that he never returned after this incident? Perhaps from this it can be gleaned that he saw some kind of denial in the scholar."

Maulana Nasiruddin, the prayer leader of Qazi Safi, was reading an abridgement of *Ihya 'ulum* and came to where it is written that, according to Imam Shafi'i, one should spend some time in special supplication at morning prayer. The Helpless One inquired if this was the practice of sheikhs. The Revered Master replied: "No, they do not, except for the followers of Imam Shafi'i, and some other sheikhs do so as well when something important crops up. They pray like that in order to bear up when experiencing some difficulty. This is why they pray like that in accordance with what Imam Shafi'i has written. That explanation is strengthened by the fact that the Apostle prayed like that in moments of crisis and afterwards abandoned the practice, meaning that he did not do so at other times." The Helpless One continued: "How does it actually work out?" The Revered Master replied: "At morning prayer the special prayer is said when the worshippers stand upright after bowing reverently in the second obligatory cycle of prayer." Again he inquired: "With regard to something sufficiently important, if someone wants to make a special prayer, but is unable to do so in the congregation, may he do so in private?" He replied: "If this is something that applies to everyone as being of common concern, the leader prays thus at morning prayer."

A discussion arose about serving the evening meal at the time for night prayer. If there is plenty of time, could the evening meal be taken? At this point, the Helpless One asked: "If there is plenty of time, and the food has been served, yet it is feared that the worshipper might miss the congregational prayer, in this situation what should a person do?" The Revered Master replied: "He should join the congregational prayer and eat afterwards."

Qazi Ashrafuddin inquired: "If someone prostrates without first purifying himself, while believing that ritual purification is necessary before doing so, yet, for some reason, acts in this way, would it amount to infidelity?" The Revered Master replied: "If a person believes that it is forbidden to prostrate before first purifying oneself, yet if, out of bashfulness or some other reason, a prostration is performed, then the consensus is that it is not an act of infidelity. On the other hand, if the person prostrates while thinking that it is lawful to do so without purifying oneself, in this situation he would become an unbeliever. The reason for this is that it necessarily contains a denial of the text of the Quran.[236] This is because the text of the Quran clearly states that purification is necessary before prostrating. Whenever a person prostrates without being purified the Book[237] necessarily implies infidelity." He further inquired: "Which is the verse which states that purification is necessary before prostrating?" He replied: "The verse which says purification is necessary before ritual prayer, because prostration forms part of ritual prayer. Indeed, it is the outstanding element of prayer. Standing and bowing are found in other contexts. Prostration is special, however, in that it is not used except for *God*."[238] Afterwards he added: "With regard to the words and actions that are described as infidelity, the underlying meaning is that a denial of some verse in the Book is involved, or the denial of something that has come down to us in an uninterrupted succession. It is on this account that such words or actions are necessarily labelled as 'infidelity.'"

The Helpless One inquired: "At the time of the call to prayer, when the muezzin says, 'I bear witness that Muhammad is the Apostle of God,' most people kiss their thumbs and forefingers and place them on their eyes.[239] What is the origin of this practice?" The Revered Master replied: "I have not seen it written anywhere,

---

236. The word is *nass,* meaning 'text'. In this particular usage, the text of the Quran is meant.

237. The word is *kitab,* meaning 'book.' In this instance the Quran is meant.

238. This has to be understood in the context of what Maneri has already said in this chapter.

239. People from the movement centred on Bareilly continue this practice.

nor is it found in the books in my possession, yet it is a common practice, and that is why people do it. Maulana Ziauddin Sunami was both a traditionist and an exegete. One day I was present when he was speaking. A man gave this very question written on a piece of paper to the Maulana. He climbed to the top of the pulpit, sat down and said: 'Such and such a question is written on this piece of paper. I have not seen it written in any book, nor have I found it anywhere, but I can say this much: whoever performs this practice will never go blind.'"[240] Again he inquired: "What was the basis for saying this?" He replied: "On account of the respect shown to the blessed name of the Apostle. Whoever hears the blessed name of the Apostle, kisses his thumbs and forefingers and then rubs them on his eyes, can expect this benefit to accrue to him."

Qazi Ashrafuddin said: "Maulana Qeyamuddin Zafarabadi has written a treatise in which he says that the prayer of anyone who says, 'God listens to the one who praises' without adding the pronoun 'Him,' is defective.[241] How could this be? Not pronouncing the final pronoun does not mean the prayer is defective. How could its omission mean it was corrupted? It is customary to cut off the pronunciation of the pronoun in the accusative case. Hence, how is the prayer defective?" The Revered Master replied: "Saying that the prayer is defective would depend on what you mean by 'listens to.' It should be understood that *God* Most Exalted responds to that praise which is directed specifically to God. By omitting the pronoun, this praise becomes general. Such general praise does not reach God. Hence *God* Most Exalted does not respond to undifferentiated praise. He responds to praise directed specifically to God. By omitting the pronoun this specific praise does not perdure. It becomes like the word 'mankind.' In this particular instance, however, omitting the pronoun is allowed. Hence the prayer does not become defective. This is the assertion of a number of people. Both these points are found in *Targhib us-Salat* [Evoking the Desire to Pray].

The Master's son went through *Sharh-i Ta'arruf* [A Commentary on Seeking Knowledge] until he came to where the qualities of the

---

240. This incident occurred while Maneri was in Delhi. Abdul Haqq, *Akhbar ul-akhyar*, p. 113, says that Nizamuddin Auliya attended Maulana Ziauddin Sunami on his deathbed.

241. The discussion presupposes a knowledge of Arabic grammar and the rules for pronunciation.

Sufi saints are described. There it is written that this might mean that they are called Sufis because they are in the front rank. The Revered Master explained: "Saying that they are in the front rank refers to the three kinds of seekers. Some seek this world; some seek the world to come; and some seek the Lord. The person who seeks the Lord is said to be in the front rank. The majority of the members of this group hold that anyone who seeks this world becomes a servant of the world; and anyone who seeks the world to come becomes its servant; while both this world and the world to come become the servants of anyone who seeks the Lord." Thereupon he recited this couplet:

> This world is the abode of calamities; the next is filled with desire:
> We are liberated from both, belonging to neither this nor that.

The Master's son thumbed through *Siraj ul-'Arifin* [A Lamp for Mystics] until he came to where it was written that a man was standing upside down and reading the Quran. The Revered Master said: "This is called *kachak* [the crown of the head], and among the yogis it is called *kapari*."[242] Afterwards he added: "This does not come all of a sudden. Only slowly, by degrees, does it become easy. They begin by getting used to reciting a single verse. Then, by degrees, they recite two and three verses until they are able to recite many." In order to illustrate this meaning he told this story: "Sheikh Muhammad al-Maliqi related that Sheikh Tamimi also, in this manner, recited the Quran completely each evening."[243] Qazi Sadruddin said: "If the top of the head is on the ground and the feet in the air, if a person does not get support from a wall or a tree, how does he do it?" The Revered Master replied: "The very best form of this penitential exercise is to perform it without any support at all. If a prop is used, it remains a penitential exercise, but of lesser value." In this connection he told this story: "It is related that Khwaja Abu Sa'id Abul-Khair[244] was informed that the Apostle had not

242. Undoubtedly Maneri witnessed yogis in this position during his sojourn in Rajgir. His giving the local name for this practice reinforces this observation.

243. Notice that this is a story Maneri had come across and not something he himself had witnessed.

244. Abu Sa'id Abul-Khair (d.1049) was born and lived in Khurasan. He lived an ascetical life—which included praying while suspended upside down—until he reached forty years of age when he began to live in a more

performed his prayer upside down. This is the example he gave. He came to the edge of a well; tied his legs together with a rope; fixed it firmly to the edge of the well; and then hung upside down in the well and performed his prayer in this fashion."

The lesson for the Master's son proceeded until these words were reached: "He prayed standing on one leg." Qazi Sadruddin remarked that there was no precedent for praying standing on one leg. He said: "This is a mistake. This is what has come down to us. Moreover it is forbidden to incline towards one side while standing in prayer. The correct procedure is to stand equally balanced on both legs. One leg should not be favoured." The Helpless One said: "Does the prayer-leader say 'Amen' after 'not those who have gone astray?'"[245] The Revered Master replied: "He says it, but in a low voice." He asked the Helpless One: "Do you remain ready for prayer at all times just as you do after your ablutions?" He replied: "Yes, this is my normal state." He then exclaimed: "Praise be to God!" Again he inquired: "After the ablution, do you perform two cycles of prayer in gratitude for the ablution?" He replied: "Yes, this is my custom." Thereupon he again exclaimed: "Thanks be to God!" The next question was: "Do you observe the fast that is customary during the days of the full moon?" He replied: "I don't observe it." He then told him: "Do so after this, because it curbs the selfish soul." Afterwards he added: "One of the practices of the sheikhs is this: although they remain ritually pure, nevertheless, before any obligatory religious duty, they renew their ablution. Hence there should be a fresh ablution before each obligatory duty."

A discussion arose about the place of prayer. Maulana Nizamuddin, the name of a spiritual guide in the mosque of the late Maulana Ruknuddin, was present. The Revered Master said: "Once this man had gone to visit Maulana Taqiuddin—the mercy of God be on him! He was engaged in a forty-day retreat at the time. It so happened that when he came to this man he placed his foot inside his prayer-cell. By chance the foot of Maulana Taqiuddin landed on the prayer mat on which he performed his prostrations. The Maulana let out a cry and began to express regret and grief. This

---

relaxed manner. He formulated ten rules for his disciples. These became a framework for the rules drawn up by later founders of Sufi orders.

245. These are the final words of the opening chapter of the Quran. It is recited during ritual prayer.

spiritual guide inquired: 'Why are you so agitated?' The Maulana replied: 'My foot landed on the prayer mat where you perform your prostrations. That is why I cried out, for it is not proper to place your foot on the spot where people perform their prostrations.'" At this point someone asked: "Was Maulana Taqiuddin a spiritual guide?" The Revered Master replied: "A number of people say that he was not, but some say that they had heard the Maulana say: 'I have the desire to go wandering with a dervish,' but this has not been verified. God, however, knows the facts of the matter."

CHAPTER 13
FASTING

The Helpless One said: "There is a tradition which says: 'Fasting is the gateway to all forms of worship.' In what sense is this so?" The Revered Master replied: "This is because what prevents a person from worshipping is his selfish soul and sensuality. Fasting is the form of worship which conquers the selfish soul and keeps sensuality in check. Since the obstacle to entering into worship has been removed through fasting, assuredly it has opened the way to worship. In this sense the Messenger said: 'Fasting is the gateway to all forms of worship.' Holy men have said: 'There are a thousand members in the selfish soul of a human being. Because of their wicked nature, all are under the sway of Satan. They all belong to him. Whenever a person ensures that his stomach remains hungry and keeps a firm grip on his gullet, he brings his selfish soul to heel and all those members wither away. They are consumed in the fire of hunger. They no longer belong to Satan. He flees from even the shadow of such a person. On the other hand, whenever a person fills his belly and grants free entrance to his gullet, he then becomes embroiled in sensual pleasures and carnal desires. Satan becomes the lord and master of all those members.' Considered in this light, fasting is certainly the gateway to all forms of worship. It is related that Luqman Hakim said to his son: 'My son, if the stomach is filled with food, you will be troubled by sleepiness; wisdom will be silenced; and your bodily members won't make any effort to engage in worship.' Nevertheless, holy men have forbidden their disciples to fast for more than four consecutive days."

Sheikh Mu'izzuddin said: "It is forbidden to join another fast to that of Ramazan and, with regard to it, the Apostle is especially privileged. If anyone else observes it, however, how would you view that?" The Revered Master replied: "If someone else observes it in order to control his selfish soul, it would be lawful. The prohibition of extending the fast, as found in the books of the sheikhs, is explained as stemming from compassion. It is meant to help us, not be a burden on us." Again he inquired: "If it can also be lawful for others, what is the point of calling it special?" He replied:

"The messengers themselves undertake whatever they enjoin upon others. If they undertake something, however, which they do not enjoin upon others, and make it their practice, and consider it to be necessary according to their spiritual state, then it applies especially to them. Such practices can be of two kinds. One is something they themselves do, but which would be dangerous for anyone else, such as wanting to keep more than four wives. There are some other things that are similarly special. The second kind are practices they themselves engage in yet, because it would be very difficult and troublesome for others to follow them, out of compassion they do not enjoin them on the community. If somebody else performs this kind of exercise, however, it would be allowable. Extending the fast of Ramazan is very troublesome. That is why the Apostle said: 'I am not like one of you. I pass the night with my Lord. He gives me food and drink.' This provides another reason for the prohibition based on compassion by drawing our attention to 'God Most Exalted gives me food and drink.' In other words, 'You are not provided with this, and so cannot bear it.' Thus it is clear that the prohibition springs from compassion, not from 'upon us.' Moreover, by evening the Apostle got rid of whatever he had received in the morning, but out of compassion and considering their weak state, he did not enjoin this on his community. If anyone else observes this practice, however, it would be allowable."

Afterwards he added: "The Sufi Path is also of this special kind. This is why the Sufis have embraced these practices. This is also what distinguishes the Sufi Path from the Law, even though their origin is the same." Later on, he commented: "I have written an explanation of this in a letter.[246] For further details it should be consulted."

This led to a discussion about the forty-day fast of that eminent leader, Moses. "It is related that it did not involve refraining from eating from dawn till sunset and then eating but, on the contrary, it meant passing forty days without eating anything. It has been related that some holy men tried to defer eating from one evening

---

246. The letter in question could be Letter 25, *The Law and the Way*, or possibly Letter 33, *Fasting*, in the collection of *The Hundred Letters*. As these letters were sent in the year 747 A.H. (24-4-1346 to 12-4-1347), it was probably written in the second half of 1346. This is an important clue regarding the chronology of *Ma'din ul-Ma'ani*.

right through till the following evening and, by degrees, managed to pass seven days without eating; then ten; then fifteen; until they finally could do it for forty days." Khwaja Suhail bin Abdullah put a question in this connection: "How could a person who has eaten only once in forty days endure his pangs of hunger?" He replied: "An interior light overcomes his pangs of hunger. The Sheikh of Sheikhs[247] in *'Awarif* states: 'I put this question to a number of pious men. By way of explanation they replied that it was an indication that anyone who attains joy in the Lord experiences his pangs of hunger being subsumed by that joy. This is well known to people.' The respected sheikh, in his *'Awarif*, also said: 'The most extreme example that I have encountered concerned a man I had been trying to meet but had not laid eyes on. He was living in a placed called Bahr. He was known as the Caliph of Ascetics.[248] He used to eat one peanut each month. I have not heard about anyone else in this community who had attained this degree of abstention. He began by reducing his intake of food to such a degree that he became emaciated. When his renunciation reached this measure the result was that he had reached this state. In this sense all are powerful, for upright people as well as frauds are included. Upright people act by virtue of their own integrity. Frauds act in the strength of their depraved desires, which lurk within them and enable them to abstain from food without too much effort. They rejoice in the adulation of the people. This is the height of hypocrisy! May God preserve us from it!" When the Revered Master reached these words he recited this couplet:

> If your fasting makes you fat,
> You had better eat your fill.

He continued: "An upright person gains in ability through continued exercise. To begin with, nobody is aware of his condition. When somebody finally does take note of it, he has already become weak, and strength to continue no longer remains within him. This is the sign that he is an upright man. On the other hand, the more people become aware of the condition of a fraud, the more he is strengthened to keep on going."

---

247. Shihabuddin Abu Hafs Suhrawardi (d.1234). He was the author of *'Awarif*.
248. *Az-Zahid ul-Khalifa*.

Maulana Latifuddin put this question: "On the Feast of Sacrifice scholars discuss the approval given to the practice of abstaining from food till the Feastday prayer is over. They call it 'fasting.'[249] How can it be correct to use the word 'fasting' for this practice, because it does not last for a month, nor are its other conditions fulfilled. Some call it a 'by law' fast, and others 'by name.'[250] The matter has not been settled. It remains in doubt." The Revered Master replied: "I recall that somewhere I have seen this fast described as 'by law' and also 'by name.' In that place it was explained that there are three kinds of fasting: one is 'by name;' the second is 'by law;' while the third kind comprises both 'by name' and 'by law.' This very fasting on the Feast of Sacrifice is given as an example of this third kind. It has both aspects, being both by name and by law. It is by name because it involves abstaining from food for a fixed period of time, and this itself is quite clear. It is by law in so far as the Law is involved in it. Anything in which the Law is involved automatically acquires a legal aspect. Moreover, although 'clothed by its coming,' yet the essence of fasting is not present, because this should be from dawn till sunset, and that is missing. For this reason it is incorrect."

Maulana Latifuddin again put a query: "What does 'Eat and drink with enjoyment what you previously renounced on empty days' mean?" The Revered Master replied: "'Eat and drink on account of something your set aside in days gone by' refers to days of fasting, those days on which you refrained from eating and drinking. What is the recompense for doing so? In heaven you will hear: 'Eat and drink.' Moreover, 'empty days' refers to days gone by."

A discussion arose about the fasting of sheikhs. The Revered Master said: "This group practises a different kind of fasting. In *Ihya 'Ulum* fasting is presented in three degrees. The first is the common fast. The second is a special fast. The third is the most sublime form of special fasting. The common fast involves refraining from eating, drinking and sexual intercourse from dawn till sunset, together with the intention of fasting. The second degree is restraining one's desires and bodily members from committing

---

249. *Saum.* This is the word for the fast observed during the month of Ramazan. Its rules are clearly spelled out. In India it is commonly referred to as *roza.*

250. *Shar'i* and *lughavi* respectively.

sin. The third and most sublime form is keeping a close watch on one's heart with regard to base thoughts and worldly anxieties, as well as restraining one's heart from becoming attached to anything except God—may He be honoured and glorified above everything! This is the fast of prophets, upright men and intimate friends. Paying attention to anything other than God constitutes breaking the fast."

Afterwards he added: "In the *Tamhidat* [Apologia] of 'Ain ul-Quzat[251] is found, by way of explanation, the following. Haven't you heard what that holy man said? 'Invisible fasting means a transition from seeing what is beneath God to seeing God.' He has also said: 'Dear friend, fast in order to see, and break your fast in order to see.' What have you understood about that type of fasting? What can be said? First of all, that God should be the initiator of that fast, and it should also be broken by God. All of this has been said in order to grasp what each person is fasting from and what it is that breaks the fast of each person." Afterwards he added: "Holy men have said that there is no knowledge among the sons of Adam except what has been brought. The rights of men on the Day of Resurrection will be vindicated except for fasting, which does not come under the law of retribution, for the Glorious and Exalted Lord, on the Day of Resurrection, will say: 'This belongs to Me!' This means there is no retribution for fasting. Some have commented that 'Fasting is for Me and I am its recompense' means that God has joined fasting to Himself. This means that fasting is one of the eternal qualities. In Quranic commentaries they are referred to those who fast and abstain because people who do this are on a pilgrimage towards the Glorious and Exalted Lord through their hunger and thirst. It is also expressed in this verse: 'Those who endure patiently will receive a recompense without measure' (Q.39:10). This is the fast referred to there, and also in this verse where it is said: 'Nobody knows what recompense lies in store for them, yet hidden, for what they have been doing' (Q32:17). This work of theirs is fasting."

Afterwards the Revered Master said: "Fasting produces innu-

---

251. 'Ain ul-Quzat was put to death in Baghdad in 1131 at the age of 33. His *Tamhidat* is a defence of what he had taught and written. His prolific writing sprang from a deep experience of God put into words by a brilliant mind.

merable benefits. Their measure can be gleaned by what has been said and written about them, yet for whom is this fasting, and who is the thirsty person referred to in this tradition: 'What is the portion of many who fast except hunger and thirst?' This refers to anyone who feels hungry while fasting, yet breaks his fast with something forbidden. It could also refer to a person who abstains from eating what is lawful and breaks his fast with lawful meat, yet does so while backbiting someone! People caught up with appearances break their fast with backbiting and lying."

At this point Sheikh Mu'izzuddin put a question: "What is the practice of the sheikhs with regard to fasting?" The Revered Master replied: "The sheikhs observe different practices. Some have fasted continually and reached their Lord. Others have fasted for a day and then broken their fast for a day. Pious people have praised this, for this exercises both patience and gratitude. Some have fasted for two days and then broken their fast for a day. Others have fasted on Mondays, Thursdays and Fridays, but not on other days. It is related that Khwaja Junaid of Baghdad fasted continually but would break his fast with anyone who visited him. He used to say that the excellence of making oneself agreeable to one's brother is no less than that of fasting. The Sheikh of Sheikhs has related in *'Awarif* that it is said: 'I have seen that Sheikh Abu Sa'id used to eat several times a day. Whenever food was placed in front of him he would eat it. He considered eating that food as being conformable to *God's* plan for him. This was because his relationship with the Lord Most Exalted was such that he had abandoned all personal choice with regard to eating, drinking and all other usages. He lived in total docility to the action of God.'" When the Revered Master reached these words, he exclaimed: "This situation is a pleasing one and constitutes an exalted stage!"

Sheikh Mu'izzuddin said that it had been related that some dervishes fasted for years but broke their fast before sunset. How could this be so in the month of Ramazan? The Revered Master replied: "The answer found in *'Awarif* is that Imam Abu Nasr Sarraj[252] said: 'There is a group of sheikhs that disapproves of this on the basis of their knowledge, even though it is an act of superero-

---

252. *Nasir* is written, but Abu Nasr as-Sarraj (d. 988) is the person referred to. He was from Tus and his *Kitab al-luma' fi't tasawwuf* is a famous early treatise on Sufism.

gation.' There are other sheikhs, however, who have praised this practice because the intention of those who do so is to bring their selfish souls into line through experiencing hunger. When those renowned for their sincerity deprive the selfish soul of enjoyment by the experience of fasting, even though it goes against the letter of the Law, they do so for a purpose. They should not be opposed, because sincerity is laudable in His eyes, whatever be its manifestation. A sincere person enjoys the protection of his own sincerity, no matter what happens." At this point he recited this couplet:

Sincerity will guide you on your quest for friendship,
Whether a thread or a turban heralds your struggle.

He continued: "The author of '*Awarif* said: 'It occurs to me that this view asserts that the selfish soul is not happy on account of fasting, whereas, in fact, its enjoyment is on account of the lack of enjoyment with regard to fasting. This is more agreeable and in conformity with the Law, and means observing the fast according to the injunction of knowledge. God Most Exalted has said; 'And do not render your actions useless' (Q47:33)!"[253]

---

253. The point of this convoluted argument is that it is better to continue fasting until sundown as prescribed by the Law.

CHAPTER 14
PILGRIMAGE TO MECCA
AND STRUGGLE[254]

A discussion about the annual pilgrimage to Mecca arose. It was the time of the pilgrimage. These words escaped the blessed lips of the Revered Master: "'Whoever stands in God's presence[255] accomplishes the pilgrimage, and whoever does not, fails to perform it.' This is the most important pillar of the pilgrimage." As he repeated these words, his eyes filled with tears. Afterwards he told this story: "It is said that a young man went on the pilgrimage to Mecca. On the ninth day of the month he was so engrossed in *God* that he was unaware that it was the ninth day. The following day he went to Mount Arafat in order to stand in the presence of God and then go to Mina to do what has been prescribed for the ninth day. Some people told him that the previous day had been the ninth, so what was he doing on the tenth? When the young man heard this he was broken hearted. The pain he was feeling gave rise to a heartfelt sigh. An enlightened one happened to be there. He said: 'I have performed a hundred pilgrimages or more. Sell me that sigh of yours for these hundred odd pilgrimages!' The young man sold his sigh for a hundred pilgrimages. Afterwards he heard a voice which said: 'Young man, you have sold your sigh for the fruit of a tree!'"[256] When the Revered Master reached these words, he commented: "Thus grieving and repenting over neglected acts of worship or devotion indicates genuine greatness." In this connection he related that a holy man was asked if he had experienced the blessings bestowed upon sheikhs of previous ages. He replied in

---

254. *Hajj* and *jihad* are the words used. *Hajj* refers to the pilgrimage to Mecca made in the last month of the Muslim calendar. Millions of Muslims assemble in Mecca to perform the prescribed devotions on fixed days and at fixed places. *Jihad* essentially connotes a struggle. It is a common yet loaded word today. Maneri will himself speak about what sort of struggle he has in mind .

255. *Wuquf.*

256. Two MSS have *bar-i zan* [fruit of a tree].

the affirmative. They asked him what he meant. He replied: "The grief of not finding."[257]

A discussion arose about the following tradition: "Whoever dies without having performed the pilgrimage to Mecca does so as a Jew or a Christian." The Revered Master explained: "This tradition applies to anyone for whom the pilgrimage is obligatory because he can manage the expenses of the journey and all the other conditions are fulfilled in him. If he fails to do so without having any excuse and dies, his death would be like that of a Jew or a Christian." Qazi Ashrafuddin inquired: "From this it is clear that he has neglected a religious duty, but how would this make him a Jew or a Christian?" The Revered Master replied: "This is an exaggeration meant as a threat. It doesn't mean that such a person really became a Christian or a Jew." Sheikh Mu'izzuddin put this question: "Having funds for the journey, a person's weakness and the length of the journey are all conditions. What about someone who trusts fully in God and has the strength to set out, even without provisions, yet trusting fully in God? According to this group, would it be obligatory for him to do so, even though he has no provisions?" The Revered Master replied: "According to the practice of this group, such a person would be obliged to go, even if he did not have provisions for the journey. According to the external Law, however, no obligation exists."

The Helpless One inquired: "If a person has all the required provisions and is therefore obliged to go, would the permission of his mother and father be required?" The Revered Master replied: "The real situation is that, if the external requirements are all present, the permission of his mother or father is not needed, nor that of anyone else. Their permission is not required, just as it is not required in order to fast or pray." Afterwards he said: "'Ain ul-Quzat has mentioned in his *Tamhidat* that the visible pilgrimage is a task for one and all, but the real pilgrimage is not meant for everybody. A person needs gold and silver for a pilgrimage to Mecca, whereas he has to throw his whole heart and soul into the real pilgrimage. For what sort of a Muslim is this pilgrimage meant? For the per-

257. Maneri's position with regard to spiritual experiences of any kind is very clear. They are meant to deepen a person's faith, not provide spiritual highs. What is essential is the steadfast pursuit of one's goal of seeking an ever deepening union with God. The interpretation of this particular enigmatic sentence is best left to the reader.

son who has been liberated from every form of bondage, 'the one who is capable of the Way.' It is said, 'Seek your heart,' for the pilgrimage is a pilgrimage of the heart. Haven't you heard that, when the Apostle was asked where God was, he replied: 'In the hearts of His servants.' In addition, 'The heart of the believer is the abode of God.' Be careful not to understand this as transmigration or becoming one, for *God* Most Exalted is completely exempt from any such thing." When the Revered Master reached these words, he recited these two couplets:

> There is no doubt at all in that person's heart:
> The image and the mirror are not at all the same.
> He is pure, as the foolish indeed have said:
> Yet purer still than what the wise have said.

Afterwards he told them this story: "It is related that Khwaja Bayazid once saw a person and asked him where he was going. He told him he was going to the Lord's House. He asked him how many dirhams he had. He said that he had seven. 'Give them to me and walk around me seven times and you will have visited the Ka'ba.'" At this point, he recited this quatrain:

> The whole world is turned towards my beauty:
> The King of the world is in my helpless heart.
> Tumult, evil, polytheism, unbelief, unity and certainty
> Hide in the recesses of the hearts that grieve for Me.

"'Ain ul-Quzat has written that everyone who approaches the Ka'ba of clay sees himself, while everyone who approaches the Ka'ba of the heart sees God." He recited this couplet:

> When He shows his essence to the people,
> In which mirror will He show his face?

A discussion arose about the actions performed during the pilgrimage. The Revered Master said: "As far as this group is concerned, every action of the pilgrimage contains a momentous secret that has been imbedded therein for pilgrims. Once a pilgrim approached Khwaja Junaid who said to him: 'Where are you coming from?' 'From the House of the Ka'ba,' he replied. 'Did you perform the pilgrimage?' 'I did.' 'When you emerged from your home and set out from where you live, did you distance yourself from all sins?' 'No.' Khwaja Junaid exclaimed: 'Then you didn't make the journey!' 'When you set out from your home and rested after each day's journey, was that rest also after having journeyed some distance along the Way to *God*?' 'No.' 'Then you have not travelled any distance along the Way to *God*.' 'When you entered the state of consecration on the outskirts of Mecca, did you doff your human qualities, such as the garment of habit?' 'No.' 'Then you didn't enter into the state of consecration.' 'When you became acquainted with 'Arafat, did you see the manifestation of your age?' 'No.' 'Then you haven't really stood on Mt. 'Arafat.' 'When you were at Muzdalifa and your aim was achieved, did you abandon all your desires?' 'No.' 'Then you weren't at Muzdalifa.' 'When you were circumambulating the Ka'ba, were you in the state of purity so that you could see the beauty of God?' 'No.' 'Then you didn't go around the Ka'ba.' 'When you were moving between Safa and Marwa, did you attain the stage of Safa and the rank of Marwa?' 'No.' 'Then you have not yet run between Safa and Marwa.' 'When you reached Mina did your desires flag?' 'No.' 'Then you haven't gone to Mina.' 'When you reached the place of sacrifice, did you make an offering of all the desires of your selfish soul?' 'No.' 'Then you haven't performed the sacrifice.' 'When you threw the stones did you throw away whatever you possessed that was tainted by your selfish soul?' 'No.' 'Then you have not yet thrown the stones, neither have you performed the pilgrimage. Go back and perform it with these qualities in order to reach the stage of Abraham!'" At this point, the Revered Master recited the following:

> Since you are busy with this matter,
> In spite of being dust, you see everything.
> Who is a man? Whose very life is faith!
> Whatever is said, this is its essence.[258]

He then told this story: "It is related that Zu'n-Nun[259] said how he had seen a young man at Mina. He was sitting there quietly while everybody else was engaged in performing the sacrifice. I glanced at him to see what he was doing. He was praying thus: 'O Creator God, everybody is engaged in performing the sacrifice. I also want

---

258. This particular translation is conjectural.

259. Zu'n-Nun—he with the fish—was the popular name of Thauban ibn Ibrahim, a Sufi from Egypt -hence, 'Misri' is often added to his name—who died in 859. There are many stories about his colourful and influential life.

to make a sacrifice—of myself—in your presence. Accept my sacrifice.' He made a sign with his forefinger and fell to the ground. When the bystanders checked him out they found he was dead.'" When the Revered Master reached these words, he recited this couplet:

> When beauties cast aside their veils,
> Lovers perish before their very eyes.

Afterwards he said: "When fighting became obligatory for believers the Apostle spent time explaining the excellence, merit and high rank of fighting. All were overcome with a keen desire to fight, to such an extent that those who were excused on grounds of weakness and inability to fight also wanted to do so. They lamented the fact that they had neither the strength nor the ability to fight and thus acquire the merit and excellence of fighting. When those who had the strength and ability to fight wanted to do so, they received the merit and rank of fighting from *God* Most Exalted. Later on, people had assembled and those excused from fighting approached the Apostle and said: 'O Apostle of God, we are the excused ones. On account of our weak condition and lack of ability, we are unable to go out and fight. We are deprived of the merit and rank of those who fight.' The Messenger replied: 'Anyone who is excused from fighting should perform the pilgrimage, for that is his way of fighting.' This made them very happy, for they were no longer deprived of the merit of fighting. The pilgrimage had replaced it, so they would perform the pilgrimage and acquire the merit of fighting. After this another group, who were not in a position to perform the pilgrimage, became upset that they had no way of gaining the merit of fighting. Moreover, they could not perform the pilgrimage either in place of fighting, for they lacked the strength to do so. They also approached the Apostle and said: 'O Apostle of God, those who could not fight were told to perform the pilgrimage. They did so and acquired the merit of fighting. We don't have the strength to go on pilgrimage. What do you have to say about us?' Thereupon the Apostle replied: 'Friday prayer is the pilgrimage of the poor.' Anyone who does not have the strength to go on pilgrimage but attends Friday prayer performs what is, for him, the pilgrimage." The Revered Master added this comment: "This was the occasion of this tradition of the Apostle."

The Helpless One inquired: "When the pilgrimage takes the

place of fighting, would the merit of the pilgrimage of the excused ones be in the same measure as that of those who fight, or would there be some difference?" The Revered Master replied: "Since the pilgrimage was performed in lieu of fighting, and Friday prayer in lieu of the pilgrimage, there would be a slight difference, for the simple reason that the pilgrimage is not fighting. The equation is a legal fiction. Hence, something which is construed as fighting would not be equal to it. With regard to something which is in reality and legally fighting, it is fitting that there should not be any difference. This is because those who fail to fight or go on pilgrimage do not do so intentionally. It is also related that the Master of the Law said that there was no choice in the matter. Those who are excused do not intentionally refrain from fighting or going on the pilgrimage. From the point of view of intention, it could very well be that there was no difference at all. For example, at the time of the expedition to Tabuk a group remained behind at Medina.[260] They wanted to go on the expedition. Because they had to be excused they were not able to set out together with the Apostle. They expressed grief and sorrow at their situation. The Apostle said: 'We have not traversed any valley or faced any adversity in which they were not participants.' Commentators have mentioned that, by virtue of their clear intention, they were close at hand, even though they were excused. From the point of view of their intention, they had set out together with the Apostle. He considered them to be equivalent to himself in crossing valleys, facing adversity and danger, and in acquiring merit and rank. In the same way, in this sense it has been said: 'For Muslim men and women; for believing men and women; for devout men and women; for men and women who are patient; for men and women who humble themselves; for men and women who give in charity; for men and women who fast; for men and women who guard their chastity; for men and women who remember God often—for them all, God has prepared forgiveness and a great reward' (Q33:35).[261]

The occasion of the revelation of this verse was that some

---

260. This expedition is described in Guillaume, A, *The Life of Muhammad: A Translation of Ishaq's Sirat Rasul Allah,* O.U.P., Karachi, 1970, pp. 602-9. It set out from Medina.

261. The actual text has 'For Muslim men and women and so on.' For the benefit of readers of other religious traditions the whole, very long and important verse, has been given.

women believers had gathered in a house. They pointed out that God Most Exalted included them in the category of men in all commands, prohibitions and other injunctions. They enumerated several illustrative verses, such as: 'Be steadfast in prayer and pay the poor tax' (Q2:110; 'Wash your faces' (Q.5:6) and other such-like things.[262] They said: 'We are given to understand that we have no distinct dignity in the eyes of the Lord Most Exalted.' One of the women said: 'I'm ready to go on your behalf to the Apostle of God Most Exalted.' After that she came to the Apostle and said: 'O Apostle of God, the women of your community have sent me to you about something which, from the present time till the Day of Resurrection, everyone who hears about it will rejoice over it and will praise me. The question put by the women is this: 'O Apostle of God, is God Most Exalted the God of women just as He is the God of men? 'He replied, 'Yes,' She protested: 'But no distinct dignity is accorded to us in the eyes of God Most Exalted because we have been included in the category of men in all ordinances.' The Apostle remained silent until a revelation came from Gabriel praising women believers: 'Muslim men and women...' In other words, Muslim men and Muslim women are equal, and men who believe are the same as women who believe. The same applies to men and women who are devout, truthful and so on. Praise has been equally bestowed upon men and women for their devotion, forgiveness and vows of devotion. Even though there may be some defect in the devotion of women, the principle of excusing factors makes the merit of their devotion the same as that of men."

262. In Arabic there is a masculine form of the verb and a feminine form. In the above quotes—and a few more—the masculine form alone is used. As this distinction is completely lost in the English translation, the other examples have been omitted, as they in no way add to the strength of the argument.

CHAPTER 15

REPETITIVE PRAYER: PRAYERS OF PETITION: RITUAL PRAYER AND SUPEREROGATORY PRAYER AT ASSEMBLING POINTS IN MECCA

Qazi Sadruddin inquired about the meaning of the tradition, 'The man of repetitive prayer is cursed.' The Revered Master replied: "This tradition has several explanations. According to one, at the time of the Apostle there was a Jew much given to repetitive prayer. People informed the Apostle of this, whereupon he recited, 'The man of repetitive prayer is cursed.' This saying was in reference to that Jew. There is a second tradition: 'The man who abandons repetitive prayer is cursed.' The explanation for this saying is that, when the Jew learnt what the Apostle had said, he abandoned his prayer in order to escape the effect of the curse. When the Apostle was informed of this, he repeated: 'The man who abandons repetitive prayer is cursed.' This saying also applied to the Jew. A second explanation is applicable to a person who is needed by the people, and those in need point this out to him. If he is slow to attend to their needs and remains preoccupied with his repetitive prayer, however, while they are kept waiting for him, of such a person it could be said, 'The man of repetitive prayer is cursed.' On the other hand, 'The man who abandons repetitive prayer is cursed' applies to a person who is engaged in repetitive prayer and other religious exercises and abandons them without any excuse. The saying is applicable in such a situation."

Sheikh Mu'zzuddin inquired whether the import of this curse was unconditional or restricted. The Revered Master explained: "There is no unconditional curse for a believer, for that is specific to an unbeliever. Here the curse is in a restricted sense, namely, to anyone who abandons repetitive prayer without an excuse. Such a person would be far from divine mercy." Afterwards he continued: "If someone has to abandon repetitive prayer or worship externally he should be preoccupied with them internally. Moreover, he should be upset over having to give them up. Hopefully *God* Most Exalted will grant him the blessings accruing to them."

Qazi Minhajuddin from the fort inquired: "If a person who practises repetitive prayer is unable to do so in the midst of people and the opportunity to pray is lost, what can be said about such a situation?" The Revered Master replied: "If a person does not pray in the midst of people because his prayer would become known to them, he should secretly become preoccupied with God. In other words, he would pray in secret. This is because any act of worship that is performed in secret is more excellent than one performed in public." Afterwards he added: "If a person does not have enough free time to pray in secret, then he himself should turn towards *God*, namely, be engaged in remembering *God*, and recite his prayers at some other time. It is said that whatever is lost during the night can be made up for during the day. In a similar way, night succeeds day, and day succeeds night, as in the Glorious Quran we read: ''He is the one who makes night follow day for those who want to be mindful or render thanks' (Q25:62). In other words, He is the Lord who ensures that day follows night in succession so that whoever wants to pray can do so, and whoever wants to work can do so. If a person knows that if he himself recites such prayers then, when other people see him praying, they also will do so and experience a desire to pray. In such circumstances let the person recite his prayers among the people so that they might also do so."

The Helpless One inquired: "If, after repetitive prayer or ritual prayer or supererogatory worship, this thought occurs to a person, 'People will applaud me and praise me for my goodness,' what should be done?" The Revered Master replied: "Danger is to be apprehended if this occurs while a person is engaged in prayer. If it occurs later on, however, then there should be no fear of danger. This is founded on the saying that there is no pretence at times of repose. When a person begins or is engaged in supererogatory prayer, however, if there were any intentional pretence, then this would be hypocrisy. Later on, however, if the question of pretence arises, the majority opinion is that there is no hypocrisy."

A discussion arose about the excellence of repetitive prayer. The Revered Master said: "The excellence consists in this. When a person given to repetitive prayer falls sick or sets out on a journey an angel writes up the merit of what he used to do when he was in good health. This is because his wish and desire is to perform the prayers, yet, because of his sickness or the hardships of the journey, he was not able to do so. This is an omission out of necessity. This is the benefit of practices like repetitive prayer. The danger is that, having undertaken such a practice, abandoning it without any excuse incurs the threat, 'The person who abandons repetitive prayer is cursed.' It needs to be explained that repetitive prayer enables believers to practise virtue and is the path of devotees. There is a famous tradition which says: 'The best work in the sight of God is that in which a person perseveres, no matter how insignificant it is.' Each person, however, should take upon himself what is within his capability and in which he can persevere. If he undertakes some practice for a while, finds it too much and abandons it, this would not be good because of the threat, 'Anyone who is engaged in worshipping God and abandons it because it proves too much incurs the displeasure of God.' For mystics, however, there is no fixed time for repetitive prayer, yet they are always repeating a prayer to their Lord. They consider it to be necessary to bring themselves forcefully back from the world and devote their entire time uniformly to their Lord."

Sheikh Mu'izzuddin inquired what was meant by 'repetitive prayer.' The Revered Master explained: "Repetitive prayer refers to a fixed time, by day or night, which comes repeatedly to a devotee. It is a time spent in intimacy with God. It could refer to a time of obligatory prayer or of supererogatory prayer. When a devotee is engaged therein at a particular time, and shows himself assiduous therein, then it becomes known as repetitive prayer. The easiest type of this prayer is to perform four cycles of ritual prayer; or to recite the thirty sections of the Quran, or one of the first seven chapters of the Quran; or to be of assistance to a Muslim in some commendable work. What all this means is that any act of worship or recitation of the Quran that is done at a fixed time is known as repetitive prayer."

A discussion about intercessory prayer arose, namely, that it should be offered before calamity strikes. The Revered Master said: "If someone prays after calamity has struck, then it is for a mitigation of the effects of the calamity. How could a prayer avert a calamity once it has already struck? A shield provides protection from arrows, but if it is held up after an arrow has struck, of what good is that?" In this connection he told the following story: "Once upon a time a king sent someone to a dervish to inform him of a calamity that had struck and to ask for his prayers. He replied that the time for prayer had passed, and the time to exercise patience had arrived. It is clear that prayers of petition should be made before a calamity strikes. Once it has struck, what other option is there than patient endurance?"

A discussion about this tradition arose: "A servant prays but the Lord does what He wants." The Revered Master said: "It is like that. A servant prays, but it is not necessary that his prayers will be automatically answered. Whatever the Lord wants, He does. Someone might come up with an objection that this contradicts the text of the Quran which says, 'Call on Me: I will answer you' (Q40:60). These words make it clear that prayers are answered. An answer is promised, and nothing can stand in the way of what has been promised. It is fitting that any necessary link should be on account of the solemnity of the promise." After giving this answer he went on to add: "With regard to this verse, many say that the will of God is implied, i.e., 'I will answer you if it is My will.' This verse came first and the tradition is in conformity with it. Those who think the verse is unconditioned and that 'the will of God' is not implied say that the prayer is answered in full. *God* Most Exalted fulfils His expressed desire, or sets aside a treasure for him in the life to come. Thus it is said that, in the life to come, someone will be granted an exalted rank and miraculous power that are not commensurate with the works he had accomplished. He will exclaim: 'O Lord, when I was in the world I did not do anything to deserve this!' A command will issue forth: 'When you were praying We were preparing a treasure for you.'"

Qazi Khan put this question: "If someone asserts that a tradition has superseded an unconditioned Quranic saying, what answer should be given?" The Revered Master replied: "The will of God which is mentioned in the tradition does not refer essentially to the answer itself, but to whether it will be granted to him in this world or stored away as a treasure for the life to come, 'doing what is possible.'" Afterwards he added: "Masters of insight, with regard to prayer of petition, have said that the prayer of ordinary people is with words; that of ascetics through deeds; and that of mystics through their states. Some say that the tongue of beginners is loosened by prayer, while that of mystics is rendered silent in prayer. This is because they witness divine manifestations, and a person is lost to himself at such times. How could such a person find a voice

in which to pray? This is what happens in some states."[263] Thereupon he recited the following couplet:

> You who speak to Him, fall silent, don't speak!
> You who search for Him, turn lame, don't move!

He continued: "A holy man has said that the benefit of prayer is
the making known of one's needs to one's Lord. If a person does
not do so, the Lord does what He thinks fit. Another holy man has
said that an ear in prayer is in part a gift, as Khwaja Kattani[264] has
expressed it: 'The Lord does not loosen a believer's tongue in asking forgiveness without opening for him the door of forgiveness.'
A mystic has said that prayer is the cause of being present, while
a gift is the cause of turning back. Remaining standing at the door
in prayer is more fulfilling than turning back from the door with a
gift. It is related that Imam Shibli said: 'Speaking at length in con-
verse with the Lord amounts to abandoning polite behaviour.' This
aphorism has been explained thus: 'This is not a general relaxation.
It refers to some special occurrences in some spiritual states. This
is because *God*—may He be glorified and exalted—has ordered us to
pray for our needs, but to refrain from speaking much as Moses refrained from speaking at length. It should be noted that *God* Most
Exalted bestowed upon him a station near to Him and allowed him
to speak at length. He said: 'Ask Me, even if it is for salt for your
flour!' Since He emboldened him, his confidence increased. He
said: 'Lord, why did You bestow poverty on me instead of a good
life?' When Moses had completed the task of watering Shu'aib's[265]
flock of sheep and had flung himself on the ground in the shade of
a tree, suffering from hunger and need, he said: 'O my Provident
Lord, compared to what was formerly bestowed upon me, I am now
in dire straits.' This was because before Moses got caught up in a
grand lifestyle he experienced a need for the unseen world. Out of
contempt for worldly needs he accounted the Lord Most Exalted
of supreme worth, for he asked for trifles from Him. This serves
as an illustrative example. This is because people seek important
favours from great kings, but are ashamed to ask for insignificant

---

263. This statement is quite matter of fact, redolent of experiential
knowledge.

264. Abu Bakr al-Kattani (d.934) was a noted Sufi of his age.

265. The biblical name is 'Jethro,' found in Exodus, 3:1.

things. When a person's status is enhanced and he is granted a special rank, however, insignificant things as well as great are sought from Him."

Afterwards he said: "Saintly people have different opinions with regard to prayer of petition, namely, whether it is better to pray for favours or keep quiet. Some say that such prayer is, at the personal level, a form of worship. Hence it is better to pray. Others affirm that simply keeping quiet and acquiescing in what *God* has already determined is more excellent than praying. Moreover, holy men also point out that situations differ. In some situations prayer is better than keeping quiet, while in others silence is better than praying. They make a distinction. They say that when your heart is troubled with many needs, then it is better to pray for succour. On the other hand, if your heart is at peace and filled to overflowing, then it is better to remain quiet. If neither of these conditions prevails, then praying for favours or remaining quiet are of equal value. In this situation it is said that it needs to be ascertained whether a person is currently under the influence of the world. If so, prayer is more fitting, since it is a form of worship. On the other hand, if a person is experiencing intimate communion, then keeping quiet is more fitting."

An esteemed person said: "If a man's destiny is already determined, what is the point of praying?" The Revered Master replied: "Averting disaster by means of prayer also comes within the ambit of what is determined, and this happens because of prayer. Seeking divine mercy can be compared to the way a shield provides protection against arrows. Prayer provides similar protection. A human being ought to employ all human means. It is not correct to abandon any such form of help, for this is what the Law enjoins. The Law stipulates that you have to make use of what has been enjoined upon you. That is what has been ordained for you." Afterwards he related this story: "As long as the Apostle was in Mecca he used to keep his companions close by him. Then this verse was revealed: 'And God will defend you from men' (Q5:67). 'No one will be able to kill you.' He told his companions that they could go, for the Lord was keeping guard over him to protect him from enemies, for He had promised to do so. When he went to Mecca, the verse regarding killing was revealed. He set out to fight the infidels after donning a double coat of mail. His companions said: 'O Apostle of God, the Lord has assured you that no one would be able to kill you, so why don a double coat of mail?' He replied: 'That is so, but this normal precaution has to be taken.'" At this stage the Revered Master recited the following:

Your Joseph is still in a well:
About to be killed, he was granted a crown.
Without seeing the bottom, how could he become the moon?
Had he not been a slave, how could he become a king?

A discussion arose about befitting forms of prayer. The Revered Master said: "Propriety in prayer demands that, after presenting a personal need to the Lord and, while waiting for a favourable response, you should not trouble *God*. You should know what is proper in such a situation. When you ask a question, you should not be in a hurry. You should be confident that there is no discrepancy in what is allotted. Realize that whatever the Lord chooses for a person is better than anything the person could choose for himself. It is said that there are four times when a person's prayers are more likely to be answered. The first is in the morning. The second is at the end of the day, namely, at sunset. The next is between the call to prayer and its commencement, as well as at the break of day. There are also the nights when people gather, such as the Night of Power,[266] the Night of the Decrees[267] and suchlike occasions. There are also some particularly holy days, such as Fridays; the ninth day of the month of pilgrimage; and the tenth day of the month of Muharram, and suchlike days."

It was the tenth of Muharram. Many people had come to kiss the blessed feet.[268] The Revered Master turned his blessed gaze towards the people present in the assembly and said: "Today you should recite chapter 112 of the Quran,[269] and pray for all your needs. God will fulfil them from His infinite abundance. You should also perform four cycles of prayer for the peace of heart of your adversaries. In the first cycle, after reciting the opening chapter

266. This is the night between the 26th and 27th Ramazan. Traditionally this is the night when the Quran was first revealed.
267. This is the night between the 14th and 15th Sha'ban, the night when God ordains things for the coming year.
268. The custom is to touch the feet of the Master with the fingers of one's right hand and then kiss one's fingertips.
269. Say: 'God is One. God is the Eternal. He does not beget, nor was He begotten. None is comparable to Him.'

of the Quran, you should recite the 112th chapter eleven times. In the second cycle, after reciting the opening chapter, recite chapter 109 three times and the 112th chapter eleven times. In the third cycle, recite chapter 102 once and the 112th chapter eleven times. In the fourth cycle, recite the Throne Verse (Q2:255)[270] three times and the 112th chapter twenty-five times. God Most Pure and Exalted will preserve whoever recites these prayers from the terrors of the grave and will grant peace of heart to his adversaries. It is related that the Apostle used to recite these prayers on six days of the year: the tenth of Muharram; the eighth and the ninth day of the month of pilgrimage; the Feast of Sacrifices; the fifteenth of the month of Sha'ban; and the last Friday in Ramazan."

Afterwards he told this story: "There was a man living in Kara with his sister's son. He was a valiant warrior. He used to dream every night. It seemed to him that the Day of Judgement had arrived and people had been gathered together. All his adversaries were hurling accusations at him. He saw all the aspects of the Day of Judgement. This continued for some time. After a while he approached a holy man and narrated his dreams to him. The holy man said: 'Perform four cycles of prayer for peace in the hearts of your adversaries.' He went and performed the prayers. After that he was not troubled by such dreams.'" Afterwards the Revered Master added: "Adversaries are like thorns in the clothing of a traveller along the Way. If a person's parents died with troubled hearts then he should renounce all those things which used to upset them so that they may attain peace of heart. If someone has said something bad about a person and he has died, then, to the same extent, he should speak well of him." Later he added: "Mystics are wont to say: 'If the whole world is happy with you, but *God* is not, how will it profit you?" He recited this couplet:

If God is not happy with someone,
The pleas of all prophets will not avail.

He gave another explanation: "Whoever has the Lord, has everything; and whoever does not have the Lord, has nothing." He recited the following:

If both worlds were given to me

---

270. 'His throne extends across the heavens and the earth, and preserving them does not make Him tired. He is the Exalted, the Almighty.'

And I lacked union, I'd be poor.

Afterwards he said: "On account of these two principles that are found in the Law, sinners have great hope. One principle is that a master is held responsible for a crime committed by his slave, and the other is that the crime of a slave against his goods is a loss. In other words, the crime of a slave falls upon his master, not on him. Here the injunction is that the master should buy back his slave it he can. If he cannot do so, he should hand him over to the aggrieved party. If the crime of the slave is against his master's welfare, he himself is the source of loss. According to the Law, the slave cannot be held for it. Since this is the command for here and now, in the world to come these two situations will be replicated. A slave's crime will be against the Lord himself, or against someone else. If it is against someone else, there is the hope of being ransomed. If it is against the Lord, there is the hope of its being written off as a loss." Several times his blessed lips exclaimed, "Praise be to God! To sum up, these two principles are found in the Law. Because of them, sinners have great hope."[271]

A discussion arose concerning special night prayers for great things and prayers for assistance.[272] The Revered Master said: "There is no mention of them in *Qut ul-Qulub* [Nourishment for Hearts][273] or in *'Awarif*. Apart from these prayers, all forms of devotion associated with gathering for prayer are found in these two books. These two practices, however, are not found." Qazi Sadruddin asked: "What is the reason why neither of these two practices is mentioned in these two books?"" The Revered Master replied: "I myself had asked two or three people the reason for this. They

---

271. The argument is convoluted. The essential thing is the perspective taken. Normally, "let the punishment fit the crime" is the perspective taken. Here it is the perspective of an infinitely wealthy and resourceful Divine Master and a poor, indigent human sinner. God can easily afford to pay any ransom or overlook any loss. It is a way of underlining God's infinite capacity to be merciful and forgiving. It is also an indirect hint at Maneri's own realization of this fact. His emotional reiteration of "Praise be to God" tends to confirm this analysis.

272. *Namaz-i lailat ur-raghaíb* and *du'a ul-istiftah*. These are not prayers commonly known to Muslims in Patna.

273. *Qut ul-Qulub* by Muhammad Abu Talib al-Makki (d.996) was one of Maneri's favourite books.

replied that they had heard saintly men say that these two practices were not well known among Arabs, but were quite well known among Persians. That is why they are not mentioned in those two books." Qazi Khan asked: "Where does the name 'night of prayers for great things' come from, and what does it mean?'" The Revered Master replied: "The word itself refers to an abundance of things. It is in the plural form. The singular refers to something good. Thus it is called 'the night of abundance' because many good things are found during this night."

Qazi Ashrafuddin asked: "Why is the month of Rajab called 'deaf?'" The Revered Master replied: "The reason why it is called 'deaf' is because fighting is forbidden during this month. That is why it is called 'deaf.' This is found in *Bustan* [The Garden] of Abul Lais, the jurisconsult. The word 'deaf' is found in *Riyahin* [Odoriferous Herbs]. Many good things have been brought together in this book."

A discussion arose about the Ten Sevenfold Cries.[274] The Helpless One said: "The Ten Sevenfold Cries are like this. First of all, 'Praise be to God' is recited seven times; then chapter 114 of the Quran; then chapter113; then chapter 112 and so on down to chapter 109; then the Throne Verse (Q2:255). How can it be that the Quran is not recited in the proper order?" The Revered Master replied: "There are instances of transposing and delaying in recitation with regard to supererogatory prayers. If it is done in some form of voluntary prayer it is allowed, as is related in *Qut ul-Qulub*." Afterwards he added: "This devotion was instituted by Khwaja Khizr who passed it on to Khwaja Ibrahim Tamimi with the injunction that he should recite these prayers at the break of day and at the time of the afternoon prayer. Khwaja Khizr said that this practice had been enjoined on him by Muhammad, the Apostle of God. Khwaja Tamimi asked Khwaja Khizr about the merit attached to this practice. Khwaja Khizr replied: 'When you see Muhammad ask him about the merit of this prayer. He will tell you.' Khwaja Tamimi explained: 'That night I dreamt that angels had come, lifted me up and borne me off to paradise. I saw what was in paradise. I asked the angels for whom it was all destined. They replied that it was meant for anyone who had done the sort of things I had done. I ate

---

274. *Musabba'at-i 'ashar*. The translation offered is that of the Arabic form as given by Constance Padwick in her *Muslim Devotions*, p.85.

the fruit of paradise and drank the wine of paradise. I saw the Messenger enter along with seventy other messengers. I also saw seventy rows of angels, each stretching from east to west. They wished me peace and took hold of my hand. I said: 'O Apostle of God, Khizr told me that he had heard about the Ten Sevenfold Cries from Muhammad the Apostle of God, who had spoken three times about the sincerity of Khizr in whatever he had narrated.' He affirmed that it was true; that he stood out among men for his learning; was the leader of the saints; and was one of God's soldiers on this earth. I said: 'O Apostle of God, if someone recites these prayers but does not see what I have seen in a dream, will he be granted what I have been granted?' The Apostle replied: 'In the name of God Who truly sent me, he will bestow all this on anyone who recites these prayers, just as it has been granted to you, even if he does not see. So, even if he does not see Khizr, all the serious sins he may have committed will be forgiven him. *God* Most Exalted will remove His wrath from that person and call him a man of virtue so that no sin will be recorded against him for a whole year. By the God Who sent me, in truth no one will read this except those created by *God* Most Exalted as fortunate, and no one will abandon it except anyone created for misfortune.'"

CHAPTER 16
REMEMBERING GOD
MOST EXALTED

Qazi Minhajuddin from the fort went through the *Wasiyat* of the Sheikh of Sheikhs until he came to these words: "On the Day of Judgement a believer will sigh for grief over every hour in which he failed to remember God." The Revered Master said: "It is related that on the Day of Resurrection everyone will be sighing for grief, sinners as well as the devout. Sinners will grieve over their sins, while the devout will grieve over the time they failed to remember and worship *God*. They will sigh every time they see the rank attained by others who were continuously engaged in worship. They will cry out: 'Why did I allow that time to slip by unutilised? How I wish I had spent all my time in remembering *God*!'" He added: "It is related that Sheikh Nuri[275] said: 'There is a chastisement for everything, and the chastisement of the mystic is to be cut off from remembering.'"

At this stage he began to describe the different types of remembering: "There are four kinds. The first is on the tongue but not in the heart. The second is both on the tongue and in the heart, although the heart, from time to time, is inattentive and gets preoccupied with something else, but the tongue continues its work. The third is when both tongue and heart remain engaged in remembering. The fourth is when the heart continuously remembers but the tongue falls silent. This is real remembering, when the heart speaks but the tongue remains silent, i.e., in that state when the tongue is silent but the heart is found remembering. This is the final stage of remembering. This is real remembering. When this predominates, even if the tongue is occupied with something else, the heart, as it were, remains. At this stage of the heart's remembering, listening occurs. It is as if when a person speaks, the ear hears, yet the heart is unaware of it. In the same way, when the heart remembers and the ear listens, yet the tongue is unaware

---

275. Abul-Husain an-Nuri (d.907) was one of the Baghdad Sufis. He was famous for the centrality of love in his life.

of it. Here the opposite takes place. To begin with, the heart was heedless of remembering while the tongue prattled on, while at this stage the heart becomes the tongue and the tongue becomes the heart." Afterwards he told this story: "A holy man had reached the stage when his heart was remembering and his ear was hearing. Later on, he heard it externally. He fled from contact with people, thinking that, just as he could hear, all the people would also be able to hear. This would lead to a commotion. This was the reason for his retiring into seclusion." In the meantime, Qazi Ashrafuddin inquired if the people could hear it or not. He replied: "No, the man engaged in remembering could hear it, and he thought that it would not be proper for people to hear as he was hearing, yet anyone else who had attained his station could hear."

A discussion arose about the best kinds of works. The Revered Master said: "I will tell you about the best and most pure works you can do in the sight of your Lord, the most sublime things in your rank, things better than gold and silver. It is also better than encountering enemies when you strike their necks and they strike your necks. The Apostle was asked what it was. He replied that it was remembering God. Another tradition says that the Day of Judgement will not come about as long as there is someone who is reciting 'Allah! Allah!' It is related that Master Abu Ali Daqqaq[276] said: 'Remembering the Lord is the proof of sanctity. Whoever is granted the grace of remembering is granted this proof of sanctity. If it is snatched from him, sanctity has been displaced.'" A dear friend asked: "Will there be worship in paradise?" The Revered Master replied: "Worship is hidden, but there it will be face to face. Moreover, remembering will perdure." Afterwards he added: "It is well known that the Apostle said: 'When you see the gardens of paradise, what will you do in them?' People inquired: 'What are the gardens of paradise?' He replied: 'Assemblies of people remembering.'"

A dear friend put this question: "If a person remembers *God* Most Exalted but experiences no joy in his heart while doing so, what should he do?" The Revered Master replied: "Khwaja Abu Uthman[277] was asked this very question, namely, 'I remember our

---

276. Abu Ali Daqqaq (d.1016?) was a Sufi who founded a *khanqah* in Nishapur and was the master of Abu Sa'id and Qushairi.
277. Abu Uthman al-Hiri (d.910) was a Sufi of Nishapur.

Lord but do not experience any joy in my heart.' He replied: 'Praise God that one of your members is adorned by means of its devotion!'" A discussion arose about the remembering of the heart. The Revered Master said: "It has been said that the Lord in one's heart is the sword of disciples. They kill their transgressions with it and thus avert calamities that had been intended for them. People asked Khwaja Wasiti[278] about remembering. He said: 'Remembering means emerging from the zone of heedlessness and entering the desert of witnessing by overcoming fear and adversity.'[279] In a number of books it is mentioned that Moses prayed thus: 'My Lord, where do You live?' God replied: 'In the heart of my faithful servant.' This saying is explained thus: 'Remembering occurs in the heart, and since *God* is utterly untrammelled by any localization or indwelling, but is absolutely permanent, He is remembered.'"

"It is said that, when a believer is completely given over to remembering God, six benefits are obtained. The first is that remembering leads to much witnessing and a person's heart quickly becomes present so that he thereby sees God. The second is that he refrains from committing sins. Whoever does not refrain from sinning would thereby indicate that he is far from God—God forbid such a thing! That would occur due to inattentiveness. Holy men say that whenever a person remembers the Lord Most Exalted with his tongue but is inattentive, the Lord remains hidden from him. He is not seen. This sort of remembering is equivalent to slander." He recited this couplet:

> If a tongue is engaged in much remembering
> But the heart is inattentive, it would be slander.

"Once a holy man was on his way somewhere. A muezzin gave the call to prayer. He gave no answer. He saw a dog. It barked. In answer, he said, 'Here I am!' People said to him: 'You did not answer the call to prayer, but when the dog barked, you said, Here I am!' The holy man explained: 'The muezzin was inattentive when he was calling upon the Lord. He was heedless. I knew that the dog was certainly remembering God. A dog's remembering without

---

278. Abu Bakr al-Wasiti (d.932?) spent some time with Junaid in Baghdad before returning to his native Khurasan.

279. The reader is left to ponder such suggestive sayings as this one evidently is.

distraction is better than a man's distracted remembering." At this stage he recited this couplet:

The dog that remembers You without distraction is a man,
While the man who remembers You distractedly is a dog.

"The dog was certainly remembering the Lord Most Exalted. Thus it is said: 'There is nothing that does not sing His praise' (Q17:44). The third benefit is that anyone who is constantly remembering God with his tongue will be kept safe from misfortunes and calamities. The fourth is that remembering God with one's tongue makes Him present. We often think of a friend, not of an enemy, as it has been said: 'Whoever loves something is always thinking about it.' Haven't you seen that Zulaikha,[280] out of love for Joseph, used to call everything by the name of Joseph, to such an extent that, one day, she was seated and the tailor was in front of her. He was stitching. Now she intended to tell the tailor to mend her garment but said: 'Stitch this garment, Joseph!' Thus it is said that friendship should be like that of Zulaikha's in order to attain one's goal as she did.[281] The fifth is that whoever takes the name of God upon his tongue is saved from the wickedness of demons, as has been related: 'Remembering God means one is borne rapidly from Satan.' The sixth is that it will be his friend in his grave and will protect him there from all torment."

The Helpless One inquired: "Which is the most excellent form of remembering?" The Revered Master replied: "The most excellent form is reciting 'There is no god but God,' according to this tradition of the Messenger: 'The most excellent prayer of petition is 'Praise be to God,' while the most excellent form of remembering is to recite, 'There is no god but God.'" The Master's son thumbed through *Siraj ul-'Arifin* [A Lamp for Mystics] until he came to these words: "When any need arises, recite 'God is Great'[282] so that the

---

280. In the Bible Joseph is purchased by Potiphar, the captain of Pharaoh's guard, and his wife tried to seduce Joseph (Genesis 39). Her name is not given, nor is it given in the Quran (Q12), where a similar account is given. Muslim tradition provides her name.

281. In neither account did she succeed, but in the Quranic account she succeeds in silencing the women who had criticised her by showing them Joseph.

282. *Akbar* is in the elative degree. This form is used, according to context, for both the comparative and superlative degrees in English.

need might be fulfilled." The Revered Master explained: "This is why dervishes recite 'God is Great.' They do so aloud while remembering God, and also in a low voice while reciting the Quran." He continued: "Some of the companions used to recite the Quran as though they themselves were listening to it. In such a situation it would become apparent to others that their prostrations stemmed from their recitation." Afterwards he added: "So many times have I told these foolish people to give themselves to remembering and reciting the Quran in a low voice in such a way that other people are not disturbed![283] When a person is seated and waiting to listen to a recitation of the Quran, then a loud recitation would be another matter. Yet if someone is sitting in quiet recollection and a person is loud in his remembering and Quranic recitation, he would be disturbing the other person and playing the role of Satan. In a similar way, at the time of formal prayer a person should pray in such a way that the person beside him should not hear what he says. None of his praising and glorifying God should reach that person's ears. The person should not even realize that there is someone beside him. Otherwise, he is playing the role of Satan. He will imagine that he is engaged in praying but will not realize that he is doing the work of Satan."

Later on he mentioned that it was related that Khwaja Hasan Basri had said: "Take pleasure in three things: in formal prayer, in remembering and in reciting the Quran. If it is found in them well and good. If not, realize that the door has been shut." He was asked if he fasted. He replied: "I fast by remembering Him, and when I think of anyone else, I break my fast."

A discussion arose about what was special to remembering. The Revered Master said: "One of its special features is that remembering does not have any fixed time. There is no determined time for a servant to remember the Lord. It can be done as and where convenient. Thus it is said that, although formal prayer is the most esteemed form of worship, at certain times it is not correct to offer such prayer, whereas remembering in one's heart can be practised in all situations. God Most Exalted said: 'Those who

More literal translations would be 'God is greater' or 'God is the greatest.' The chosen rendition is analogous to 'God is Love.'

283. This is one of the rare instances of Maneri's use of the first person singular. He is obviously annoyed by any inappropriately loud recitation of prayers.

remember God standing, sitting and in all their activities.' Regarding this a holy man said: 'I heard that Sheikh Furak said: Stand up to remember and desist from making claims while remembering.' One of the special features of remembering is that *God* Most Exalted has made this promise with regard to remembering Him: 'And remember Me; I will remember you' (Q2:152). It is related that Gabriel said to the Messenger: 'The Lord has instructed me to give your community something which I have not given to any previous community.' He replied: 'What is it, brother Gabriel?' He gave this answer: 'And remember Me; I will remember you (Q2:152). This has not been said to any other community except this one.'"

A discussion arose as to whether remembering or reflecting was more perfect; or whether there was no difference between the one and the other. The Revered Master said: "A holy man asked Master Abu Ali Daqqaq whether remembering was more perfect or reflecting. He asked the holy man what he thought. He said that he thought remembering was more perfect than reflecting. He asked him why he thought so. He replied: '*God* Most Exalted is praised by remembering, not by thinking. What involves the praise of God is more perfect.' Sheikh Abu Ali approved of this answer."

CHAPTER 17

THE MASTER-DISCIPLE RELATIONSHIP, AND WHAT BENEFITS IT

A discussion arose about the master-disciple relationship. The Revered Master said: "It is written in books that *wilayat* and *walayat* are both found in the Quran. Commentators have said that *wilayat* refers to governing a country or province, while *walayat* refers to assistance or victory. Some followers of the Way, however, say that *wilayat* is both ordinary and special. The ordinary meaning is clear, and the special meaning is when a spiritual master helps bring a disciple to *God*. Some others say that, although it is special, nevertheless the fact that a disciple attains *God* is due to the will of God, for God Most Exalted has said: 'God chooses whom He will for His mercy' (Q2:105). Just as the Messenger cannot cause anyone to be accepted who has been rejected from all eternity, in a similar way, a guide cannot cause a person who has been repudiated from all eternity to attain union. On the other hand, when a person has been accepted from all eternity, this becomes clear through the invitation of the messengers. Similarly, if the wealth of union, nearness and miracles has been determined from all eternity, this becomes clear through a person's service and association with a guide. The promulgation of the divine guidance is based on this." At this point the Revered Master recited this couplet:

> Every gift that you possess, O dervish,
> Is from God: don't attribute it to begging!

"The task of a guide consists in no more than explaining the Way according to the command of *God* and overseeing the disciple's training. He points out to him all the hazards of the Way. He also tells him what to do and what not to do. This is the task of a guide. Nothing more than this can be expected from any guide. Actually bringing a person to *God* is the special prerogative of *God*. The result of the first saying—leading a disciple to *God*—would fall within the ambit of a special *wilayat*, but according to the second saying, the meaning would not come within the ambit of a special *wilayat.*" After this, he related the following story: "Khwaja Shibli was the son of a minister. He used to issue orders in his own city. Khwaja Junaid was living in the same city. After a while, Khwaja Shibli came to Khwaja Junaid and said: 'I want to attach myself to you and pledge my fealty to you.' Khwaja Junaid said to him: 'You are the son of a minister of this city and issue orders. Whatever I command, you would not be able to carry out, so how could I accept your pledge of fealty?' Khwaja Shibli replied: 'I shall carry out whatever is indicated to me.' Khwaja Junaid again repeated, three times in all, what he had said, and Khwaja Shibli replied each time that he would carry out whatever he was commanded to do. After this Khwaja Junaid said: 'I would order you to shave your head and wear an old, patched garment, but you would not be able to do this.' He replied: 'Of course I would!' Immediately Khwaja Shibli stopped issuing orders. Khwaja Junaid ordered him to shave his head and don an old, patched garment. He then said: 'Take this purse and go to all those places where you issued orders and where people hold you in esteem, and begin begging there.'" When the Revered Master reached this point, he recited the following verses:

Intellect is a man well versed in control:
Love is a pain royally inflamed.
Love provides a potent stimulus for living,
Just as lips discover the excellence of honey.
If you have any love of goods,
In their midst, what profit do you have?

"Khwaja Shibli did as he was instructed. He took the purse and began to beg. Some people gave him a leaf of gold; some gave him silver; and others gave him something similar. People kept this up for some time. Every day he would bring whatever he had received and present it to Khwaja Junaid. As the days went by some gave a small coin or the other, while others gave him nothing at all. People thought he was mad. The day finally came when no one gave him anything at all. He came to Khwaja Junaid with an empty purse and showed it to him. When Khwaja Junaid took the purse, he found it was empty. He said: 'Why is the purse empty today?' He replied: 'No one gave me anything today.' After a little while, Khwaja Junaid said: 'Up till this point the work was mine. I have completed my work. Now it is up to what *God* wants. The final step is seclusion to be preoccupied with God.'" He went on to explain:

"The point is that the guide has done whatever he could for his disciples." Afterwards he commented: "One calamity that might befall a disciple is to be deceived by his guide. Even if this happens, he should still have a right intention. The first step for him to take would be to forget his guide."

In this connection he related this story: "A disciple asked permission from his guide to be released from serving him in order to go his own way. The guide gave him certain instructions. The first instruction was that he should forget his guide, for the cause of attaining to *God* is the will of *God*. The guide is the occasion. What should happen is that the cause becomes totally involved, not the occasion. If the occasion were fully involved, the cause would be completely veiled for him.[284] If there were only an occasion but no cause, then a disciple could never attain his goal. This point should be kept in mind." He thereupon recited the following couplet:

How can you remember your first guide?
On arriving, you won't remember anything.

This dispensation applies to all intermediaries, as has been said:

When you attain the state of union,
A broker's words lose their taste.

A discussion arose about who should be called a disciple. The Revered Master said: "A disciple is a person who submits himself to his guide in word, deed, heart and body." He went on to explain: "'In word' means that his speech is in conformity with what his guide says regarding the essential principles and derived teaching of religion. 'In deed' means that he does nothing, whether in a religious or worldly matter, contrary to what has been sanctioned by his guide, even if it be an act of devotion! 'In heart' means keeping his heart unstained by any blameworthy quality, just as his guide does. 'In body' means keeping his senses and bodily members pure and without any stain of sin, just as his guide has done. When he has conformed himself in all these ways, then he can be called a disciple. The majority of disciples keep their eyes on their guide, imitating all his activities and periods of quiet. He does not pursue

---

284. It is worth recalling that Maneri himself, after spending time with his guide, Najibuddin Firdausi, in Delhi, went off into the jungle of Bihiya in order to be completely alone with God.

any studies apart from what is needed. What he acquires in an hour by submitting to his guide could not be acquired in a thousand years as a result of his own efforts."[285] A dear one asked: "Is there a hierarchy in the tasks given to a disciple so that he progresses from one to the other?" The Revered Master replied: "Spiritual masters have insisted that disciples should, at all times, keep themselves occupied. The order of precedence in what he does runs like this. He should begin by devoting himself to ritual prayer. If he grows tired of this he should turn to reciting the Quran, for this is an important dimension of prayer. If he tires of reciting the Quran, he should occupy himself with remembering God, because this is implied in reciting the Quran. If he tires of this he should turn to contemplation and meditation, for this is implied in the former. The former involves the moment of the tongue, while the latter does not."

---

285. The exaggeration is obvious, but the essential point remains valid. The greatest obstacle to progress is one's selfish soul, the inordinate demands of one's ego. Submission to a guide is humbling.

CHAPTER 18
THE MOULDING
OF A DISCIPLE

A discussion arose about the moulding of a disciple. The Revered Master said: "If a person wants to engage in the work of religion all by himself, and mould himself, then he will not be able to do so, even if he is a scholar of considerable learning. Even though it is possible for a person to mould himself and to fulfil the tasks of religion, yet this is an inferior way of acting. Whoever wishes to devote himself to the work of religion has two choices. He will need either a messenger, who will instruct him and guide him along the whole path of religion; or he will search for a guide, for guides are the successors of the messengers. He should throw himself at his feet in order to carry out whatever he tells him to do, without making any distinction with regard to how to act, defects, how to speak, duty or obligation. Together with this indifference, as he treads the path of religion, the novice must put into practice whatever his guide tells him to do. This is the way he will mould himself. He has no need to distinguish between what is obligatory and what is necessary. The whole purpose of knowing all these categories is to put them into practice. By actual doing, that aim is achieved. The guide gives the novice express instructions about his duties and obligations, as well as remedies against corrupting influences and dangers along the Way, and so forth. If he wants to become a guide himself in order to instruct others, for this purpose he will be directed to engross himself in studies in order to be able to distinguish between duties and obligations, as well as other matters." In this sense he stated quite clearly: "A disciple cannot mould himself except through the instruction of a guide. It could happen, however, through the grace of *God*, that a person is brought to this stage at the very beginning, but this is extremely rare." He added: "Prophets and righteous people are famous for that special grace, and a special grace will certainly produce special qualities."

Sheikh Mu'izzuddin asked what grace[286] meant. The Revered

---

286. *Faiz* has the basic meaning of abundance, of being brimful and

Master explained: "Grace refers to what *God* Most Exalted bestows superabundantly and generously by way of a special gift and spiritual wealth. He does so without the recipient's having sought it, or having endured any struggle to acquire it. Moreover, it will not cease right up until the Day of Resurrection. This is why it is said that grace will never cease." The Helpless One inquired: "Does a guide order a particular occupation for the disciple at his request, or does he do so on his own initiative without any request made by the disciple?" The Revered Master replied: "If the guide is a man of insight and of spiritual experience, he will perceive and understand how far the disciple has progressed; where he has reached; and what he is capable of achieving. What is the need for him to wait for a request from the disciple before telling him what to do? If he does make a request, however, there is no harm in doing so. Not making a request would not involve any loss either. This is because the guide will not leave him by himself."

Again, the Helpless One inquired: "Could it happen that the guide does not give him an instructions?" The Revered Master replied: "Guides simply could not do such a thing! This is because they are obliged by virtue of their role as exemplars and leaders. The basis for this is that disciples and followers must necessarily have the path of religion explained to them, especially by informing them about what they have to do." The Helpless One continued: "In some instances it is seen that the disciple makes no request, nor does the guide give him any instructions. Since the disciple makes no request, why doesn't the guide give him any instructions?" The Revered Master replied: "This is because of the lack of spiritual capital, good fortune and aptitude of the disciple, since these have not been apportioned to him. In this situation, he gives no instructions.[287] Where is the pain that descends and, taking hold of a person, so changes him that he seeks relief from all that exists; blinds him to it; and leads him forward, sick and afflicted, so that he seeks treatment?[288] Nowadays it is all ambition.

---

overflowing. That is the kind of divine grace which is intended here.

287. The simple fact is that not all those who think they are called to seek God by following a Path of full obedience to a guide are called to do so. An experienced guide will come to know who is actually called, and will guide him, and who should be gently directed to another calling in life.

288. It is worth recalling that Maneri had become an eminent scholar in Sonargaon; had experienced intercourse and fatherhood; had returned

This is the basis of all activity."

Later on, he added: "Nowadays the work is rooted in ambition. Somehow, they hear that it is an honourable work to become a disciple. They then hurry off to become one. They get their heads shaved and become disciples. Guides also suffer from ambition. It suddenly occurs to them that it is a good thing to have disciples. This makes them feel happy. They then begin to gather disciples. If they are asked a question about what it means to be a dervish, or about a saying of the dervishes, they are nonplussed and are unable to give an answer. What instructions can a person, who himself does not know, give to someone else? Both guides and disciples are victims of ambition. The world, however, is not bereft of guides. There have been guides; there are guides; and there will be guides. The Messenger has assured us of this. Nevertheless, we see that nowadays, for the most part, both disciples and guides are fired by ambition."

A discussion arose about 'to him' and 'upon him'.[289] The Revered Master said: "'To him' refers to whatever is meritorious for a servant, while 'upon him' refers to whatever involves chastisement for a servant. Dervishes say that disciples, at the very least, should be able to distinguish between 'to him' and 'upon him,' so as to know to which category anything that comes to him belongs. If something belongs to the category of 'to him,' he should accept it. If it comes under 'upon him,' he should distance himself from it. According to their terminology, this is the essence of meaning. In other words, this saying constitutes a compendium of the knowledge of the world. By means of this basic distinction, guides issue their instructions. For example, it is related that a disciple bound himself to a sheikh. After having done so, the sheikh instructed his disciple, saying: 'Whatever you would not choose for yourself, do not choose for another; and desire for others what you desire for yourself.' After a while the disciple came to the sheikh and said: 'I bound myself to you and you have not given me any instructions.' The sheikh replied: 'Since you have not yet learned the first les-

---

to Maner with his small son, Zakiuddin; but had gone to Delhi in search of a guide. He felt the need for guidance to assuage the deeper yearnings of his being. His quest led him to Sheikh Najibuddin Firdausi who lovingly guided him into an ever deeper union with God. The example of Al-Ghazali also comes to mind.

289. *Lahu* and *'alaihi.*

son, how can I teach you the second one?' The disciple could not grasp his meaning. He said: 'I don't know what the first lesson was.' The sheikh replied: 'On the first day didn't I tell you not to choose anything for someone else if you would not choose it for yourself; and also to desire for others what you desire for yourself? This was your first lesson.'" The Revered Master exclaimed: "Just look at this first lesson! These two sayings encompass all commands!"

A discussion arose about purification and refinement. The Revered Master said: "It is not proper for a beginner to act on his own initiative, as he did before being purified and refined. Whatever he does should be at the instance of his guide. This is because he is not yet conversant with the subtleties and secrets of the enterprise. Before he is purified and refined, he is full of satanic and selfish impulses. For example, whenever food is placed in front of him he is happy and eats it out of habit and the pleasure he experiences. He does not eat it because it is needed for his well-being. Another person may hear that it is good to lead a life of retirement, and that many people have embraced such a life. In the meantime, he is experiencing difficulties at home. Bearing the sorrow of home life seems a great burden to him. He cuts himself off from his wife and children and embraces a life of solitude. What is going on? He says; 'I have become a recluse. I have chosen solitude.' The fact of the matter is that home life has become difficult for him, and the burden has proved to be too much to bear, yet he is unaware of this. In a similar way, a disciple might be smitten by a desire to travel and change the place where he lives. He feels impelled to travel. This self-centred desire makes him happy and he sets out on a journey. What profit will he gain by such a journey, unless it has been prescribed by a master of the heart?" He then recited the following:

> Whoever is obedient worships with abandon,
> Whether the act be difficult or easy.
> An hour spent in obedience to a command
> Is better than a life devoted to one's choice.
> Whoever himself initiates prolonged austerities
> Would be a dog in his alley, not a somebody.
> A dog endures many pains, but to what profit?
> Where there is no command, nothing but loss ensues.
> Hardship, endured for a moment out of obedience,
> Reaps a whole world full of merit.

What is commanded is correct: take refuge therein!
May Your servant not incline towards vacillation!

After this, he continued: "This applies to anything that is laid aside
or taken up. As for anything a person does at the instigation of his
selfish soul, whether he does it or not is one and the same. What
does it profit him if it is not done at the command of a spiritual
guide? According to the limits already mentioned, a beginner does
not even undertake voluntary exercises without the permission of
his guide, even if they be acts of devotion. Moreover, since voluntary exercises are worship, and whatever is worship has to be undertaken, what need is there for any permission? The answer given
is that a beginner, before being purified and refined, is unable to
distinguish between a divine and a satanic inspiration. He is not
yet conversant with the subtleties and secrets of the enterprise.
Whatever he does is to please his selfish soul, or according to habit.
He will consult his guide because he has become acquainted with
the subtleties and secrets of the work. He can detect the difference
between a divine and a satanic inspiration. He can immediately
put his finger on its source! This is because of his experience. Severing the link to the selfish soul, the guide tells the beginner what
to do, so that nothing he does is bereft of merit.

The whole point at issue in this matter is what *God* Most Exalted has said: 'O you who believe, do not be forward in the presence
of God and His Apostle' (Q49:1). Imam Kalbi has provided this explanation: 'Do not go ahead of the Apostle of God, in word or deed,
unless he commands you to do so.' With regard to his guide, a novice should be bereft of personal choice. He should relinquish control over his personal choices and anything he possesses, and act
according to the suggestions and commands of his guide. The benefit of such behaviour has been described in this way. The guide is
a trustee for the novice with regard to inspirations, just as Gabriel
is a trustee with regard to revelation.[290] Moreover, just as it is inad-
missible for Gabriel to be guilty of deception regarding revelation,
a similar stricture applies to the guide with regard to inspirations.
Similarly, just as the Messenger did not speak out of desire, in the
same way a guide, who is a follower of the Messenger, clearly does
not speak out of selfish desire. Thus it is said that a guide, because

---

290. Gabriel is credited with transmitting the divine revelation
contained in the Quran to Muhammad.

of what he says, is a listener, so much so that it is related that one day, Khwaja Abu Sa'id Abul Khair was conversing with his friends. He said: 'I am a listener in this conversation.' One of the novices found this comment hard to accept. He expostulated: 'By virtue of what he says a speaker is undoubtedly a learned person. How can he be a listener?' In this frame of mind, he went home. When he fell asleep that night he dreamt that someone was saying: 'What is astonishing about this? Haven't you seen a diver plunge into the sea in search of precious stones and pearls? He collects them in his pouch, a hundred pearls and precious stones, but he does not look at them. When he comes out of the sea he examines those pearls and precious stones together with the people who happen to be on the shore.' The novice understood in a dream what his guide had been hinting at. In this way his difficulty was clarified."

The Helpless One inquired: "Is the guide aware of the anxieties that a novice experiences?" The Revered Master replied: "He knows about it by virtue of an enlightenment that is bestowed upon him. It can also happen on occasion, however, that he does not know, on account of his being preoccupied with something." Afterwards he told the following story: "In *Kashf- i Mahjub*[291] [Revealing What Lies Hidden] it is related that an enlightened person said: 'On one occasion my guide was performing his ablutions. I was pouring the water for him. A disturbing thought occurred to me, namely, that the Lord had already apportioned wealth and favours for a servant, or He had not done so. If He had not, then a servant would never receive them. If, however, they had been apportioned, he would certainly receive them. What's the point of novices' performing all these services for their guides? By virtue of enlightenment concerning these disturbing thoughts, my guide lifted his head and said: 'My son, it is just as you were thinking. Nevertheless, when the Lord apportions wealth and favours to anyone, He brings him to this Way. This becomes his way of acting.' In a word, it becomes his wealth and favour."

The Helpless One again inquired: "Just as a guide exercises influence over the states of a novice when he is awake, does he exercise a similar influence over him when he is asleep?" The Revered Master replied: "Yes, it can happen in both states. When a guide

---

291. This is the form found in the text. The title is normally given in its Arabic form, *Kashf ul-Mahjub*.

has reached this stage, 'I am his hearing and seeing,' the influence of the guide over the novice occurs in both states. This is because *God* Most Exalted is aware of the states of servants whether they are awake or asleep, so anyone who shares His seeing and hearing will also share a similar awareness with regard to him."

The Helpless One inquired: "Some people say that novices consider their own guides to be better than others. What would you say about this comment?" The Revered Master replied: "This is not so. How can there be any question of his knowing that one is better than another? All guides are the same. A novice should have enough belief in his own guide as to realize this: 'What my guide says and does is divinely inspired. No word of his proceeds from his selfish soul. Indeed, what he does and says is *God* acting and *God* speaking. Drawing close to him means drawing close to *God*. In other words, if I am perfectly in tune with my guide in whatever he does, I attain *God*, just as he has.' God rightly knows best, however.

CHAPTER 19

SHAVING ONE'S HEAD: CUTTING, DIVIDING AND PARTING ONE'S HAIR: AND WHAT IS FITTING IN THESE MATTERS

Qazi Sadruddin inquired: "How many times did the Apostle have his head shaved?" The Revered Master replied: "He had it shaved once. Otherwise, he simply divided it. This he did by taking hold of the hair at the nape of his neck and making a knot of it on his forehead. His followers, however, simply parted their hair." The Helpless One inquired: "This parting is done by drawing some hair to the left and some to the right. The followers of Ali, however, make two plaits. Has this been handed down or not?" The Revered Master answered: "It has not come to my attention anywhere." There was a earnest seeker who had his hair cut. He said that he wanted to have his head shaved, but his mother wanted him only to cut his hair. The Revered Master said: "Although shaving the head is better, nevertheless, because his mother only wants him to cut his hair, this would be better, because here two rights are brought together." Afterwards he continued: "The Apostle instructed pilgrims to Mecca to get their heads shaved. Some of his companions asserted that it was enough to have a haircut. The Apostle again prescribed shaving, while the companions spoke up for a haircut. The Apostle again insisted on shaving the head, and the companions still favoured a haircut. For the fourth time the Apostle prescribed shaving the head, and added 'a haircut.' If shaving the head were not better than having a haircut, the Apostle would not have repeatedly insisted on it. The relative merit of shaving the head as compared to having a haircut has thus been established, as one of preference, not of radical difference. Nevertheless, shaving the head is preferable to having a haircut."

Later on he added: "At the time of the Apostle and of earlier generations there was no pledging of fealty, shaving of the head, or getting one's hair cut. There was simply association and the bestowal of a robe. Haven't you read that the Apostle sent his own blessed robe to Khwaja Uwais Qarani?[292] Cutting the hair, shaving the head and pledging fealty appear in later generations. It is said that they date from the time of Khwaja Junaid when they began to be practised again. They were not speaking about pledging fealty, nor actually placing hand upon hand. There was no instruction about formalising the relationship between guide and novice. Discipleship was then established by placing the hand upon the hand. In some places it was said that, since there was no shaving of the head, cutting of the hair, or placing hand upon hand, Khwaja Junaid himself initiated these practices. The response given to this accusation is that Khwaja Junaid was simply following these practices. Unless they had come to him from the Apostle or from his companions, and he had established their origins, he would not have started using them, for no one had accused him of initiating these practices. In this way it is known about their origin and that they were being followed."

Later on, he told this story: "When Sheikh Nizamuddin was alive Sheikh Ahmad Amun visited him. He asked him for a headband. Sheikh Nizamuddin gave him one. There was no pledging of obedience or getting his hair cut. After the death of Sheikh Nizamuddin, Sheikh Ahmad went to Delhi. He expressed his desire to pledge obedience to Sheikh Mahmud.[293] He asked him if he was anyone's disciple. He replied: 'I received a headband from Sheikh Nizamuddin, but did not give my hand in pledge of obedience.' Sheikh Mahmud replied: 'There is no need to do so. That constitutes a pledge of obedience.' A number of Sufis were present in that assembly. They began to discuss the matter amongst themselves. 'That headband was a holy relic. How could it be a pledge of obedience?' Finally, Sheikh Mahmud also began to consider the matter. He said to Sheikh Ahmad: 'I shall mention this matter to other sheikhs and we shall discuss it among ourselves. I shall also dili-

292. Uwais Qarani is a legendary figure from Yemen who was supposedly a contemporary of Muhammad. He was first mentioned by Dostowai (d.770) and plays an important role in the history of Sufism. Those Sufis who had no personal spiritual guide are often known as 'Uwaisis.' He remained in Yemen, according to the legend, and never met Muhammad.

293. Sheikh Nasiruddin Mahmud Chiragh-i Dehli, the spiritual successor of Sheikh Nizamuddin Auliya, is meant. He was the leading Sufi in Delhi until his death in 1356.

gently search the books of the sheikhs to see what is found there.'
That is exactly what he did. Sheikh Mahmud searched the books
and consulted other sheikhs by informing them about the problem
that had arisen and asking their opinion. Finally, a consensus was
reached by all the sheikhs and dervishes that it was not a pledge
of obedience. 'Make your pledge of obedience. That headband was
a holy relic.'" Afterwards the Revered Master added: "The point of
this story is that, since hand was not placed upon hand, nor were
scissors employed, the command about formalizing discipleship
was not carried out."

He then related another story in this regard: "Abu Ishaq was
a member of the order of complete transparency.[294] He was living
quietly in his village. One day he was by himself. Suddenly Khwaja
Abdullah Khafif[295] arrived beside him. Because of his perfect spiritual insight he called out to Abu Ishaq, telling him to come forward and become his disciple. Khwaja Abu Ishaq had no idea how
a person became a disciple. He said: 'How do I become a disciple?'
Khwaja Abdullah replied: 'Come, place your hand upon mine, and
say: I have become your disciple.' Khwaja Abu Ishaq did as he was
bidden. He placed his hand upon his and said, 'I have become your
disciple.' Until hand was placed on hand discipleship had not been
established. Khwaja Abu Ishaq then asked: 'What do I do now? How
should I occupy myself?' Khwaja Abdullah Khafif replied: 'You do
not have to do anything but this. Do not eat until you have giv-
en a portion of your food to a dervish. First give him a portion
of your food and then you yourself eat.' Since this is what he was
commanded to do, he made it his practice. He continued to act
in this way. After some time three dervishes arrived in his village
and made to continue their journey without stopping. Khwaja Abu
Ishaq said: 'They did not stop in this village. If I can manage it, I'll
bring some food for them. He came home. He saw that he had three
nans.[296] He picked them all up and ran after them until he caught

---

294. The Persian is: *az farzandan-i tafiya-i saped ban.* The import of the
phrase seems to be that Abu Ishaq had no knowledge whatsoever about
Sufi orders but was leading an exemplary, pious life in the village. The
proffered translation is an attempt to convey this.

295. Khwaja Abdullah Khafif was a famous Sufi of Shiraz. He travelled
extensively but ended his days in his native Shiraz, where he died in 982.

296. *Nan.* In Iran, a single bread of this type is quite substantial. In India,
it is much smaller.

up with them. He said: 'I have brought something to eat.' They sat down at that very spot. He brought out the three nans and placed one in front of each person. They started eating and talking among themselves. 'This man has done his job. We should also do ours.' At this point one of them said: 'I shall give him the world.' The second one said: 'The poor fellow will be destroyed! I shall give him the world to come.' The third one said: 'The dervish is a young man. Both should be given.' They said: 'We shall give both.'"

Afterwards the Revered Master continued: "What can be said about the work of the world to come? What are its limits? So many goods and possessions were accumulated that a kettledrum was played five times a day at his door.[297] The practice still takes place at Khwaja Abu Ishaq's tomb, long after his death. The expense that was involved in providing food is still being provided. An incredible amount of revenue pours into the tomb complex from ships. In that area, whoever sets sail makes this vow: 'If I return safely, I shall donate so many thousand gold coins to the Khwaja's tomb.' On account of this, hundreds of thousands of gold coins are donated every year and are spent on food." After this, the Revered Master recited the following:

> For whomsoever He is, tomorrow He will be for him:
> Seven rivers will flow for him beneath the bridge.[298]
> Be a real man here, so that it may be revealed to you!
> Don't turn from the Way, that it may be shown to you!

He said: "Just see Sheikh Abdullah and the degree of his perfection!" He then recited this couplet:

> Your mind should be brighter than the sun,
> To discern the state of each madman.

A discussion arose about why sheikhs, when having their hair cut, have only three strands of hair cut. What does it mean? The Revered Master said: "Sheikh Ahmad Bangali had asked me this very question, namely, why do sheikhs get only three strands of hair cut? I could not find the answer to this question in any book. Fi-

297. It was a common practice to beat a large kettledrum five fixed times a day in front of the residence of an important man, prince or king, both as an indication and a reminder of his importance.

298. The reference is probably to *sirat*, the bridge over hell. The abundant waters would save a person from the fires of hell.

nally, it occurred to me—but God knows best—that a possible reason for cutting three strands of hair could be connected to what
is described about three veils. The first is creatures, for they are a
veil with regard to devotion and worship, because a person tends
to get absorbed in them. The second is the world, for it veils the
world to come. The third veil is the next world, for it veils the
Lord. Hence, every time three hairs are cut, these three veils are
removed. Cutting each hair indicates the removal of a veil. Some
sheikhs get four hairs cut: one from the forehead; one from the left
and another from the right side of the head; and one hair from the
back of the head. The meaning given to this—but God knows best—
is that some speak about four veils. We have already seen three of
them. The fourth veil is one's selfish soul. The cutting of each hair
indicates the removal of a veil. One point has to be noted here,
however, and it is that the selfish soul is a creature. It is included in
the category of 'creatures.' For this reason, the selfish soul is not a
fourth veil." After a while, the Revered Master proposed an answer
to his own difficulty: "'Creatures' form a general category, while
'the selfish soul' is something special. Another possibility—but
God knows best—is that the world has four supports. Hence the
cutting of four hairs means one is severing one's ties with those
four supports." In relation to this, he recited the following:

> The story of dust is a diverting sport:
> The pure world is pure devotion.
> Along this Way, if you don't act like that,
> Exert yourself fully: you won't suffer any loss.

A discussion arose about the benefits of shaving one's head. The
Revered Master said: "In an account of the sayings of Sheikh Nizamuddin[299] I saw three things that you yourself should do but not
disclose to your enemies. They are extremely beneficial. What he
said, and not to be told to enemies, is to be diligent in what is profitable, but sparing in sharing it with others.[300] Shaving the head
is one of those three things. The second is to drink water before
eating a meal. The third is massaging the soles of the feet with oil.

299. Nizamuddin Auliya is meant.
300. Dushmanan ra nabayad farmud mubalaghat ast dar manfa'at wa
tahris ast dar haqq-i digaran. This is the Persian text. The sentiment
which seems to be expressed is very surprising in a Sufi text, especially
when one reads the three practices being referred to.

There are many benefits in shaving one's head. For example, ritual impurity can occur while taking a bath if a single hair on one's head is not washed. Such a doubt is also removed. Yet again, if you have a head of hair, the selfish soul becomes slothful, and prayer is thrown into jeopardy. Moreover, so much time is consumed in looking after one's hair that there can be a falling off of prayer."[301] At this point a dear young man came and was honoured to kiss the ground. He expressed his desire to become one of the Revered Master's disciples. The Master complied with his request. He then expressed his commitment. Qazi Ashrafuddin inquired: "Why do sheikhs, at the time of commitment, cut some of the hair on the candidate's head?" The Revered Master replied: "It is said: 'No one becomes a disciple until his guide has cut some of the hair on his head.' Cutting the hair is meant to ensure the soundness of a person's commitment. As to whether shaving the head is required, God knows best. It occurs to me that in some books it is mentioned as indicating that our heads are full of desires and pleasures which act as a veil between us and the Lord. We cleanse our heads of all that." After this, he recited the following:

> As long as this world grips you, you can't attain the next:
> As long as you focus on self, you cannot attain God.
> If you want to attain that stage,
> It will be difficult until you shave your head.

He commented: "That dear young man used to come in wholehearted search of what *God* wanted, namely, whether mercy was destined for him at this time." He went on to explain the origin of the robe and scissors. "The origin of the scissors is found in the narrative of how Adam ensured that each of his sons became engaged in a particular trade and employment. Several sons came along and he saw to it that each of them was employed in a particular trade. Finally the messenger Seth was born. From the very beginning, Seth was enamoured of living in seclusion. Adam was carefully considering what trade would be suitable for him so that he could tell him what he should do. It so happened that Gabriel appeared and said: 'Seth is a Sufi.' Thereupon the messenger Seth embraced seclusion. It so happened that people began to associate

---

301. The warning seems to apply to extreme cases of an elaborate hairstyle, not to a normal person's hairstyle.

with him and visit him. The number of visitors increased. Again, Gabriel appeared with a pair of scissors for Seth and instructed him thus: 'Use these scissors to cut the hair of anyone who wants to be associated with you in order to establish a relationship between you and that particular person.' This is the origin of cutting the hair.

With regard to the Sufi garb, however, there is a difference of opinion. Some trace it back to Abraham. It is said that when accursed Nimrod placed Abraham, the Friend, in a catapult and sent him flying towards a great fire, he had first been stripped naked. Gabriel descended with a garment from heaven and put it on him, so that the fire turned to perfume for him. Some others link it to our Messenger. They say that, on the night of ascent, when our Messenger received a robe from the Respected One, *God* Most Exalted put a question to him for his friends to answer. He also made known the answer to the Apostle. He instructed him to give the blessed robe to the person who gave the correct answer. Thereupon the Apostle went first of all to the Commander of the Faithful, Abu Bakr, the Righteous, and put this question to him: 'If I give you this robe, what will you do?' He replied: 'I shall acquire and cultivate truth and purity.' He then asked the Commander of the Faithful, Umar, the same question. He replied: 'I shall cultivate justice and equity.' He then asked the Commander of the Faithful, Uthman, the very same question. He replied: 'I shall bestow gifts liberally.' Each one answered from his own disposition. Finally, he asked the Commander of the Faithful, Ali: 'If I give you this robe, what will you do?' The Commander of the Faithful, Ali, replied: 'I shall become a veil covering the people and concealing their faults.' The Apostle took hold of the robe and said: 'Put it on, because I was instructed to give it to the person who gave this answer.'" Later on the Revered Master added: "This explains why this group conceals the faults of people. If a person's fault is out in the open, they try their level best to convert it to what is good. They keep trying to bring out any possible good contained therein." At this point, he recited the following:

Whoever reveals the faults of sinners,
Aligns himself with oppressors.
If all without exception were prayerful,
The secret of love's playfulness would lie hidden.

No amount of asceticism equals a Muslim's worth:
Nothing at his tomb can equal his value.[302]

He said: "In *'Awarif* it is mentioned that Abu Dir'a[303] relates that
his father said, concerning Umm Khalid, that she said a number of
robes were brought to the Apostle. Among them was one that was
short and black. The Prince of the world said: 'Does any one of you
know whom I shall clothe with this robe?' The companions stood
around silent. He commanded: 'Bring Umm Khalid to me!' Umm
Khalid reported: 'I was brought into his presence. He clothed me
with that robe.' The Apostle said: 'Attend to this and change it!' He
repeated these words. She went and stitched a border of gold and
red. He examined it and exclaimed: 'O Umm Khalid, that is a very
fine border!' Two types of robes are obtained, the robe of commitment and the robe of blessing. The discussion now is about the
robe of commitment. The robe of blessing is similar to it. The robe
of commitment is for a genuine disciple. 'Whoever is like a people
will be included among them.' This is no small matter."

He said: "Donning the Sufi garb establishes a bond between
the guide and the disciple. It entails the disciple's handing over of
control of his selfish soul to the guide, just as the community en-
trusts itself to the Apostle of God in the words of the Ancient Book,
wherein *God* Most Exalted has said: 'But no, by thy Lord, they will
not believe until they make you the judge in their disputes. Then
they will find no resistance within themselves with your judge-
ments and will accept them wholeheartedly' (Q4:65). The occasion of the descent of this verse was when a dispute rose between
Zubair bin Awam and another person about the passage of water to
his date palms. He came to the Apostle and requested him to give
a judgement. The Apostle told Zubair bin Awam to provide water
first to his palm grove and then to let it flow on to his neighbour.
That man was enraged at hearing this and said: 'The Messenger
has decided in favour of his paternal uncle!' And God Most Exalted
sent down this verse. He learnt from this verse the correct way of
behaving with the Apostle of God, as it is stipulated in the verse

---

302. Maneri is speaking about a genuine Muslim, a person whose whole
life is lived in submission to God, not about a person who simply claims
to be a Muslim.

303. The name is not clear. Different forms are given in different
manuscripts.

that he should accept what he says. This applies exteriorly and has to be applied interiorly as well. This is also the condition of the disciple with his guide once he has entrusted himself to him."

Afterwards he added: "This clothing by the guide is based on the example of the blessed Apostle, just as *God* Most Exalted has said: 'Those who swear allegiance to you swear allegiance to God. The hand of God is above their hands. Anyone who breaks his word does so at his own peril' (Q48:10). To sum up, clothing with a robe is a sign of his entrusting himself to his guide and of his being accepted, and of his coming under the sway of God and of the Apostle, and imitating the Apostle means bringing his way of living to life again. Concerning the Apostle of God it is related that Walid bin Abbad bin Samat said: 'I pledged allegiance to the Apostle of God, swearing to pay attention to whatever he said; and to carry out whatever he commanded, whether it be difficult or easy, bearing grief or bringing comfort. If somebody says something that should be contradicted, I will not contest against him. In all circumstances I shall speak the truth, and I will not be afraid of anyone who blames me for anything.' The Sufi garb indicates imitation and entering into association. The aim of all association is to enable the disciple to achieve the fulfilment of all his good aspirations. It has been related that most guides think that happiness will never be revealed to anyone who is in search of safety." At this point the Revered Master recited the following:

The association of men of insight is like the fragrance of a rose:

> The admonition of well-wishers is like the flavour of wine.
> Journeying together with friends is pleasant:
> Without friends, a journey can be hellish.
> Wise men have expressed it well when they said:
> One companion for a house, but many for a journey.

The Helpless One inquired: "If a worthless sinner, or somebody in the grip of satanic suggestions or evil inclinations, has the inclination and desire to have his head shaved, but says, 'When I have emerged from rebelling and disobeying, and my evil inclinations, then I shall follow my desire and get my head shaved.' What would you say about this line of thinking?" The Revered Master replied: "This is like a person who said, 'Until I acquire the probity of Abu Bakr I won't take part in ritual prayer!' Tell me, when will he acquire the probity of Abu Bakr and thus begin to pray? Take care not to entertain such thoughts! Whenever such thoughts do occur, no matter what the circumstances, don't entertain them! Holy men have forbidden such things. They are all temptations of Satan. They say that whoever comes, no matter what state he is in, this garment should be given to him." Afterwards he added: "One should exert oneself fully and not lose hope on account of so much rebellious behaviour. If no improvement takes place, at least he will become similar in appearance to dervishes. He will attain the wealth of 'The person who resembles a people becomes one of them.' In the family of the famous men of Chisht, this is the way of proceeding. Everyone who comes is given this garment, even if he is a worthless fellow. The reason for this is that putting it on is a first step. The robe makes him feel ashamed. He knows it is the robe worn by those whose lives are pure. He turns aside from the path of sin and approaches a guide." At this juncture he recited the following:

> If you have sinned, by repenting you return:
> So repent, for this door will never be shut.
> It is like a sorrow-less ocean of His grace:
> In His immensity your sins are a drop of mist.
> Everyone who has experienced such forgiveness
> Experiences no change because of pollution.

After this, he added: "By virtue of the blessing of this garment, it can so happen that he can emerge completely from his sinful situation. In order to overcome these temptations and dangers he calls them exaggerations. They are satanic in origin. They hold him back from what he wants to do." He recited the following:

> Despise the world as Moses did,
> Then settle accounts with this Pharaoh.
> In both worlds real men rejoice in Him,
> Passing their lives in His protection.
> Anyone at all, tell me, what is better than He,
> That you may rejoice therein for a single breath?

CHAPTER 20
GOD'S SAINTS

A discussion arose about this tradition: "My saints are beneath my domes." The Revered Master said: "'Domes' is the plural of 'dome,' which can mean 'skirt.' Thus, 'My saints are beneath my skirts.' Here, 'skirt' means 'protective honour.' This is the opinion of a number of saints. Ordinary people think of hiding something precious in the folds of their garments." He then related this story: "Khwaja Junaid got up one night, performed his ablutions in order to go to the mosque of Shuniziya, for that was a holy place. When he reached the door he saw someone of a horribly disagreeable appearance standing there. He said: 'Who are you? I feel like rejecting you.' He replied: 'I am the one you have very often desired to see.' The Sheikh realized that it was the Devil. He exclaimed, 'Indeed!' He then asked: 'Why did you want to see me?' He replied: 'I wanted to ask you a question.' He said: 'What is your question?' The Sheikh replied: 'It is this: Do you have any hold over God's saints?' 'No.' 'How is that?' he went on to inquire. He replied thus: 'When I try to ensnare them with this world, they flee to the next. When I try to ensnare them there, they fly to the Lord God, where I have no access.' Once again the Sheikh put a question: 'Have you become aware of their secret?'[304] 'No,' he replied, 'except for one time, namely, while listening to songs, if they are overcome by ecstasy. That is when I discover what has been manifested to them.'[305] After saying this, he disappeared. Mulling over these words, the Sheikh entered the mosque. A voice came to him from a corner of the mosque. 'Be careful, my son, not to be deceived by the words of this enemy! The Lord's saints are so precious to Him that He does not reveal even to Gabriel what He manifests to them, so how could He reveal it to that enemy?' He looked and saw that it was his guide, Sari Saqati,[306] and rejoiced."

---

304. The 'secret' is what happens in moments of ecstatic union with God.

305. This attempt at satanic deception will be quickly unmasked by Junaid's guide.

306. Sari Saqati (d.867) was a prominent Sufi of the Baghdad circle. He was a dealer in second-hand goods.

Qazi Ashrafuddin inquired: "Does a saint know that he is a saint by manifesting miraculous powers?" The Revered Master replied: "Some say that they do know, but mostly they say that they do not. This is because their miracles are not free of duplicity and deception, even though they have differentiated between miracles and duplicity. They give thanks, however, that sometimes it is a miracle. It is because of this basic fact that they always retain a lowly opinion of themselves. In no way do they consider themselves to be an abode of miracles, nor do they see themselves as such."[307] At this point he recited this couplet:

You call me an ascetic, but I am a lost idol-worshipper:
This rosary in my hands deceives you: it is a sacred thread.

"In *Kashf ul-Mahjub* it is asserted that it is childish to hold that saints do not know they are saints. This is because so much profound understanding occurs between them and *God*—may He be glorified and exalted—that is not found in anyone else. They are also endowed with the ability, by means of the light of intimate knowledge as well as the light of faith, to discern between what is miraculous and what is duplicitous." After a pause, he continued: "Mostly people think they do not know. This is because they are not free of doubts about being deceived or duped. There were several ascetics who initially performed miracles yet ended up in duplicity and deception, such as Balaam, son of Beor, as well as the ascetic, Barsisa.[308] Both of them were renowned for their unparalleled knowledge and as workers of numerous miracles. It finally so happened that they all turned out to be duplicity and deception." When the Revered Master uttered these words he groaned in anguish. All present in the assembly were so moved that they wept.[309]

---

307. This is a reflection of Maneri's own inner disposition.

308. The first is the well-known biblical figure who was called upon to curse the Israelites and ended up blessing them. The second figure is found in Muslim literature from the tenth century onwards. Both typify the man with a saintly reputation who is duped by Satan and ends up bereft even of faith in God.

309. We are left to imagine the scene. From the reaction of those present it is very clear that Maneri had been deeply moved at the thought of the downfall of holy men. His reaction can be interpreted as a spontaneous, heart-felt prayer to be spared a similar fate! His abhorrence of all claims, together with spontaneous expressions of genuine humility, are more

Several times he repeated these words: "Where should I go? Whose door should I approach? To whom should I speak?" He then recited the following couplet quite a number of times:

For years I have stood at His threshold, but He has ignored me:

So many years of my life spent grieving for Him have proved futile![310]

A discussion arose about the perfect man. One of those present inquired what 'perfect' meant. The Revered Master explained: "'Perfect' is of two kinds. One refers to focussed perfection, while the second refers to liberated perfection. The focussed perfect man has four accomplishments to his credit: mastery of the Law; perfect adherence to the Sufi Path; an experience of Reality; and an abundance of mystical knowledge. A liberated perfect man has eight accomplishments. Four of these are the ones just described. The other four are: valuing obscurity; rejecting high office; going into seclusion; and enjoying contentment. The focussed perfect man makes claims and exercises leadership. What this means is that, after completing the work of his own perfection, he then looks around in search of any better or more fruitful activity. He hones in on that of leading a person from unbelief to faith; from a life of sin to one of devotion; from preoccupation with what is other than *God* to being wholly taken up with God; or of liberating someone from the clutches of his infidel soul and leading him to the reality of belief in One God. This is what claimed his attention. 'Scholars are the heirs of the prophets' really applies to them.[311] A perfect man is called learned; a spiritual

---

indicative of his sanctity than some of the outlandish stories subsequently circulated about him.

310. In the printed copy, H.L.9849, Maneri invites those present to join him in reciting the opening chapter of the Quran for a good end to their lives. This is not found in the older MS 1219.

311. Notice that the scholar who sets about helping others has experiential, as well as scholarly, knowledge of God. When the learned Muzaffar Shams Balkhi became a disciple Maneri sent him back to Delhi for further studies. "Whatever knowledge you have acquired was for the sake of rank and position. You did not obtain a number of its fruits. Return to your studies with sincerity of purpose, doing them for God's sake. Be thorough, so as to be granted fruit in abundance which would be the cause of making progress along the Way." This extract is from *Manaqib ul-Asfiya,* p.148, as found translated in Paul Jackson, S.J., *The Way of a Sufi: Sharafuddin Maneri,* Idarah-i Adabiyat-i Delli, 1987, p. 89.

master; a guide; a sheikh; a leader; a Solomon; a Khizr; and a Jesus. He is called a Solomon because he knows the language of birds. He is called a Khiz because he knows what real life is. He is called a Jesus because he brings the dead to life, at the command of God Most Exalted. This means bringing someone to a well-ordered life, e.g. from unbelief to faith, or from a sinful to a devout life. If someone inquires as to which of these two is the more excellent, the answer normally give is this: If you focus on calling people to *God*, this follows the prophetic model. In this respect, the focussed perfect man has a greater perfection. On the other hand, if your focus is on the fact that the liberated perfect man is wholly preoccupied with *God*, then he would have the greater perfection. This is in accordance with the saying: 'He who cuts himself off from all, becomes united to the All.'"

In this connection, he related the story about Asma'i[312] who was walking along and happened to see a beautiful young woman. She inquired: 'How are you?' He replied: 'I am wholly taken up with you!' She exclaimed: 'If you are wholly taken up with me, I shall devote myself entirely to you, but you should know that I have a sister who is more beautiful than I am.' He asked her: 'Where is she?' 'Right behind you!' he turned around and looked behind him. She gave him a slap across the face, saying: 'If you were wholly taken up with me, how could you look at another?'"

A discussion arose about the renown and concealment of saints. The Revered Master said: "Saints are of two kinds. One kind is well known, while the other remains concealed. Anyone who becomes famous belongs to the first category, while a person who remains concealed is included in the second. 'Their bodies are in this world, but their hearts are in the next world.' They are present, but hidden." He went on to say: "Here are some verses about the qualities of saints. They should be committed to memory. If these verses are memorized and you see a person with these qualities, you will immediately realize that this man belongs to that group." Several times, in order to encourage those present, he said: "You should memorize these verses and also keep them fresh in your memory! An old woman recited some verses to Khwaja Zu'l-Nun Misri.[313] The story is that

---

312. Asma'i (d.828) was a philologist of great importance in the history of Arabic poetry and philology. He compiled early Arabic poetry, mainly by listening to Bedouin reciters. The critical method he formulated proved influential.

313. Zu'l Nun Misri (d.859 or 861) was born in Upper Egypt, which explains

an old woman approached Zu'l-Nun Misri one day. He asked her: 'Where did you come from?' She replied: From men 'whom neither trading nor selling can distract from remembering God' (Q24:37). He then asked her where she was going. She replied: To men 'who forsake their beds to pray to their Lord' (Q32:16). Zu'l-Nun Misri was overcome with yearning for them. He said to the old woman: 'What qualities they had!' It was then that he recited these verses in praise of their qualities:"

> This group is totally concerned with God:
> They have no other interest except the One.
> The aim of these people, whether novices or adepts,
> Is to devote themselves totally to God.
> They struggle with the world and against fame:
> They are not in search of fine food or offspring.
> They are not concerned about what they wear,
> Nor do they aim to settle down anywhere.
> Their whole effort is directed towards nothing,
> Except that Path which is filled with enemies.
> They are hermits living in wild and deserted places:
> As they mount higher, they encounter new enemies.[314]

Qazi Ashrafuddin put this question: "Khwaja Zu'l-Nun Misri was aware of the qualities of saints. What was the point of putting these questions to the old woman?" The Revered Master replied: "Perhaps it was because, even though he knew about them, he was experiencing a certain confusion. One should also remember that members of this group do not want anyone to become aware of their secret and go astray. There is safety in such behaviour. This is exemplified by the following couplet:"

> My heart is given to You, yet I seem to look at others:
> So that people won't know my gaze is fixed on You.

'Misri.' The first part of his name means "He of the fish." The story about his nickname is that he was on board ship when a jewel was lost. He was suspected of theft and thrashed. Finally he cried out, "O Creator, Thou knowest!" Thereupon thousands of fish put their heads out of the water, each with a jewel in its mouth. He took one and gave it to the merchant who had lost a jewel. He became a famous and influential figure in early Sufism.

314. The original language of these verses is Arabic. The translation was made with the assistance of friends.

After this he explained the meaning of the above verses as far as the words are concerned. I have written down as much as I can remember. After explaining each couplet, he gave other possible meanings of the words. He explained the first couplet thus: "They are people who are steadfastly committed to *God*. They have no commitment to anything else. This means that, except for a resolute commitment to the Lord, they have no other ties." In addition to the meaning of this couplet, he gave this hint to those present in the assembly: "You should act accordingly, for it is a way of recognizing the members of this group, according to the saying of the sheikhs: 'A poor man is one who does not depend on anything except God.' If this world and the next were brought to him in their thousands, he would not think of himself as rich until he had attained *God*. If he relies ever so slightly on anything else, he would not belong to this group." He illustrated this by pointing out that the hunger of a starving man is assuaged by bread, not by both worlds. At this juncture, he recited the following:

> If both worlds were to be given to me,
> I would be a beggar unless united to You.

When he had explained the meaning of this couplet, 'Their struggle is with the world and against fame,' he went on to say: "Those who visit taverns and flaunt reproachable behaviour do so to deflect attention from their noble state and to ensure that nothing can hinder them on their path of seeking." When he had explained, "that Path which is filled with enemies," he commented: "When they speak about setting out they mean that, although their destination is far off, yet it is only two steps away. In one stride they bypass this world, while their second stride takes them beyond the next world. When both have been traversed in this fashion, they attain to *God*. Although the way is long, members of this group traverse it in two strides. That is also the meaning of this couplet:"

> Sufis celebrate two feasts in one breath:
> Spiders tear the flesh of flies into strips.

Qazi Ashrafuddin remarked: "In a number of places it is written that a certain dervish attained to *God* at his third stride. How could this be?" The Revered Master replied: "This is a good example. Both worlds had been traversed in two strides, while his third stride took him to *God*." At this point, he recited the following:

A hundred thousand men get lost forever,
Yet only one may fully fathom secrets.
If you don't enjoy union with the Friend,
Arise and grieve over your separation.

The Revered Master said: "In the record of Sheikh Nizamuddin's discourses I have read that Sheikh Fariduddin once went to a mosque. He saw a dervish seated in the mosque. He recognized him for what he was. This was done by means of his qualities, not by what his face, hands and feet looked like. Thereupon Sheikh Fariduddin turned around and went home. He wanted to prepare a meal for him, but found nothing in the house except for some maize. With his own hands he immediately ground it, cooked it himself and brought it. Afterwards the dervish smiled and asked him what he wanted. Sheikh Fariduddin told him what he wanted.[315] His need was met by the dervish." When the Revered Master finished his story, he explained: "He recognized him on account of this. If the Sheikh had not recognized him, how could his need have been met?" He thereupon recited the following:

Sensitive hearts mix only with their own:
Nothing can be seen except with the eye.
Clay can see only what is made of clay:
It befits the pure to see only the pure.

Qazi Ashrafuddin inquired: "How can a quality which is internal be recognized?" The Revered Master replied: "By means of words, deeds and their saintly state they recognize, through spiritual intuition, the group they belong to. Moreover, in their saintly state they learn things that cannot be grasped through words. It is because of this that it is said that 'words provide only a hint of one's spiritual state.'" The Helpless One put this question: "Saints are admissibly sinless. This very point is found in the writings of ancient

---

315. This incident could not be traced in *Fawa'id ul-Fu'ad*, the record of the discourses of Sheikh Nizamuddin Auliya, complied by Amir Hasan Sijzi. Moreover, it does not fit the tenor of the stories about Fariduddin as found in this *malfuz*, for he is portrayed therein as the most eminent Sheikh of the period. This was Nizamuddin Auliya's experience of him. Maneri clearly says, "I have read" in the *malfuz* of Sheikh Nizamuddin... Was it a fabricated malfuz already in circulation a bare fifteen years or so after the death of Sheikh Nizamuddin?

authorities. In the recorded discourses of Sheikh Nizamuddin, however, we find that saints are unconditionally sinless. Jurisconsults say that prophets are necessarily sinless, while saints are admissibly sinless. How can saints be simply described as 'sinless'?" The Revered Master replied: "The point about their being called sinless is that they will be protected, for both words convey the same meaning. The only difference in this context is that, whereas for saints it is taken for granted, for prophets it is of necessity."

A discussion arose as to whether or not saints are aware of what is contained in the preserved tablet. The Revered Master explained: "Saints catch a glimpse of the preserved tablet, but how could they possibly be aware of everything inscribed on that tablet?[316] They are aware of only what is given to them. In other words, any particular saint can be aware to the extent that God Most Exalted bestows awareness upon him. There is no question of an awareness of all the divine commands, for the secrets of the Lord are such that no limit can be ascribed to them." After a while he added: "Awareness is granted to saints according to the stage of their spiritual development. Thus one is granted awareness of one secret; another of two; another of three; another of four and so on, according to their spiritual development. For example, even Israfil[317] has knowledge of events of only one whole year, not of all the commands inscribed on the preserved tablet. In some books, however, it is written that a reflected image of the preserved tablet is found in the hears of saints. In other words, the image of whatever is in the preserved tablet is formed in the hearts of saints. They draw a comparison with two mirrors. If you line up two mirrors so that they face each other, it so happens that whatever is in one mirror has its reflection formed in the second mirror. The same applies to the hearts of saints. The image of whatever is in the preserved tablet is formed in them. This downloading would occur according to their degree of spiritual development, namely, they would be aware according to the measure of awareness granted by divine grace, but God knows best and grants rewards." He then recited the following:

---

316. In Q85:21-22 the Quran is said to be "in the preserved tablet ." Several references to a book in which everything is recorded, e.g. Q:10:61; 22:70 and 27:75, are commonly understood to refer to the preserved tablet as a record of the totality of divine knowledge, which is clearly beyond human comprehension.

317. Israfil is the angel of death.

If you wish to attain to that stage,
Yet even a hair remains, it will be difficult.
If you breathe, you are not of one breath:
If but a hair remains, you are no confidant.

Afterwards he said: "The point of all this is that whatever *God* Most Exalted has caused to pass through a person's heart should not be in opposition. The principle behind this is that it cannot happen that their external behaviour exhibits any opposition to *God*, or that any inner movement of theirs is without His good pleasure. *God* Most Exalted also by way of work, order and grace, sees to it that, in their pure interiors, nothing occurs which would displease Him. This is the basis for proper behaviour."

A discussion arose about the breasts of saints being the successors of the call of the prophets. The Revered Master said: "It is written that, 'if prophecy has passed away, tradition remains.' The explanation of this saying is that the breasts of saints are where inspiration occurs. If revelation ceases, inspiration remains in its stead. This is what perdures. In other words, if there are no prophets, saints, as their successors, are at hand. It has been related that, if revelation has ceased, nevertheless the tradition regarding inspiration's taking its place remains."

A discussion arose about the wonderful deeds of Ain ul-Quzat. The Revered Master said: "He had so many insights revealed to him while intoxicated by *God*! Whatever he has written in his letters has been inspired entirely by what he himself has experienced and witnessed. It indicates what has brought delight to him. In some of his letters he has written that there are countless thousands in quest of paradise, but not a single person in quest of *God*." He went on to say: "A traditionist benefits by arguing with another traditionist, while a person lost in God loves another such person." After a while he continued: "Once Ain ul-Quzat was in a trance. In that state he prayed thus: 'O God, my prayer is that I may be burnt.' Lo and behold, that is what actually took place! He was burnt. It so happened that, while he was being burnt, he cried out, 'Ah!' People criticized him for this, pointing out that he had prayed to *God* that he might be burnt, so why did he cry out while this was happening? He replied: 'I do not cry out because of my affliction. It is a cry of satisfaction that they are burning me so promptly!'" At this point, the Revered Master recited the following couplet:

He is about to be killed, and this astonishes me:
How good is the wielding of that sword of His! ∘

After this he added: "Even though one and all have written something or other about intimate knowledge, yet few have written
as Ain ul-Quzat has in his *Tamhidat* regarding the way of acting;
required dispositions; and the fundamentals of religion. His writings provide a solution for many difficulties. In order to grasp the
meaning of his words, however, a person has to be aware of the
principles and regulations of this group, otherwise some of his
sayings would not tally with the accepted ways of acting."[318]

Someone wanted to hear about '*Awarif*. The Revered Master
said: "'*Awarif* is an esteemed book in which there is an accurate
description of Sufism; the injunctions concerning the Way; and
the religious outlook of this group. Although its author was quite
mature and capable of writing in a better and more advanced manner than he did, he adapted himself to the level of disciples and
beginners. Moreover, he was famous for his abundant knowledge
and the mystical insights that he enjoyed, so much so that Sheikh
Nizamuddin is recorded as having said that every blessing and accomplishment that a man is capable of had been bestowed upon
the Sheikh of Sheikhs by *God*—may He be glorified and exalted—
except for a taste for musical gatherings. This was missing, but the
Letters of Ain ul-Quzat contain a different story!"

A discussion arose about the glorious deeds of Khwaja Bayazid
Bastami. The Revered Master said: "One winter's night, on account
of a nocturnal pollution, Khwaja Bayazid Bastami had to take a pu-
rificatory bath. He was all ready to do so when his slothful selfish soul pointed out to him that it was the middle of the night.
He should have his bath later on. It was winter, after all! As soon
as Khwaja Bayazid perceived what his slothful soul was up to, he
immediately got up and, clad in his patched garment, plunged
into some water. It so happened that, in a short time, the patched
garment covering his body became dry." He then reflected: "This
power emanated from his sanctity. It is not within the capacity of
human beings." He recited the following:

---

318. Maneri's esteem for Ain-ul Quzat is self-evident. It seems that his
exquisite prose "put into words," so to say, much of what Maneri himself
had experienced. His words became 'alive' for him, at many levels.

Whoever gains complete control of this dog,
Has dust which is better than the blood of others.
This unruly selfish soul is like an infidel:
How could killing it be at all easy?
This dog is responsible for its own depravity:
No one has benefited by heeding what it says.

A discussion arose about the death of Khwaja Junaid. Qazi Ashrafud-din inquired if Khwaja Junaid had related anything about his death,[319] or had any expression deserving of death escaped his lips and result-ed in his being killed. The Revered Master explained: "He was not killed, nor did any word deserving of death escape his lips. He was an esteemed Sufi sheikh. All the Sufis sheikhs agree on this. He is also acceptable to all the Sufi confraternities, and was renowned for his sobriety. Even though thousands of meaningful insights found ex-pression in him, other types of expressions were never found on his lips. He shared in the sobriety of all the prophets. If thousands of in-sights come to mind and some travellers along the Way, at the begin-ning of the appearance of the King, utter something when overcome by what they experience, it is because of the effects of their intoxica-tion. This is before they enter the desert of sobriety. There are many examples of such utterances. For example, some have said: 'Who un-der heaven is like me?' Or, 'I have planted my foot on the necks of all the saints.' Or, 'I saddled my horse and set out on a journey. I said: Is anyone prepared to come out and fight me? No one came forward!' There are many such examples. Sufi sheikhs can speak with author-ity about such matters. They have passed beyond the constraints of intoxication and have stepped into the wide expanse of the desert of sobriety.[320] How could such things emanate from them? The follow-ing couplets give apt expression to that perception:

When the mind is constricted you lose your heart,
Since the wine of intoxication stifles the mind.
Don't become a proud flute intoxicated by a single cup!

---

319. There is a story that Junaid, when he felt his death was imminent, bade his disciples prepare a meal, for he wished to die while they were at table.

320. *Az tangi-i sukr bargashte and wa befarakhi-i sahra-i sahw qadam nihade and.* The repeated phrase, "the desert of sobriety" seems to flow from Maneri's personal experience and finds an echo even in modern times, e.g. in the letters of Mother Teresa of Calcutta.

Seek the wine with strength that knows no limit!

Afterwards he said that Khwaja Mansur Hallaj had been killed and went on to say: "Anyone who has attained the state of perfection does not experience change. This means that nothing makes its appearance in such people which in any way could harm them, even granted the fact of the fickleness of the selfish soul. This is because it is a constituent element of our human nature, yet it does not exercise any authority over them. It cannot do any harm to men of eminence. When overcome by a spiritual state, however, they could utter something which, outside their circle, might appear to be contrary to the Law. What is it all about? When an overpowering spiritual experience occurs some of them are incapable of bearing it. Of necessity they blurt out something. It is according to human nature to spit out something a person is incapable of digesting!"

After this he said: "I inquired of Sheikh Zada Chishti—may God keep him safe—when he was here whether in our own day and age there were any such personages where he comes from whose utterances were such as to render them liable to be put to death.[321] He replied: 'There are! Anyone who utters such things is promptly put to death. There is no delay.' I also asked him if there were any people who commented on what Ain ul-Quzat had written. He replied: 'There are! In Hamadan there is a revered Sayyid who is writing a commentary on each and every word written by Ain ul-Quzat. As no one has objected, he is able to carry on his project. If someone does object, however, he will have to keep quiet." At this point the Revered Master commented: "In this way it becomes known that it is not proper to object to the utterances of eminent persons."

He went on to describe the glorious deeds of the eminent Sheikh Zada: "Sheikh Zada has been travelling for twenty-five years. He was more than forty years of age when he visited us. He was very well versed in spiritual matters. He repeatedly exclaimed: 'It was the poetry of Khwaja Attar which inspired me to travel. It happened like

---

321. Sheikh Zada Chishti was presumably from Chisht near Herat in Afghanistan. He visited Maneri around 1335 while he was staying in the cave in Rajgir. This is recorded in the sixteenth assembly of *Khwan-i Pur Ni'mat*. He speaks about how an earlier Sheikh, Maudud Chishti (d.1133) had gone by foot twice to Harv to help a person in need of his support. The text indicates that Maneri's visitor was a widely experienced traveller, with its reference to Hamadan and to 25 years on the move.

this. When I was young my father used to read the Quran every evening. He would sit me down beside him. When he became tired of reading the Quran he used to place the *Diwan* [Collected Poems] of Khwaja Attar in front of him and read his poems. Tears used to well up while he was thus engaged. Whenever this happened he would lay his blessed hand upon me. I quietly took note of the places in the *Diwan* where he relished the poems and wept. In the morning I would open them up and look at them. When his glance fell upon me he used to ask me about the poems I was studying and say that, God willing, when my time came, I would study his poems. At that moment, however, what could I understand?'"

A discussion arose about the glorious deeds of Sheikh Nizamuddin. The Revered Master said: "There is no doubt about the eminent stature of Sheikh Nizamuddin. He was an eminently spiritual man. In an account of his discourses I read that Amir Hasan[322] had said: 'I do not get much consolation in my extended prayers of petition.' Sheikh Nizamuddin replied: 'Glory be to God! You at least have the consolation of being able to say: O God, I beseech You that I may ask nought of You except You!' This is an indication of his wholehearted striving. If there had been anything else, it would have indicated another desire." At this juncture he added this comment: "This is similar to what the Apostle, on the night of nearness and the miracle of his approaching to within two bows' length, said: 'O God, I take refuge in You from You!' If there had been anything else in his pure mind except *God*, he would have said: 'O God, I take refuge in You from such and such!' Since he said, 'From You,' it became clear that nothing apart from *God* remained in his pure mind and in his wholehearted striving." At this point he recited the following:

The finest quality of the king of the world is high resolve:
The winds and feathers of the bird of souls is high resolve.
The bird of high resolve, when in league with the Lord,
Passed beyond the world and religion as well.
If you are not a man of such resolve,
Stay far off, for friendship is not for you.
Every heart that is bereft of high resolve
Will not be graced with a kingdom without end.

---

322. Amir Hasan Sijzi was the compiler of the account—*malfuz*—known as *Fawa'id ul- Fu'ad,* as already noted.

CHAPTER 21
THE SECRET THOUGHTS OF HOLY MEN

A discussion took place about the inner perception of holy men. The Revered Master said: "It is said that holy men know the spiritual state of anyone and the status he will attain. They have this inner power of perception. They say: 'Today a fortunate or a wretched man has been born.' This is according to men of perception, which is what they are." Maulana Nizamuddin, the son of his maternal aunt,[323] inquired: "How do they know?" The Revered Master replied: "They are informed about the states of felicity or wretchedness, together with whatever is associated with them, whether manifest or hidden, yet in accordance with right action. This is how they know, even though, in contrast to this, divine providence is all-embracing." He then related the following:

> We know what brocade is and how long it is:
> We can discern whether love is genuine or feigned.

He then related this story: "There was a holy man who used to send his son to study so that he could make progress in learning. One day the holy man said: 'Whoever brings me the good news of an approaching traveller will be given whatever he asks of me.' It so happened that his son first saw a traveller approaching. He came and said: 'I bring you good tidings about an approaching traveller. You had said that you would give whatever he wanted to the person who brought you the good news of an approaching traveller.' The holy man replied: 'Tell me, what do you want?' His son replied: 'From now on, don't send me to study!' When the holy man heard this, he considered the matter carefully: 'If I say that I won't send him, then my son will remain ignorant. If I send him, I will break my promise.' After reflecting in this way, he said: 'All right, do not go and study, but on condition that you memorize *The Victory*.'[324] After this, he stopped going to study.

Some time later the holy man died. His disciples gathered to de-

---

323. *Khala zada.* The word for a maternal uncle is *khali.*

324. The text has *Inna fatahna,* the beginning of *sura* (chapter) 48 of the Quran, called *Al-Fath* (The Victory).

termine who should succeed him. They agreed among themselves that his son should take his place. In this way his son became his successor. Day by day his fame increased and he became famous. Later on, along with some disciples, he set out to visit a particular city. He drew near to the city in which were many disciples of his father. When they heard that their Master's son was approaching, they turned out to welcome him. They also informed the king of that city of his approach. The king also welcomed him. He became famous in that city also. Everyone showed him great respect except for a group of scholars who accorded no importance to him; neither did they go to visit him. They said: 'How could anyone who has not studied the Quran or acquired knowledge enter upon this Path? What possible wisdom could he have?' News of this reached the king. He summoned the scholars who repeated what they had said: 'He has not studied the Quran or acquired knowledge.' The king summoned everyone into his presence. The Sheikh's son arrived together with his disciples. The king turned to him and said: 'The scholars are saying that you have not studied anything.' The disciples spoke up: 'Let him be tested!' The scholars replied: 'To begin with, he has not studied. If he has, let him recite a chapter from the Quran!' They replied: 'Which chapter should he recite?' They came to an agreement that he should recite *The Victory*. In accordance with his father's wish, he had memorized it. He began to recite it and continued until the end. All were overcome with embarrassment and became convinced."

After a pause, the Revered Master commented: "The whole point of this story is the insight of the Sheikh. He was able to foresee that eventually such a situation would arise. This is why he insisted that his son should memorize this chapter." He told another story in this vein: "A dear soul related how, when Sheikh Ruknuddin[325] had travelled to Delhi for the first time, some religious luminaries agreed among themselves to put him to the test. They would visit him in order to do so. They agreed among themselves to call on him at a particular time and put five questions to him. They came to the Sheikh. They put their five questions to him. He

325. Sheikh Ruknuddin (d.1335) was the son of Sheikh Sadruddin (d.1285), who was the son of the famous Sheikh Baha'uddin Zakaria (d.1262) of Multan. They formed the first three generations of the Suhrawardi Silsila (religious order) in Multan.

gave an elaborate reply to each question until all five were com-
prehensively answered. Some to those scholars immediately became his disciples, while others refused to repent of their action.
The people present in the assembly asked him why he had begun
to weep. He replied: 'I have been waiting for this day for thirty
odd years.' Those present asked him for an explanation of what
he meant. He explained: 'When I was trying to hurry up with my
studies, I reached this lesson. No matter how hard he tried, I could
not grasp what my teacher was saying. I noticed that my father,
Sheikh Sadruddin, was standing behind me. He told me to get up.
He would explain those five problems to me. I got up and followed
him home. One by one, he explained all five problems to me in
such a way that I understood them. Finally, he told me to remember them well, for I would have need of them. I was wondering how
they would prove to be useful for me. After more than thirty years
it has become clear to me that this was the situation he had been
referring to.'"

Malik Zainuddin Majd ul-Mulk[326] arrived to pay his respects to
the Revered Master. He was telling a story about a mendicant who
had called on Sheikh Alauddin in Ajodhan. The Sheikh did not offer him his hand. The mendicant spoke up: "I have mingled with
the holy men of Chisht and performed many services for them.
They granted me whatever I needed from them. Why do you not
offer me your hand?" Sheikh Alauddin replied: "I have given you
my heart, so what need is here for me to give you my hand?" At
this point, Majd ul-Mulk interjected with: "Shaking hands is prescribed for us because the Apostle used to proffer his hand, so why
didn't Sheikh Alauddin do so?" The Revered Master replied: "My
answer to this would be that, for holy men and those treading the
Sufi path, it could be justified on the basis of a spiritual state. If
they see something in such matters which results in laxity with regard to their selfish soul, they shy away from such things. It could
have happened that Sheikh Alauddin, by following the convention,
would have experienced laxity with regard to his selfish soul. That
is why he did not proffer his hand."

Qazi Mu'inuddin had accompanied Malik Majd ul-Mulk to the

---

326. Malik Zainuddin Majd ul-Mulk was the governor of Bihar. He is
referred to on a number of occasions in the manuscript evidence. He held
Maneri in high esteem.

assembly. He made this comment: "Tradition is neglected when the Apostle used to proffer his hand, but this person did not do so. This is setting aside Tradition." Again he replied: "As far as appearances are concerned, there is a breach, but not with regard to meaning. This is because perfecting religion consists in confirming Tradition. Since perfecting religion was his whole intention in this matter, in appearance there was conflict, but not according to inner meaning. Such things are beyond words, and this is like some matters pertaining to the Law. For example, at the dawn prayer, a person who has missed part of the prayer might apprehend that the sun is on the point of rising, and the prayer-leader has not yet given the valediction. If he stands up before the leader does so in order to perform the missed portion of the prayer, this would be the correct way to fulfil his obligation.[327] To all appearances this would be a breach of Tradition, nevertheless, since it is being done to fulfil a religious obligation, the inner purpose would be achieved. You could not call it a breach. The same applies to those who have not observed a Tradition in order to fulfil religious obligations. Appearance-wise there is neglect, but not according to the inner meaning."

Qazi Mu'inuddin observed: "Such an action would necessarily involve the breaking of the heart of a believer. It would also show scorn, because all the person wants to do is to kiss his hand. If he does not offer his hand, his heart would be broken." He gave a similar reply: "In no way does he intend to break the heart of a believer. If it happens, it should not cause alarm. An opinion should not be based on this, just as if you carry out an injunction of the Law with regard to a particular believer, and your whole intention is to implement the Law, in these circumstances the heart of a believer would necessarily be broken.[328] Since it is an unintended consequence, it does no damage. Subversion occurs when a person does something intentionally, for 'a man subverts by means of his intention.' His intention was not to break the heart of a Muslim. On the contrary, his intention was to fulfil the obligations of his religion."

Afterwards he added: "A traveller reaches a stage along the

---

327. One is obliged to complete the dawn prayer before the sun actually begins to rise, as prayer is strictly forbidden at the actual moment of sunrise, sunset or noon. This is to obviate any possibility of sun worship.
328. The implication is that some form of punishment is involved.

Way when, as an act of obedience, fasting and ritual prayer are set aside. For this group, for example, if a person realizes that what he has to do will become clear to him in a tavern, whereas fasting and ritual prayer have become a veil for him along the Way, he immediately abandons them and proceeds to a tavern. This takes place with regard to a sincere traveller. This is because ritual prayer and fasting are for the sake of achieving one's aim. Their perception is: 'At this moment I shall achieve my aim in a tavern.' At that very moment they abandon fasting and ritual prayer in obedience to some obligation. This is an obligation arising from a spiritual state, not from the Law. Sometimes it happens that members of this group, as they travel along their way, find it difficult to distinguish between abandoning something on the basis of an obligation arising from a spiritual state, yet not clearly in accordance with the Law, and introducing an innovation. In this instance, an innovation is introduced by abandoning an obligation. In the eyes of the Law, there is no difference."[329]

One of those present in the assembly asked: "Can you give an example from the Law?" The Revered Master replied: "For example, if someone sets out to pray four cycles of prayer and, arriving at the third, stops praying, being confused as to whether it is the fourth cycle, or only the third. In such a situation the worship-

---

329. One division of Sufis is into *ba shar'* (with the Law) and *be shar'* (without the Law). This refers to a Sufi's permanent disposition. Maneri is clearly in the former, Law-abiding group. The present discussion is about Law-abiding people, sincere Sufis whose holiness is widely acknowledged. It may happen that, in a particular situation, such a person becomes convinced that he should do something else, perhaps perform some urgently needed service that would entail breaking his fast or failing to observe the normal ritual prayer. Perhaps Maneri has someone like Shibli in mind. He himself was punctilious in his observance of the Law. For example, the *Wafat Nama* [Death Account] records how, at the noon prayer on the very day he died, as he was performing his ritual ablutions, he forgot to wash his face. When this was pointed out to him, he began all over again. Zain Badr Arabi records: "When Sayyid Zahiruddin and the others present in the assembly saw all this they were amazed at the care and punctiliousness shown in such a condition." We also need to recall that, in letter 46 of his *Hundred Letters,* Maneri wrote: "Tomorrow, all the prescriptions of the Law will be cancelled, but these two things remain forever—the love of God and the praise of God."

per is obliged to sit at the completion of the cycle. He should then stand up and perform one more cycle of prayer. If in fact this was the third cycle, then sitting at the end of it would have been an innovation. On the other hand, if he thought it was the fourth and sat down, his missing a cycle would be a breach of obligation. In this situation, as mentioned, the obligation is to sit, even though it is an innovation, because it is the third cycle, so that no breach may occur, and similarly if it is the fourth. A traveller, eager to perfect his religion, is perplexed. On the one hand a breach occurs, while, on the other, an innovation is introduced, for his action necessarily involves this, even though he was obliged to break the prophetic custom. No harm is seen to be done. This is similar to what is stated in the Law, namely, cutting short ritual prayer, once it has begun, is an innovation. In spite of this, if a person is overcome in spirit, any resulting deficiency in prayer is condoned. This corresponds to the custom regarding having begun to help someone. Similarly, when the prayer-leader has taken his place, this thought might occur to the worshipper: 'If I give preference to what is customary, I shall fall behind the leader by one cycle of prayer.' In this situation his observance of what is customary would be defective. He therefore acts in unison with the leader. This would be only an apparent breach, but not with regard to its inner meaning. No harm results from such behaviour, because it is done in order to observe an obligation as completely as possible. According to the Law, this is what custom is all about."

Afterwards he said: "If you see that, with respect to this group, the apparent introduction of an innovation or the abandonment of a custom has come into existence through one of them, you should immediately realize that something has come to his attention. Acting in this way is a fundamental article of faith for them, for they observe the principles and injunctions of the Law; are righteous travellers, and are also masters of inner meaning and insight. For every innovator and lust-driven person, however, this is not what being a Muslim is all about. For such a person it is sheer heretical behaviour."[330]

---

330. Maneri has introduced an important distinction in the whole realm of spiritual discernment. In addition to the objective, observable act, one has to take into account the spiritual state of the person making the judgement. The "innovator and lust-driven person" is obviously bereft of any inner life of the spirit. He can only judge externally. Moreover, Maneri

A discussion arose about the situation arising when a holy man goes to the territory of another holy man in order to settle there. When he arrives, he settles down there. "Zakaria Gharib described how a holy man had arrived at Maulana Fariduddin's place in order to settle there. After a few days, he died. Similarly, a dervish arrived at Sheikh Khizr Paradoz's place and said to Sheikh Khizr: 'You have occupied this place for quite a number of years. Now get up so that I can reside here for some time.' Sheikh Khizr rolled up his prayer mat and came away from the place. The dervish took up residence there and made himself comfortable. He was there for some time and then died. No agreement was reached. Something similar happened to a number of holy men. No matter what the provocation, members of this group do not get involved in disputes." The Revered Master said: "Even though there are no disputes, nevertheless human nature remains. Since this is so, all those things associated with human nature also remain. Things that engage him would include what the Law permits. For example, it would be perfectly in order to seek justice against an oppressor. It was extra grace which, in this situation, pushed for justice. No clear necessity flows from this situation, but he should refrain from any improper use of things. 'Another order came from God' made its appearance. There are many similar examples."[331]

Afterwards he added: "In this manner it is mentioned that 'the appointed time of this dervish has supplanted that of another,' and 'his station has fallen below this one's.' Human nature is certainly operative here. 'This one's appointed time has supplanted, and that one's time has been supplanted.' It is for this reason that such situations as these come about. Such things do happen among dervishes." By way of illustration he told this story: "Sheikh

---

has subtly pointed out what experience commonly confirms, namely, that those loudest in condemnation of, for example, sexual deviations, are often themselves guilty of sexual sins. The "members of this group," by contrast, are spiritually mature people, as he maintains, with a long-honed docility to the divine action within themselves. Maneri's thought on this whole subject is clearly expounded in letter 96, *The Forty-Day Retreat*, in his *Hundred Letters*.

331. Maneri clearly refers to the drag of human nature on a person, even one with a reputation of being a holy man or a dervish. He usually attributes lapses to a person's *nafs*, his selfish soul, which becomes increasingly subtle in proportion to a person's growth in holiness.

Ali Zada told one of his disciples to go to Lahore and settle down there. At that time Sheikh Zanjan was living in Lahore. Sheikh Zanjan and that disciple were both disciples of Sheikh Ali Zada. This thought occurred to the disciple: 'Sheikh Zanjan is in Lahore, and my Sheikh is sending me there. Perhaps this has not occurred to him.' When this thought occurred to him he came to his Sheikh and said: 'Master, Sheikh Zanjan is already in Lahore. How can I go to the same place?' Sheikh Ali replied: 'What is all this to you? Just go!' He set out. In the very evening he reached Lahore, Sheikh Zanjan died. The following morning he saw the funeral procession of Sheikh Zanjan coming out of the city." He told another story in the same vein: "Sheikh Haidar Zada was settled in a particular city. One day he was seated along with his disciples. Suddenly the holy man turned towards his disciples and said: 'Get up! Let us go somewhere!' His disciples were dumbfounded. They said: 'Master, what has made you suddenly decide on such an undertaking?' The Sheikh replied: 'Genghis Khan is about to reach this city.[332] He is bringing a dervish with him. He is coming under the protection of that dervish. I engaged that dervish in a hidden struggle, but he threw me to the ground. I am no longer able to protect this city.' Those who firmly believed in that holy man set out together with him. A short while afterwards Genghis Khan reached that city, captured it and enslaved the populace."

332. Genghis Khan swept through the Muslim Empire of Khwarizm between 1219 and 1225. Many people fled to India to escape the slaughter and destruction wrought by 'the scourge of God.'

CHAPTER 22

THE GENEALOGICAL TREE OF
THE SHEIKHS AND SEEKING THEIR
INTERCESSION IN TIMES OF NEED

A discussion arose about the genealogical tree of the sheikhs. The Revered Master said: "You should learn by heart the genealogical tree of the sheikhs. You should recite it after completing your obligatory prayers. This is a source of many blessings." At that very moment he indicated to those present in the assembly that they should write it down. He himself dictated it in this Order: 'In the name of God, the Merciful, the Compassionate! Khwaja Najibuddin Firdausi; Khwaja Rudnuddin Firdausi; Khwaja Badruddin Samarqandi; Khwaja Saifuddin Bakharzi; Khwaja Najmuddin Kubra; Khwaja Ziauddin Abu Najib Suhrawardi; Khwaja Wajhuddin Abu Hafs; Khwaja Muhammad bin Abdullah al-Ma'ruf; Khwaja Ahmad Siyah Dinawari; Khwaja Abul Qasim Junaid Baghdadi; Khwaja Sari Saqati; Khwaja Ma'ruf Kakhi; Imam Ali Reza; Imam Musa Kazim; Imam Ja'far Sadiq; Imam Muhammad Baqir; Imam Zain ul-Abidin; Amir ul-Muminin Husain; Amir ul-Muminin Ali bin Abi Talib; The Prince of Apostles and Seal of the Prophets, Muhammad bin Abdullah bin Abd ul-Muttalib'—may he direct my works in the right direction!"

The Revered Master thereupon turned his gaze towards those devotees who were present and said to them: "You should recite this daily after the obligatory prayers. If a person is confronted with some weighty religious or worldly matter, he should perform his ablutions; two cycles of prayer; and then recite the genealogical tree. His spiritual forbears will be his intercessors. God Most Exalted will fulfil his needs—God willing!"

CHAPTER 23
STRUGGLING
AND GAINING MASTERY[333]

Qazi Ashrafuddin commented: "Once I heard the Revered Master say that struggling is the cause of union."[334] The Revered Master replied: "Some people say this, but the majority are of the opinion that it is not the cause, because a cause is such that nothing should come between it and its effect. Moreover, many people tried hard yet did not acquire what they desired." At this juncture Maulana Abul Qasim opined that in this verse, "And those who strive for Us, We shall guide them to Our paths" (Q29:69), the will of God is implied.[335] The Revered Master commented: "One opinion is that the will of God is implied. Some, however, think that struggle is the cause, and understand from this verse that there is a causal link. Moreover, they hold that struggle is a conditional cause. They mean to say that, if someone seeks and struggles, yet does not acquire what he desires, the reason is that the condition has not been put in place. The failure is attributed to this reason. This is similar to the verse, 'Call on Me and I will respond to you' (Q40:60). One opinion in this matter is that the will of God is implied, while the second is that the petition is conditional. If the condition is present, the request is complied with. As for all those people who present petitions which receive no response, the reason is that their petition did not include the requisite condition."

Qazi Mu'izzuddin inquired: "What about a person who agrees with the opinion of the one who says the will of God is implied and says that wherever seeking and struggling exist, yet nothing is acquired thereby, since these are not a cause, but rather because seeking and struggling are not even a condition?" The Revered

---

333. *Mujahada* and *riyazat*. The basic meaning of *riyazat* is 'breaking in (a colt)'. This conveys the sense of a means, not of an end. The basic idea is to enable a person to be perfectly responsive to "the divine reins," rather than earn a reputation for extravagant ascetical practices.

334. Union with God is meant.

335. *Muzmar*, i.e. the will of God is implied as the cause.

206

Master replied: "If this were so, it would be by virtue of a special dispensation of the will of God, as has been said: 'God chooses whomsoever He wishes for His mercy' (Q2:105). Other verses similar to this do not help us. Moreover, seeking and struggling belong to time, which is preceded by eternity, so time cannot be a cause with respect to eternity. Thus it is known that seeking and struggling are not a cause. Someone has said that a special dispensation applies with regard to prophethood, namely, *God* Most Exalted chooses for prophethood whomsoever He wishes." He himself gave this answer: "This interpretation is different from the one given by the ancients. An error has occurred." Afterwards he added: "Whatever exists is bound by the will of *God* Most Exalted. 'God chooses whomsoever He wishes for His mercy' (Q2:105). His will is the determining factor, not goods, life or anything else. Men offer up their lives to acquire what they have desired. This occurs through something determined which, in fact, is not decreed from this side.[336] No one is even aware of it." The Revered Master then recited the following couplets:

> Regarding Your acceptance, O Unfettered by any cause,
> What is the difference if a handful of dust is good or ugly?
> O Unique One, for anyone devoted to Your threshold,
> The cloak of Joseph symbolizes seeking life in You.

When those present in the assembly heard these words of explanation they were overcome with grief and tears filled their eyes. Qazi Ashrafuddin inquired: "Since *God* Most Exalted has determined events by means of His will, should a person engage in seeking and struggling or not?" The Revered Master replied: "By no means should they not be undertaken!" He then repeated several times: "They have to be undertaken, not read about! This is because all the commands of religion come down to two fundamental principles: one is what is to be known, and the other is what is to be done. One has to know, for example, about belief and unbelief, obedience and disobedience. Since these are ordained by God, they should be known. They should not be concealed. As regards what has to be done, some examples are the injunctions to believe; to be obedient; to shun infidelity; and to keep far from disobedience. All these things have to be put into practice. There can be no talk of

---

336. This world of time is meant, as opposed to that of eternity.

abandoning them, because here it would not be correct to conceal them." At this point he recited the following:

> The intellect is meant to help us be obedient:
> Love and faith are meant to be experienced!
> The minds of lovers before Him are all awhirl,
> Intellects hidden in sleeves, and lives in hands.

"Just as when a person does not know and does not believe, he becomes an unbeliever, similarly, when a person does not do something and knows that this is a sin, he becomes a sinner. If he does not know that it is a sin and says that it is something good, then he himself becomes an unbeliever. This is because, after hearing what he has said, some foolish people have abandoned struggling, asceticism and ritual prayer. There is also the situation of a person who, when in an ecstatic state, has spoken out in criticism of asceticism and ritual prayer. What have such people done? They have provided a person's selfish soul with an excuse for abandoning ritual prayer and asceticism—let us seek refuge in God from such! That criticism of asceticism and ritual prayer takes place in a state of ecstasy. The whole aim is to refrain from focussing on such practices and indicates the calamities that could be associated with them.[337] In everything that is said about such things the criticism is not aimed at the things in themselves, but at refraining from fixing one's attention on them in view of the possible attendant calamities. For example, it is related that Imam Shibli said: 'In reality, there is no asceticism in the world.' This is not a denial of asceticism, because it is confirmed by the Book, the practices of the Prophet, and the consensus of Muslims. No denial itself is found. It means not focussing on asceticism, and being aware of the calamities that could be associated with it so as to be saved from being overly impressed by it. This is one of the principles of the people of the Way, namely, they notice the defects in what they do, as well as those of their selfish soul, but do not dwell on their own virtues and devotion."

Afterwards he added: "These are the words of the group whose members have no strength except in *God*, even though seeking and struggling are not bereft of benefits. In fact, they bring about many

---

337. The 'calamities' referred to apply particularly to severe ascetical practices, for there is a danger of taking pride in them.

benefits, but the strength of their practitioners is not derived from them. For this reason their attention is not fixed on these things. They have also very truly said that, if they focus their attention on seeking and struggling, they won't make progress, but will remain stalled by the wayside." Qazi Ashrafuddin again inquired: "If a person, in order to overcome[338] his selfish soul, removes one of his members, or asserts that something similar has to be done to gain control, how would you view it?" The Revered Master replied: "Removing a member is not the way to overcome one's selfish soul! If anyone does so, he becomes a sinner, because anyone who mutilates his body, which is the mount of the seeker on the Path to *God*, becomes a sinner. In fact, no more is required of a seeker than this: if his selfish soul deviates to the right or the left along the Path to *God*, he should bring it back onto the straight Path by means of the whip of struggle with self, while remaining within the confines of the Law." Yet again he inquired: "If some insect bites your body in such a way as to irritate your selfish soul, and if you are able to bear it, what comment would you make?" The Revered Master replied: "This would be laudable. This sort of thing is acceptable."

Again he inquired: "If someone, in order to cut down on his sleep, ties a rope around his neck and suspends himself by means of it, what would you say about it?" The Revered Master replied: "This sort of thing has not come down to us. At the time of the Apostle, a virtuous woman, either to cut down on her sleep or to struggle against her selfish soul, tied a rope around her neck and suspended herself by it. News of this reached the Apostle. He ordered the woman to stop, for such things should not be done."[339] Afterwards the Revered Master added: "A person should choose for himself those things that he can practise with constancy. If someone suspends himself for ten days, or fasts for ten days[340] in order to

---

338. Literally *kushtan*, "to kill." Maneri's thinking is in terms of controlling, not killing, one's selfish soul. The analogy of the mount aptly illustrates this. You break your horse in. You do not kill it.

339. Rather than focussing on the fatal consequence of such an action, it might be more helpful to take note of its condemnation. Maneri can draw from his own experience in the jungle of Bihiya to correctly evaluate the merit of different ascetical practices.

340. This fasting is outside the prescribed Ramazan fast. It might indicate a total fast from food for ten days as a spectacular ascetical exercise.

remain hungry, it then so happens that he returns to his previous way of living, and no gains are achieved. He should undertake very small things in which he can persevere."³⁴¹ Afterwards he added: "There are twenty-four hours in a complete day. Sufi masters have apportioned these in such a way that a certain number of hours are devoted to worship and others to sleep. Out of these twenty-four hours they have set aside eight for sleeping. These eight hours have been further divided into how many hours he should be set aside in the day, and how many during the night. They have allotted two hours during the day and six during the night. They have even specified when those two hours of siesta should be taken, namely, during the free period after the mid-morning meal, yet before noon. It is necessary to get up before noon in order to be ready for the noon prayer. A person should compose himself in readiness for this prayer. The time to sleep during the night has also been fixed. A person should sleep for six hours after night prayer. If a person sleeps longer, that amount of time is lost. Sufi masters talk about two mornings. The first is when a person rises after his night's rest, while the second is when he gets up after his siesta." He added: "After completing the noon prayer he should perform supererogatory prayers by reciting Quranic verses which are supplicatory in nature, such as: 'Lord, burden us not with what we have no strength to bear' (Q2:286) and what follows, as also 'Unless You pardon us and have mercy on us, we shall be the losers' (Q7:23), and verses similar to these. This is because they evoke much spiritual relish. The verses that have this effect should be repeated, even though another cycle of prayer remains.³⁴² This is because saintly men, when this relish is experienced, become overcome with holy desires. The same thing applies after night prayers. If supererogatory prayers are undertaken, verses similar

---

341. Maneri's position with regard to asceticism is very clear. He is against all forms of spectacular, non-sustainable and attention-drawing practices. He advocates the patient acceptance of the trials of everyday living; fidelity to what is enjoined by the Law, such as the annual month-long fast; and small, unobtrusive practices that anyone can easily observe for an extended period and which can help, so to say, to keep a person "tuned in" to God.

342. It should be kept in mind that this discussion is about personal prayers of devotion, not canonical prayer. The advice to linger where spiritual relish is experienced is a well-attested principle.

to these should be recited.[343]

[Qazi Sadruddin inquired: "Granted six hours rest of a night and two during the day, is it really necessary to adhere to the timings given?" The Revered Master replied: "Sufi masters consider the time as fixed. They have not made it free." The Helpless One inquired: "Have Sufi masters prescribed some sort of order with regard to struggle with self, beginning with this and then moving on to that?" The Revered Master replied: "Yes indeed! They ascertain what exactly is needed for each particular person and order its acquisition. The foundation of this work demands separation. If a person is single, the master will prescribe the extent of this separation. If he is a family man, the master will take this into consideration in prescribing the degree of separation. The first thing a master enjoins is the baptism of a forty-day retreat.[344] If he sees good progress in that forty-day retreat, he will enjoin a second one. If he observes a tendency to over sleep during the retreat, he prescribes a fixed schedule for sleep. If he notices a preoccupation with food, he prescribes exactly how much he should eat." The Helpless One again inquired: "When the master enjoins something on a beginner, does he do so at the beginner's request, or on his own initiative?" The Revered Master replied: "If he asks the master, then he does so at his request; but if the master himself sees his need, he does so on his own initiative." At this juncture Khwaja Jalaluddin Hafiz Multani, who happened to be present, opined that the first task of a beginner was the remembrance of God which acts as a polisher of hearts. The Revered Master commented: "This very remembrance is enjoined in the forty-days retreat. During this time all the things that the beginner has previously done or witnessed will all come crowding into his heart. The master enjoins this remembrance to drive them all out. For example, at this moment you are engaged in conversation with me. If you go outside, all these things will occur to you. Then you will become engrossed with something other than God. In order to set aside such thoughts you should engage in remembering God. Sheikhs go so far to say that, if they feel drowsy and fall asleep, even in that state their tongues should continue to move in remembering God."]

---

343. Manuscript differences are encountered at this stage. MS Acc. 1219 in the K.B.O.P.L. does not contain the material indicated within square brackets, but it is found in the 1884 printed version and the Aligarh MS.

344. Letter 96 in *The Hundred Letters* is fully devoted to the topic of the forty-day retreat.

At this stage he related this appropriate story: "A group of itin-erant dervishes arrived at the hospice of Sheikh Ruknuddin. He told them to occupy themselves in remembering God. In the eve-ning all of them began to remember God in a very noisy manner. The master's disciples were all in their own cells occupied with prayer and remembering God. This uproar was very disturbing for them. One of them came out of his cell in an angry mood and ex-claimed: 'If you are remembering God you should do so in such a way that you can hear what you are saying but don't make such a noise!' They lowered their voices. In the morning, they all came to the Revered Sheikh and said: 'Master, at your command we spent the night remembering God. One of your disciples came and an-grily told us to keep quiet.' The Sheikh[345] called for that disciple and said: "Why are you forbidding them at the very time they are experiencing what is already yours? Let them all have a similar experience themselves!"[346]

The Revered Master elaborated: "Gaining self-control is essen-tially the same for a believer and an unbeliever. It is mentioned in several places that, by gaining self-control, hermits also attain a spiritual lustre." In this connection he told the following story: "There was a hermit who continued struggling for self-mastery in his cell for sixty or seventy years. At that time forty years had been fixed for attaining this goal. After forty years the work is accom-plished. News reached Khwaja Ibrahim Khawass[347] that a particu-lar hermit had spent sixty or seventy years at this task. Khwaja Ibrahim exclaimed: 'Forty years have been fixed for this task. This extra time is not without significance. I'll go and ask him what this is all about.' After coming to this decision, he went to meet him. The hermit was engrossed inside his cell. When Khwaja Ibrahim reached the place, before he could even put his question to him, the

345. In some copies this comment is inserted: "He did this on his own initiative."

346. In the Printed work and one MS the following is found: At this stage the aforementioned Jalaluddin commented: "It has been well said in Hindavi that a holy man said: 'It is a good thing, but difficult.'" Thereupon the Revered Master commented in Hindavi: 'The country is good but distant."

347. Ibrahim Khawass (d. 904) was famous for his trust in God, and his endless wandering. The stories that follow, in a slightly modified form, are well known.

hermit stuck his head outside his cell and said: 'There is no meaning!' Khwaja Ibrahim replied: 'Why have you spent so any years beyond the prescribed period?' He answered: 'Because I have tied up this dog of a selfish soul and am keeping guard over it.' When Khwaja Ibrahim heard this he lowered his head in prayer, saying: 'O Lord, You have granted this stranger so much understanding! You can turn him into a friend.' After Khwaja Ibrahim had prayed thus in his mind, the hermit made this comment: 'What impertinence! Go and attend to yourself!'"

He told another apposite story: "There was a hermit who heard about the fame and reputation of Khwaja Ibrahim Khawass. He resolved to go in search of him. Now Khwaja Ibrahim was always on the move. He had no fixed abode. He had attained that stage of complete trust in God. Strengthened in this way he used to travel without a camel or provisions. The hermit went in search of him, inquiring as he went along, until he found him. He said to him: 'I want to travel along with you.' The Khwaja replied: 'You cannot travel along with me, for I have complete trust in God.' The hermit continued: 'Are you still preoccupied with your belly?' When Khwaja Ibrahim heard these words of his, he exclaimed: 'This is a profound statement!' He allowed him to travel with him. Three nights and days they travelled, but nothing came their way from the unseen. They were breaking their fast with water. At the end of three days and nights, the hermit exclaimed: 'O Sheikh, people talk about your knowledge in so many cities. What have you got to show for it?' The Sheikh performed two cycles of prayer. He then bowed his head to the ground and prayed thus: 'O God, You are able to prevent my being put to shame in the eyes of this stranger!' Thereupon two glasses of water and two lengths of bread[348] appeared on his prayer mat. He placed one glass of water and length of bread in front of the hermit, and one in front of himself. With these they broke their fast. They then proceeded for another three days and nights, during which they received nothing. The Sheikh thought to himself: 'Just as he spoke to me, so shall I speak to him.' He said: 'Now it is your turn. Let's see what you can come up with!' The hermit performed two rounds of prayer according to the custom of his religion, and then, bowing his head to the

---

348. The Persian has *nan*. In Iran, this refers to a length of bread almost three feet long. In India, it is about six inches long.

ground, prayed thus: 'O God, if this man has any standing in Your court, provide us with something from the unseen!' At that very instant four lengths of bread and four glasses of water appeared from the unseen. Khwaja Ibrahim and the hermit broke their fast together. Afterwards Khwaja Ibrahim Khawass asked the hermit to tell him what his prayer had been. The hermit replied: 'I had nothing to recommend myself. I called upon you as my intercessor. I said: O God, if this man has any standing in Your court, provide us with something from the unseen!' He then added: 'The doubts I had about your religion have disappeared. Bestow Islam upon me now!' Khwaja Ibrahim bestowed Islam upon him. He immediately became a Muslim. Praise be to God for it!"

He told yet another story: "At the time of the Apostle there was a hermit who was preoccupied with religious practices in his cell. One day the Apostle passed in front of his cell. He asked him how far he had reached. He answered thus: 'I have reached the stage where I can see the throne of God.' The Apostle replied: 'That is the throne of Satan!'" When the Revered Master reached these words, he said: "Yes, efforts at self-control which do not stem from Islam are all satanic in origin—but God knows best!"[349]

---

349. It is good to recall that stories, such as the present ones, are meant to convey religious instruction of some sort or the other. They are similar to parables. Maneri's attitude to the asceticism of non-Muslims is discussed in *The Way of a Sufi: Sharafuddin Maneri*, pp.150-160.

CHAPTER 24

SHOWING DISPLEASURE TOWARDS ONE'S SELFISH SOUL: A DESRIPTION OF ITS PERSISTENCE: AND A PEEK AT ITS HIDDEN NATURE

It was said that a person could not catch a glimpse of God until he severs ties with his selfish soul. The Revered Master spoke up: "Spiritual masters have written about veils in various books. They mention four: people; the world; Satan; and the selfish soul. People hinder our devotion to, and worship of, God. This world conceals the world to come. Satan downplays religion. One's selfish soul acts as a veil with regard to the Lord. Four veils can be enumerated but, if you examine the matter, they all stem from one root, one's selfish soul. One gets overly preoccupied with people because of one's selfish interest. Being immersed in worldly affairs also flows from self-interest. Agreeing to what Satan proposes also stems from selfishness. Hence it is clear that the selfish soul is the root of all these distortions. This is the origin of the adage, 'The selfish soul is the greatest of all idols.' In fine, whoever has brought his selfish soul to heel has been liberated from them all."

> Tread underfoot whatever you hold as precious,
> In order to lay hold of the very water of life!

He continued: "Haven't you heard about what was said concerning Khwaja Bayazid Bastami? One night he saw the Lord of Glory in a dream. He inquired: 'O God, which path leads to You?' The reply came: 'Abandon your selfish soul and come along!' He did not say, 'Pray!' He did not say, 'Fast!' He did not say, 'You have to spend the night in vigil!' He did not say, 'Ignore the world!' or 'Ignore people!' No, His order was, 'Abandon your selfish soul!' This is an indication that the selfish soul is the root of all veils. If there had been a greater veil than the selfish soul, He would have ordered its abandonment. This is the reason why travellers along this Path, on their own initiative, undertake difficult things, even performing

215

base and blameworthy acts, in order to bring their selfish soul all the more quickly to heel. Qazi Umda—but God knows best—embraced this way of acting."

Afterwards he continued: "When a person's selfish soul is completely tamed, all sorts of laudable qualities appear in him, such as accepting what comes from God; trusting completely in Him; confiding in Him; patience, gratitude and similar qualities. The result is that these qualities become connatural to him. This means that they come into play without any undue effort on his part,[350] just like other natural dispositions, for example, hunger and thirst. A person experiences them spontaneously, without exerting himself. This is the basis for the adage, 'Habit is a fifth sense.' The difference between acquired dispositions and natural ones is that a person has no control over natural dispositions, in contrast to acquired dispositions, over which he retains control. This means that the effort associated with such activity has been removed, with the result that a person is recompensed and praised on account of it."

Zakariya[351] spoke about the astonishing states of Qazi Umda. Once he applied henna to his hands, put his arm around the neck of a harlot, and began to walk around the bazaar. While doing so, he once called upon Maulana Mahmud. He said to him: "O Sheikh, take a turn like this through the bazaar! If you aren't up to it, then give your turban to this harlot!" The Revered Master spoke up: "Some people have tried to explain it in this way. They say that, by means of these actions of his, he breaks free of custom and habit. Such a person is a genuinely holy man. When people enter upon the Way, things which lie within them, which constitute idols, sacred threads and veils, and have hitherto remained hidden, are brought out into the open. The purpose of doing so is to thrust them to one side. If a seeker along the Way hears that someone has engaged in such behaviour, he immediately understands that this is what is happening, namely, that the whole purpose is to thrust such hindrances to one side. Since Qazi Umda had broken free of the customs and habits that bind people, he was able to give open expression to this fact, such as by applying henna to his hands— but God knows best! The explanation could be that, when the idol

---

350. The printed version has what seems to be additional material, not found in MS 1219. It has been omitted.

351. The printed version adds 'Gharib.'

and sacred thread that had lain hidden within him were brought out into the open, he saw them face to face. He recognized what was manly about himself and what was lacking. 'At the moment, I do not have this quality. In my inner being I am not a man, although my appearance is that of a man. I am thus both a woman and a man. In view of this, I must be a hermaphrodite, just like so many others. I am simply one of them, so that my inner reality may be given an external expression.' This is a great work. Not all are capable of doing it." At this juncture, he recited the following:

> For the person who is escorted by love,
> Unbelief and faith remain outside the door.
> Set aside what pertains to the Way or thinking,
> To enable your heart to become God's abode.

The Helpless One commented: "When what is internal is manifested externally, how can it be thrust aside? On the contrary, what is internal is strengthened." The Revered Master replied: "This is the way it is thrust aside! Many other interpretations concerning this are given besides this one. They are based on experience. Would to God hypocrisy would find no hold on a person or haughtiness remain in him!" Afterwards he added: "There is what is external and what is internal, and seekers are of three kinds. The first seeks this world. The second seeks the world to come, while the third is in quest of the Lord. The person who seeks this world spends his time accumulating its goods. The person who seeks the world to come assiduously follows the injunction of the Law with regard to external matters. He acquires the world to come. The person in quest of God, however, cannot attain his aim until his inner dispositions are correct." At this point, he recited the following:

> Be pure in order to become a man of religion!
> Be like that, in order to become like this!
> Even though all your intention be pure,
> All of this has no resemblance at all to *God*.

He continued: "Their first priority is to attend to their inner dispositions. This is their work in hand. Nothing else has to be undertaken. Time has to be put to good use. The task, however, is that of inner purification." At this point, the Revered Master recited the following:

> By bathing, one seeking Him makes an impression:

On God's part, ritual prayer is not accepted.
Until you travel the pathless way to 'no's' confusion,
You cannot attain the haven of 'except God.'
Don't become important in your own estimation
By performing many prayers and much fasting.
No matter how much you wander, you will be turned aside:
These two drops will not make a lord of you.[352]

A discussion arose about how to oppose one's selfish soul. The Revered Master said: "It is recorded that Khwaja Sahl Tustari[353] said: 'No act of divine worship can be compared to that of opposing the lustful tendencies of one's selfish soul.' A dervish once put a question to a mystic: 'What is the remedy for the afflictions of the selfish soul?' He replied: 'When you oppose your selfish soul you are applying a remedy for the ills it inflicts!'" The Revered Master thereupon recited the following:

How long will you discuss what it means to arrive?
What does it mean to be chosen on the path of religion?
Put an end to evil and you will be chosen!
Trample self under foot and you will arrive.

"The meaning of the saying, 'The very thing that was an affliction for the selfish soul has become a remedy' is that, what was detrimental for a person at the initial stage has become for him, at an advanced stage, quite profitable. For example, allowing a disciple to move freely in the beginning would be harmful and distracting for him. On the other hand, if an advanced soul is free to move around for a worthwhile purpose, it would be beneficial for him, not harmful.[354] This is the freedom of action enjoyed by holy men."

In this vein he narrated the following story: "The son of a widow became the disciple of a holy man. The holy man ordered the disciple to live in privacy and to cut down on his intake of food.

---

352. Many textual differences make this translation tentative. There is much confusion about whether or not some verbs are negative.

353. Sahl Tustari (d.896) is the subject of many extraordinary stories. He contributed to the development of ideas about sainthood and was strong on the need for continual repentance. He came in contact with Al-Hallaj. He spent his final years in Basra, where he died.

354. The presumption is that the selfish soul of the advanced Sufi has been brought to heel. He is thus enabled to freely choose what is good.

The result was that he became lean and weak. His mother was informed about the situation. She exclaimed: 'What sort of a sheikh is this? He himself sits at table and eats plenty of good food and kills my son through hunger and thirst!' She covered her head and came to the hospice. It so happened that the holy man was at table. The table was covered with a variety of food. She said: 'What sort of a sheikh is this! You are eating all this good food and killing my son through hunger!' The sheikh thought to himself: 'This is a woman. If I try to explain the situation to her, she may or may not understand. It is necessary to do something in reply.' He lifted up his eyes to heaven and prayed: 'Lord, if my food is indeed fit and proper, give his poor woman a sign to put her heart at rest!' When he finished his prayer every cooked pigeon, chicken etc. that was on the table immediately came to life and flew away. The holy man exclaimed: 'Mother, I am killing your son so that he might be able to eat like this!'" The Revered Master then recited the following:

> If you want this ruby, you will have to dig for it!
> Love of this kind demands nothing less than life itself.
> You have not experienced the vagaries of heat and cold:
> You have not reached the door of this Hidden One's abode.

Mubarak Qusuri came forward to kiss the Master's footprints. He began to speak: "When I became a disciple of my sheikh, he said to me: 'What do you have in mind at the moment? You are of royal stock. Are you fully involved in your possessions or in some other preoccupation?' I replied: 'My present commitment is to service. I am ready to do whatever you indicate to me.' He elaborated: 'It is better for those who enter upon this Path to sacrifice everything.' "I have accepted this. In fact, this is what I have in mind."" The Revered Master interjected: "These words indicate that he has no doubt that it is better to give up everything, if a person remains firm in this resolve. On the other hand, what if someone has 'given up' everything on several occasions and distanced himself from all his possessions, yet afterwards gets involved in affairs once again, so that his attention is drawn to them, and yet he again repents of his conduct? What's the point of this type of renunciation? On the contrary, it would be better if the renunciation were done in a measured manner so that what is really needed is not renounced. This would ensure stability in the work and smooth progress. You are of noble birth and have participated in the assemblies and gatherings of your friends and equals. If you attend such assemblies and take your seat beside such people and see the way they live their lives, you would then become greatly disturbed and unhappy. You would immediately be upset. What profit would all this be? Before such a situation arises everybody says: 'I have abandoned everything! I have become an ascetic and a servant of God!' What happens when these claims are put to the test? If a person is neglectful and unhappy when called upon to implement such claims they would prove to be false. The selfish soul is guilty of many such deceptions by means of untried claims. It should not be trusted."

Thereupon the above-mentioned Mubarak spoke up: "Master, there is no desire for anything within me!" The Revered Master replied: "This is the deception of the selfish soul, for it pretends that it has renounced everything and fixed its gaze on the world to come. Those who are familiar with its deceptions can discern whether such a claim is true or false, for the selfish soul is steeped in deception, while the qualities of the heart are all genuine. Whatever the selfish soul says is false, whereas the heart utters nothing except the truth. This is the basis for the assertion that every work that is actually accomplished has been inspired by the heart. It also gets a person's limbs moving! This is because the impulse comes from the heart. Since the qualities of the heart are all genuine, its utterances are truthful. How could any action arise that is contrary to what has been said? If the qualities of the heart are genuine, how could a manifest lie appear? The answer given is that, if there is a conflict, the selfish soul must be involved! It has acted as a usurper by taking up lodgings in a person's heart. It robs the heart of many things. It deceptively adds to the heart. What is said actually emanates from the selfish soul. This explains the discrepancy between deed and word. There is an example that bears witness to this. A demon once occupied the throne of the prophet Solomon. It was issuing orders and, through deception, made itself completely like the prophet Solomon. Everyone who approached it thought he was approaching Solomon and paid obeisance to him. While carrying out 'his' orders, people were actually carrying out those of the demon. No one suspected that Solomon was actually a demon. The deception was complete. The deception of the selfish soul is of this nature." He then recited the following:

You are not the one who rules over your kingdom,

For your demon is in the place of Solomon.
If you once again place a signet ring on your finger,
Demons and fairies will all hearken to your command.

"Only those well versed in mystical knowledge are aware of its deceptions. Apart from them, others do not have this insight. If they desire something, yet do not obtain it, they say it was not meant for them. This is 'contraction.' If they obtain it, however, they are happy. They call this 'expansion.' Both contraction and expansion are states of the heart. First comes the heart, then its states, which appear as contraction and expansion. These stem from the selfish soul. It is unhappy when it does not get what it wants." Afterwards he added: "Consider those people whose renunciation is total and are free of all their previous attachments. If they suddenly focus their attention on something, it means their hearts have been corrupted. Before this, such a person was saying: 'I have renounced everything.' He had put an end to all his desires, but now that he has set his heart on something, he has corrupted his heart." Sheikh Mu'izzuddin inquired: "Can the selfish soul deceive people at all stages?" The Revered Master replied: "This can happen if the selfish soul has not been overcome. It can deceive people at every stage. At no stage at all can the masters of insight be said to be immune to its deceptions, even though it has become submissive and obedient to them."

A discussion arose about the deceits of the selfish soul. The Revered Master said: "It is related that Khwaja Usman Maghribi said: 'As long as a person sees something good in his selfish soul and thinks appreciatively of it, we deduce that he has not set eyes on its deceits. Anyone who does so remains vigilant.' Thus it is said that, if the Devil had kept a sharp eye on himself, he would never have said, 'I am better than he' (Q7:12)."[355] At this point, he recited the following:

For intelligent people, it is as clear as the day
That foolish people, night and day, are unlucky.

He told this story: "One day a man walked past a holy person. The holy man drew up his garment out of his way. The man said: 'Sheikh, why did you draw your garment around you? My clothes

---

355. The comparison is with Adam, made of clay, while he himself is made of fire, a superior element.

are clean, not dirty.' The sheikh replied: 'I suspected that my garment was dirty. I did not want it to touch your clean clothes. They would have become polluted." The Revered Master added: "This is the sort of opinion holy men have of themselves, especially those who are masters of insight, in spite of all their holiness." In this vein he continued: "In the world of purity, no one could match the Chosen One. In spite of his being so great, in his prayers of petition he used to say: 'O Lord, these are my hands with which I have sinned against myself. Forgive my sins, which are great, for no one can forgive such sins except the Glorious Lord!' We all know that these 'offences' of theirs are not sins at all. Nevertheless, because they thought that their behaviour was not all that it should be when they consider what is due to their Lord, they think of themselves as sinners. Holy men have said that Unitarians and believers should not consider themselves as more pure than others. The very moment they think like this they lose the Way! Nevertheless, they should compare themselves with upright men so that they can travel the right road. They come back to it. It is also true that men are rendered blind by their faults. You should ask pure souls about their faults. By learning about their faults you will become aware of your own." At this stage, he recited the following:

> All this knowledge forms a compact body:
> That of the Path to *God* is something else!

A discussion arose about veils. The Revered Master said: "There are two veils, one of darkness and one of light. Whatever is associated with the dark veil is blameworthy, such as hypocrisy, haughtiness, envy, hatred and similar such things. The veil of light consists of all praiseworthy qualities, such as prayer, fasting, trusting in God, striving to please Him, sincerity and similar such things. The veil of darkness is thrust aside by means of abandonment, while that of light is lifted by not paying attention to it. A person should utilize praiseworthy qualities, but not get caught up in them." Afterwards he said: "It is related that Khwaja Abu Bakr Tamastani said: 'The greatest blessing is to escape from the clutches of one's selfish soul, for it is the greatest veil between you and God." A dear soul inquired: "Is the selfish soul the veil of both the novice and an accomplished traveller, or is there another veil for the latter?" The Revered Master replied: "If an accomplished traveller focuses his attention on his stages and states, then this becomes a veil. This is because a stage has assumed prominence for him. He is happy with it and cultivates it. He becomes enamoured of it and settles down therein. This is a veil for him, as is anything of a similar nature. On the other hand, such a person has passed beyond his selfish soul. How could his selfish soul possibly be a veil for him?"

By way of explanation he told the following story: "On one occasion some people spoke to Khwaja Junaid in this fashion: 'It is said that there are three veils—people, the world and the selfish soul.' He commented: 'These are the common veils. There are three other special veils. If a worshipper fixes his attention on his worship, it is a veil for him, preventing him from seeing the Worshipped One. If an ascetic becomes enamoured of his miracles, this veils the Revered One from his gaze. If a mystic gets preoccupied with anything other than *God*, this will become a veil between him and *God*." Thereupon Maulana Nizamuddin and Shamsuddin Samir inquired; "If someone settles down happily in a particular stage, would this stem from his selfish soul or not?" The Revered Master replied: "This is because some defects continue to remain in a traveller. There is no one in whom such things do not remain.[356] The harm is in proportion to what remains. The basis for saying this is that there are beginners, mediocre disciples, and accomplished travellers. Beginners, from the point of view of their stage of being beginners, are equal but, as far as degrees are concerned, there is disparity. Similarly, from the point of view of mediocrity, mediocre disciples are equal, yet there is disparity from the point of view of degrees. In the same way accomplished travellers, even though their stage is the same, yet there is a disparity of degree among them." Again he inquired: "Is there any obstacle between a stage a person is on the brink of entering and the one in which he is already firmly grounded?" The Revered Master replied: "It is said that anyone who has attained a particular stage and has become firmly established in it, and is pleased with it and finds contentment therein, then this very pleasure and contentment become an obstacle for him. This applies to stages involving spiritual experience and divine manifestation. If a person on an ordinary journey alights at a particular stage on his journey and rests contentedly there, then there is no way he can reach the stage that lies ahead of him." At this point, the Revered Master recited the following:

---

356. *Nist kasi ki dar way in ham namande* (MS 1219).

Move forward in order to pass beyond the kingdom:
By remaining where you are, you will quickly slip back.

A dear soul inquired: "The Lord is referred to as being 'secluded.'[357] This is a current saying. What does it mean?" The Revered Master replied: "Both 'secluded' and 'veiled'[358] mean that they cannot be seen. It is correct to say that the Lord is secluded, whereas it is not correct to say that He is veiled. This is because 'veiled' refers to a veil which prevents us from seeing what is referred to as 'veiled.' This is a quality denoting subjection. 'Secluded,' on the other hand, means 'not showing yourself to another.' This is a divine quality. The Lord is not 'veiled' from people, but people are 'veiled' from the Lord!" He then recited the following:

Whoever is hidden behind the eternal veil
Is like the tract traversed by the sun.
He would be a light moving towards the Light,
A Light far brighter than that of the sun.

He went on to say: "In the *Ihya* it is stated that our intellects are extremely weak, while the beauty of the Divine Lord is infinitely dazzling and His self-concealment is utterly overwhelming. It is his incomparable sublimity that is the reason for His being concealed. Take the example of a bat. It sees by night, but not by day.[359] This is not because the light of day is somehow hidden, but rather because of the extreme brightness of daylight. The bat has weak eyes. The light of the sun is as nothing as far as it is concerned. It is like twilight. The extreme brightness of the sun, in conjunction with the weak vision of the bat, explains the inability of the bat to see. Pure indeed is that Lord Who is secluded by the pre-eminence of His light and concealed from the vision and eyes of others by His own dazzling appearance! Those people who are themselves seeking intimate knowledge of Him are as utterly confounded as 'a person seated upon an ass, and yet still looking for the ass!' It is

---

357. *Muhtajib.*

358. *Mahjub.*

359. In fact, bats 'see' by what is called 'echolocation.' This in an incredible 'radar' system involving the analysis of returning signals in a few thousandths of a second. As far as the topic under discussion is concerned, however, we can prescind from this, and take Maneri's example at its face value.

just like something that is plainly visible, but when you start looking for it, it becomes very hard to find. The secret of this work has
been well expressed as follows:

> You are plainly there, hidden from no one at all,
> Except from those who cannot even see the moon.
> You are hidden, because Your brilliance veils You:
> Who can see You, when none can see the veil itself?

Those deeds of God that have become clear for mystics, even though
unimaginably brilliant, lie hidden. It is not fitting to display the
full brilliance of the external manifestation. Indeed, full and complete disclosure is not possible except in the world to come. With
regard to the divine activity, no boundary can be fixed for each and
every devotee. For some of them it is revealed. A mystic has said:
'I do not utter, O Lord! O God! except when I feel the need to do so
weighs more heavily on my heart than would a mountain.' This is
because such a call would be from behind a curtain, and no one
calls out to someone sitting beside him!" At this point, the Revered
Master recited the following:

> If a dove is not seen, a person calls out to it:
> If You yourself are present, why call out?

He said: "With regard to the explanation of this verse, 'For those
who do good there will be a reward and more' (Q10:26), it has been
said that *God* will remove the veil, but He will not be seen. How
could this be explained?" He himself offered this explanation: "In
the Commentary of Maulana Fakhruddin Razi[360] it is mentioned that
it is really impossible to speak about a veil with reference to God.
A veil refers to a body placed between two other bodies. Moreover,
for us 'veil' is a loaded word. 'God has not created in human eyes the
capability of seeing Him.'" A person in the assembly said: "It is well
attested in books that the Apostle said: 'God has seventy veils of

---

360. Fakhruddin Razi (1149-1209) was much travelled; a venerated
teacher; and an esteemed scholar, who was also not without enemies. He
brought an acutely philosophical bent of mind to his numerous writings.
These included his famous Quranic commentary, *al-Tafsir al-kabir* [The
Great Commentary], which is quoted here. The quotation illustrates his
philosophical approach. Maneri's personal reaction to this commentary
is found in *Khwan-i Pur Ni'mat*, in the thirty-ninth assembly, p.137: "So
many arguments are above the capacity of a man like me!"

light. If they are torn away, the vision of the sublime splendour of His countenance would be attained.' A second tradition says: 'Light is His veil.' How are these to be understood?" The Revered Master replied: "These have also been explained in his commentary, namely, that everything that has been made obligatory is because it has an effect on something else. Whatever perfection has been obtained has an origin. What is acquired comes from an efficacious source. There can be no doubt that the strength of any such perfection as found in its source is far superior to anything in which it is acquired. There can also be no doubt that the bestower of all perfections and graces is the Lord. All perfections, when compared to God, are nothing. Thus it is clear that the perfection of any human being, compared to the perfection of God, is inferior. It is said to be as good as nothing. It cannot be doubted that the strength of the human spirit and body is not from the ornament of that perfection,[361] nor is it possible to study about that perfection. On the contrary, human spirits and everything associated with them are vanishing and becoming nothing in the very lowest stage of that perfection. This is what is intended by the tradition, 'If they were to be torn apart, the vision of the sublime splendour of His countenance would be attained.'"[362]

---

361. The basic idea behind this statement is the affirmation of primary causality to the exclusion of secondary causality.

362. One manuscript finishes with, "But God knows best!" This addition underscores the difficult nature of Razi's abstract line of argumentation. At bottom, it is a comparison between absolute being, i.e., God, and contingent being, i.e. creatures. The former necessarily exits, while the latter totally depend on the former for every moment and aspect of their existence. One can thus stress the "as good as nothing" dimension of contingent beings—as emphasised here—or rejoice in the fact that God has created us for union with Him in this life and the vision of Himself in the life to come. This is the main thrust of Maneri's teaching, which can be ascertained from a perusal of his *Hundred Letters.*

CHAPTER 25

CUTTING ONESELF OFF FROM PEOPLE AND FROM ONE'S VERY SELF: AND WHAT PERTAINS THERETO

The topic of cutting oneself off from people and from one's very self arose. The Revered Master said: "The saying, 'It takes two steps to reach God' is explained in various ways. The following explanation, however, seems to be the best. The first step refers to cutting oneself off completely from people in order to attain to one's self. The second step is held to mean that, when a person has reached his self, he will not attain to *God* until he has severed all connections with his self. When he has accomplished this, he will attain to *God*. Just as before severing his ties with people he had steps to take with regard to self, in a similar way, before he could sever his ties to his self, he had steps to take with regard to *God*." At this point, he recited the following:

> Whoever has passed by this is now engrossed:
> God forbid that you should say that he is *God*!
> If you have traversed what I described, you are not *God*,
> But you have become immersed in Eternal Reality!
> How can an engrossed person actually become God?
> How could such words be anything but excessive?

"Another explanation is that one step is the abandonment of this world, while the second is the abandonment of the word to come. In other words, although the Path is a long one, a person can reach *God* in these two steps. This the meaning of the following couplet:"

> At one breath Sufis celebrate two feasts:
> Spiders tear the flesh of flies to shreds.

Zakaria Gharib spoke up: "Master, although there are many holy men in the town, yet your whole way of acting is found to a much lesser degree in others. The holy men that are found today, since they intermingle with the people, certainly act in a way that is customary." The Revered Master responded in this fashion: "People around here have great confidence in this group and are faithful followers. For this reason they are unsettled by so much interaction with the local people. In this state of affairs, holy men have said that, when people begin to flock to someone, he does something to conceal the truth. He does something which is seemingly against the Law, but which is essentially in conformity with it. The whole purpose is to flee from the attention of the people and devote oneself totally to following the Way. This is called 'asceticism within asceticism.' In other words, when a person abandons the world he becomes an ascetic. His asceticism becomes clear to the people round about. When he wants to escape from this stage of asceticism he does something deliberately to conceal his stage and escape from the attention of the people. When he has escaped their attention, he has emerged from the first stage of asceticism. This second stage is an extremely difficult one because it involves the renunciation of being held in high esteem. This is more difficult that renouncing the world. This is why some have said that name and fame are like an iron girdle. Breaking out from such a girdle would be extremely difficult." At this juncture the Revered Master recited the following:

> None but God can open up this work for you:
> You cannot attain to God if you cling to anything.
> Importuning God is all sorrow and affliction:
> Pass beyond them all and God becomes your all.

Afterwards he said: "When holy men see someone belonging to this group they immediately know how steadfast he is. Through an inspiration from on high they perceive whether his steadfastness is completely centred on *God*. If they discern the slightest attachment to creatures they immediately exclaim that it will be astonishing if he attains his goal." He thereupon recited the following:

> What does love have to do with unbelief or faith?
> How can lovers be involved in this fleeting life?
> Each person who is firmly established in love,
> Has passed beyond unbelief and beyond Islam.
> People will call it apostasy, and call him an apostate:
> Yet his love is better than either unbelief or faith.

The Helpless One inquired: "How does one cut oneself off from people?" The Revered Master replied: "Much has been said about this but, in *Sharh-i Ta'arruf*, the best explanation of cutting oneself off from people is that they do not dwell on the injury or gain that comes from people, and regard the praise or reproach of people as one and the same. When this happens, even if a person is in the midst of people, nevertheless he has emerged from their midst. Thus it is said: 'Externally they are with people, but inwardly they are taken up with their secret, not with people.' A person could be far from people, even to the extent of living in a cave in the depths of the earth. He could still be influenced by some gain or damage at the hands of people, take pleasure in their praise, or be afraid of their reproaches. If this occurs, then even though he is far from them according to appearances, in reality he is still among them." Afterwards he added: "It is related that Khwaja Usman Gharibi said that anyone who chooses solitude in preference to living with people should be free of all considerations apart from remembering God, and have no other intention than that of pleasing his Lord. He should also be free of all the designs of his selfish soul about accumulating goods. If he does not enjoy this freedom, his retreat into solitude would plunge him into temptations and serious trials."

He went on to say: "If a person is praised by the people, yet is not united to *God*, how would it profit him? If people reproach him, however, yet he is united to *God*, what loss would he suffer? If angels, heaven and all the worlds call him a Muslim, yet there is something amiss between him and *God*, of what benefit would this be? On the other hand, if all the worlds call him an unbeliever and an apostate, yet everything between him and *God* is good and praiseworthy, what harm could accrue to him?" He thereupon recited the following:

When the all-pure God is pleased with His servant,
If others are not pleased with him, what is there to fear?

"Cutting oneself off from people does not mean living in solitude yet, at the same time, having a heart which is inclined towards people, rank and spiritual eminence. This is of no benefit. On the contrary, if a person is living among people and yet his heart is with *God*, no harm would result thereby." At this point he recited the following:

O Sana'i, be less fulsome in your praise!

Make yourself acquainted with how to behave!

The Helpless One inquired: "If a person cuts himself off from people but has no knowledge at all, would he know the reality of his situation?" The Revered Master replied: "He should have some knowledge; or there should be someone to show him the Way and explain to him the dangers that lie lurking along it. Other than this, he would come under the influence of this threat: 'Satan is with the solitary person.' For no reason at all should a weak person be allowed to live a solitary life. A person cannot travel this path without a companion. Even if he is a learned man, as long as there is no one at his side, he would not attain his aim. Common experience bears this out." He then recited the following:

> Without knowledge, the work is a fruitless burden:
> An egg without a sperm produces nothing.
> Take pity and become like Jesus:
> What can you do for one who sits alone?

Qazi Minhajuddin from the fort went through the *Wasiyat* of the Sheikh of Sheikhs until he came to the words, "Enlarge your house!" The Revered Master said: "'Open wide your house' contains a hint about living in seclusion. In other words, a person considers the whole world as his own home. This is because he has a different aim. Consider the whole world as your home until the stage of diligent service of Divine Unity is attained!" The Revered Master continued: "A disciple should discern whether it would be better for him to live in seclusion, or in close association with a holy man. If he thinks that a solitary life would be more meaningful for him, he should embrace solitude. If he opts for companionship, he should choose it. It has to be pointed out, however, that solitude involves many dangers. It would not be safe for everyone. Either a disciple should have an experienced and capable guide to attain his aim, or he should himself possess abundant knowledge. This is where the hint of the Lord of the Law comes into play: 'Satan is with the solitary person, but far away from two people.' If a person lives by himself without a sincere guide or an abundance of knowledge, then this warning applies to him, namely, that 'Satan is with the solitary person.' It is said that a beginner has no other option at the outset of his religious endeavour than that of sequestering himself from his peers; while, at its accomplishment, he emerges from seclusion as someone who has experienced divine intimacy for himself."[363]

He continued: "The duty of a servant is to ensure that, when he wants to embrace solitude, his intention should be that he is doing so to keep people safe from his wickedness, not to keep himself safe from the wickedness of the people. This is because the first intention stems from the baseness of the selfish soul,[364] while the second involves perceiving oneself as superior to other people. Whoever holds his selfish soul in utter contempt is humble and submissive, while the person who considers his selfish soul to be superior is proud and haughty." The Revered Master told this story: "Once upon a time a mystic saw a hermit. He said to him: 'Are you a hermit?' 'No, I am a dog-keeper. My selfish soul is a dog that goes around biting people. I have removed it from among them to deep people safe from its vicious behaviour." At this point, he recited the following:

Kill your selfish soul and become a believer!
Wrestle with it in order to be safe!

And:

Until one born of men becomes a man,
Whether fairy, office or demon, all have a sting.
Your selfish soul is your enemy: turn it to dust!
God's Ka'ba is the heart: keep it pure!

---

363. This important sentence, *Gufte and charah nist mar murid ra dar aghaz-i hal 'uzlat az abna-i jins-i khish pas dar nihayat-i hal az khalwat ta mutahaqqiq gardad be uns-i haqq*, sums up the discussion. We recall that Maneri had become an outstanding scholar in Sonargaon; had been lovingly guided along the Sufi Path in Delhi by Najibuddin Firdausi; and had then gone into the jungle of Bihiya to be 'alone with the Alone,' the only Teacher left to him. This is the progression of which Maneri is speaking. When Sheikh Zada Chishti visited him after he had moved to a cave in Rajgir, he urged him to "take up the burden of the people." This led to his weekly visits to Bihar Sharif for the Friday prayer so that people could meet him, and he eventually had to take up residence there, where he spent the rest of his life in worshipping God and "bringing comfort to hearts." The topic is discussed in letters 94, 95 and 96 in his *Hundred Letters*.

364. This base creature, as we see in the following example, has to be kept away from people.

Afterwards he said: "There is a difference of opinion among sheikhs as to whether solitude is superior to companionship; or whether companionship is more beneficial than solitude. Some say that companionship is superior to solitude because sin finds an entrance in solitude. This happens because, if a solitary person is tempted, he gives in and quickly falls into sin in the absence of anyone to prevent it. On the other hand, sin does not find an entrance in companionship. This is because people restrain each other from sinning, not to mention their shame at what others might think of them. This is why Khwaja Yahya Mu'az Razi[365] used to say: 'Solitude is the table companion of the righteous.' Another holy man is reported as having said: 'Power is not conferred on a solitary person but on the powerful.' As for people like us, however, coming together is considered profitable. This is because seeing each other's devotion and worship acts as a stimulus. Nevertheless some, who consider solitude superior to companionship, say that seclusion acts as a restraint upon a person in so many different ways. To begin with, the eyes are prevented from looking at forbidden things; the tongue from speaking forbidden things and making slanderous remarks; and the feet from going to what is forbidden. Many other similar benefits are obtained.

In contrast to this, for a person who is associating with others, there is every chance that, when two people get together, they fall into slander. This type of behaviour takes place because two people have come together. They tell stories to each other. As they tell story after story, they fall into many unsavoury things, such as we hear that Khwaja Junaid said: 'Whoever wants his religion to attain fruition and make things easy for his heart and body should seek seclusion from human beings, for this is a period of dreadful uncertainty, and an intelligent person will seek solitude while it lasts.' It is also related that Sheikh Abu Ali said: 'I heard that Shibli used to say that penury and intimacy were found with human beings.' He was asked: 'O Abu Bakr, what is the sign of penury?' He replied: 'One of the signs is becoming intimate with human beings.' In other words, until a person becomes a pauper, he does not experience intimate friendship with people." He returned to the

---

365. Khwaja Yahya Mu'az Razi (d. 871), from Rayy, near Tehran, was famous as a preacher who was overwhelmed by the mystery of God's love.

theme of abstaining from idleness: "According to the dictionary meaning, 'idleness' means 'being without anything to to.' Hence, if one is in seclusion, it is necessary to remain active and not fall into idleness. It is imperative to keep oneself occupied and refrain from sinning. Seclusion is profitable for such a person as this." He again returned to these words: "Idleness deadens the heart, so he passes his time fully engaged in what leads him nearer to God—may He be glorified and exalted!" The Revered Master reiterated the point: "A solitary person in seclusion should shun idleness because it deadens the heart. He should keep himself fully occupied in prayer; fasting; remembering God and reading the Quran. Every day and every night let him be engaged in prayer, remembering God and reading the Quran. In this way he will be occupied at all times." At this point the Helpless One inquired: "If a person who is occupied in these tasks experiences a certain dreariness and tedium, what should he do?" The Revered Master replied: "At such a time he should associate closely with some pious man so that he can become like him. When he settles down with him he should tell him about what has been happening to him. This is because by telling him all of this you could say he also shares in it."

The Master's son went through *Siraj ul-'Arifin* [A Lamp for Mystics] until he came to these words: "If a person does not embrace a sequestered life and is preoccupied with bodily worship, then association would be better for him." The Revered Master explained: "This means associating with pious people. It would be better to be in their company than being preoccupied with bodily worship. This is because a person who embraces a sequestered life would ideally be living an interior life and would attain his goal. Bodily worship by itself, however, is not capable of attaining the goal. Instead of such a preoccupation with bodily worship, it would be better to associate with pious people, because this would facilitate an interior life. This is the correct way to achieve one's goal. Understood in this way, preference should be given to associating with pious people." Afterwards he added: "A single interior effort is of more value than a hundred external ones." He then recited the following:

When the sun is not shining, stars sparkle brightly:
Your lamp, however, cannot turn night into day.

CHAPTER 26
ASCETICISM
AND FEARING GOD

Sheikh Mu'izzuddin was reading *Ta'arruf* [Seeking Knowledge] and came to the place where a holy man was asked what asceticism was. He replied: "When you have no fear of the power of the world, whether you be a believer or an unbeliever." Thereupon the Revered Master commented: "Yes, when he is not concerned about the world, he makes use of whatever exists, whether he be a believer or an unbeliever. Everything is one and the same for him." He thereupon recited the following:

> The world is the stepping-stone to cupidity and avarice:
> It is the legacy of Nimrod and Pharaoh.
> *God* Most Exalted said: It is called nothing!
> You have become entangled in its snare.
> What about the activity of the world? It is useless!
> What do you mean, 'useless?' It's an imprisonment!
> Whoever becomes lost in a particle of 'nothing'
> Has no chance at all of becoming a man!

He then came to where it is written that Khwaja Shibli was asked what asceticism was. He said: "Woe to you! Asceticism is abstaining from something that really exists, but how can you abstain from something that does not exist? Asceticism means abstaining from something you can actually give a name to, whereas the world itself is really nothing." The Revered Master commented: "What can you call the world? It is nothing! This explains why, when God Most Exalted addressed the world, He said: 'O nothing!' If someone remarks that the world is beautiful and is something, he then goes ahead and calls it something. What does addressing something which does not exist mean?" He himself proffered an answer: "By itself the world simply has no value at all, even though it exists. This is because its existence depends on the creative activity of Another. The existence of something which depends on the creative activity of Another can by no means be said to really exist."

At this point Qazi Ashrafuddin asked the meaning of "Existence is what is found between the two non-existences." The Revered Master replied: "This simply means that the existence in question, first of all, did not previously exist, and will end up ceasing to exist. This sort of existence is found between two non-existences. The poet Labid,[366] a contemporary of the Apostle, expressed it thus:

> Beware of the emptiness of everything except God,
> And that all blessings, without a doubt, fade away.

As soon as the Apostle heard this verse, he said: 'Truly no Arab has spoken as has Labid!' Here it was also pointed out that everything except *God* certainly exists, so how can it all be called null and void? The Apostle attests to this. It can be explained in this way. The reality of existence belongs to God who exists by virtue of His essence. No other being came into existence by itself. Existence was granted to all of them by God Most Exalted. Of themselves, they are nothing. Their existence is established by the existence of *God*, while *God* himself exists by virtue of His very essence. Other beings, by virtue of themselves, are worth nothing. Their existence is called 'existence' metaphorically, and it has to be admitted that a metaphor, in comparison to reality, carries no weight. It has nothing to show for itself. Beings other than God seem to exist, but have no reality. This is because they are accidental and will ease to exist. Khwaja Nizami[367] put it thus:

> You are the refuge of heaven and earth:
> All are nothing! You are The Existing One.

This couplet also gives this same meaning. Although all beings exist, nevertheless, they do not exist. Someone said that there is no reality. While at prayer, the Apostle prayed: 'O God, show me things as they are!' This petition wants the reality of things to be made manifest." Afterwards he continued: "The first thing mystics do when they see something is to ascertain its reality. They find non-existence in everything they see. That is why they cannot be

---

366. Labid was a very famous Arabic poet who became a Muslim when he met the Prophet as a member of a delegation from his tribe, around 630. He lived to a ripe old age, dying about the year 660.

367. Nizami (d. 1209) is known particularly for his famous love poem, *Khusrau Shirin*. Maneri quotes him on three occasions in his *Hundred Letters*.

completely as ease with anything. How could they be, since they all partake of non-existence? This is also why mystics are always on the move, never standing still." He then recited the following:

> Come heart in hand and gaze at His glory:
> Make your soul a mirror and gaze at His beauty.
> If it happens that a door is opened for you,
> Then you will see the sun, even from the shade.
> The path you travel is obstructed: prefer life!
> Throw away your eyes and begin to see!

"Whenever ordinary people look at anything the first thing they see is its apparent existence. This is why they love it and become attached to it." Afterwards he said: "Imam Shibli is said to have prohibited asceticism. It is known that both the Quran and the traditions speak in affirmation of asceticism. How could Khwaja Shibli prohibit it? People answer this by saying that Imam Shibli's intention was not to prohibit asceticism itself, but to prohibit fixing one's attention on it. In other words, asceticism should be practised, but not made much of. Similarly, whatever holy men have prohibited refers to not paying much attention to such things." When he came to these words, "A holy man was asked what asceticism was," he exclaimed: "It means abstaining from a privy and from nothing, but how can this be done?" At this point the Revered Master continued: "The reason why the world is called a privy and nothing is because when Adam was placed in paradise he ate the grain of wheat. After doing so, he felt a natural urge. Paradise, however, is not a place for fulfilling such human needs. He was told that the place for such actions was the world. This was why he had to be taken outside. This was how Adam was expelled from paradise, and it is why the world is called a privy."

Coming back to the question about asceticism, he said: "In reality, there is no asceticism, because it is exempt from two conditions. It is either abstaining from something which has been decreed from all eternity, or from something which has not been so decreed. If it is from something that has been decreed, this itself is not possible. Moreover, if it is from something that has not been decreed, then that has no profit either." Sheikh Mu'izzuddin spoke up: "Since asceticism is affirmed in both the Quran and the traditions, what weight can be given to this assertion?" The Revered Master replied: "Quite so! Moreover, renunciation is necessary for a person, or he should have the intention of renouncing some-thing if the need arises. That is something else. It is the readiness to abandon something which is important." Once again, with ref-erence to the meaning of asceticism, it was said to be "renouncing something that was necessary." The Revered Master said: "There are both necessary things and others that are not necessary. When a person renounces something that is needful for him, that is as-ceticism. With regarded to what is not necessary, there is a differ-ence of opinion. Some classify unnecessary things as those with-out which the selfish soul cannot become firmly established. For mystics, however, the one thing you cannot abstain from is *God*. Except for this One Necessary Thing, everything else is granted to a servant." When the Revered Master reached these words, he recited the following couplet:

> If nothing is mine, either in this world or the next,
> Yet I have You, I have all, even if nought else be mine.

Qazi Minhajuddin from the fort began reading the *Wasiyat* [Testa-ment] of the Sheikh of Sheikhs. At the very beginning were the words: "My son, I command you to fear God!" The Revered Master said: "Fear of God is of two kinds. The first is genuine fear of God, while the second is 'prohibiting' fear. Genuine fear of God consists of loathing ingratitude[368] and embracing faith. 'Prohibiting' fear, on the other hand, submits to the whole gamut of commands. It shows itself averse to everything that is prohibited." Qazi Ashra-fuddin inquired: "What is the meaning of adding 'God' to the no-tion of fearing?" The Revered Master replied: "According to the dictionary, the word simply means 'fearing.' Adding 'God' to 'fear-ing' is simply providing the object of the described activity. This is what was meant by the command to fear.[369] This group explains the fear of God as refraining from anything that could detract from a person's being purely dedicated to God. This is also found

---

368. *Kufr.* The word is usually translated as 'infidelity' or 'unbelief.' Because of the emotional context, it seems appropriate to use the basic meaning of *kufr*, which is 'ingratitude.' The underlying idea is, "God has done so much for you, and you don't even have the decency to acknowledge this fact! You ungrateful wretch!"

369. Many words, when used in a religious context, refer either to God or to divine activity. Thus *taqwa*, which simply means 'fearing,' when used in a religious context, means 'fearing God.'

in the Quran (Q2:194). It is this fear of God that is intended. It is also reported that, at the time of the Commander of the Faithful, Umar, whenever he came to the words, 'fear God,' while reciting the Quran, anyone listening immediately had to recite, 'There is no god but God.' It is also related that he was going along on horseback one day. Someone called out, 'Fear God, O Commander of the Faithful!' He dismounted and rolled around in the dust." At this point, he recited the following:

> How brightly they shine, those who gaze at the moon!
> How they belittle religion, those who seek after office!

The discussion again was about fearing God. The Revered Master said: "Regarding the explanation of this word, it has been said: 'Fearing God means obeying Him and not sinning; remembering Him and not forgetting Him; and being grateful to Him, not ungrateful." Afterwards he said: "It is related that Khwaja Hariri said: 'Unless a person's relationship to God is one of fearing Him and focussing on Him, he cannot attain to His revelation and manifestation.'" Qazi Sadruddin inquired: "What does it mean to say, 'He does not give a command between himself and *God*?'" The Revered Master explained: "It is a matter between him and the Lord. It involves the command to fear God and be focussed on Him. In other words, he should advance by fearing God and focussing on Him, not through external commands and long explanations." Afterwards he added: "It is related that Khwaja Nasirabadi said: 'Whoever is assiduous in fearing God longs to escape from the world.' Some people have said that the fear of God has various manifestations. For ordinary people, it means abstaining from polytheism. For more advanced souls, it means refraining from committing sins. For saints, it means not trying to win favour with God by means of their deeds. For prophets, it means turning from Him to Him.[370] In this vein the Apostle, on the night of ascent, prayed in this fashion: 'I take refuge in Your forgiveness from Your punishment.' He went forward and arrived at the divine qualities. He prayed: 'I take refuge in Your pleasure from Your displeasure.' When he reached the divine essence, he exclaimed: 'I take refuge in You from You!'"

---

370. This possibly means turning from God, revered on account of His providential relationship to me and others, to God, as He is in himself.

CHAPTER 27
FEAR AND HOPE

A discussion arose about fear and hope. The Revered Master explained: "This latter is of two kinds. One is genuine hope, while the other is wishful thinking. Some write 'foolishness' for 'wishful thinking.' Hope refers to something after a person becomes engaged in serving God. This involves operationalizing the preconditions of serving God and observing the divine commands, as well as being careful to refrain from what is forbidden. Hope is based on this foundation. Wishful thinking, on the other hand, means that a person is not worried about acts of devotion or about any divine command, nor is he bothered about refraining from what is forbidden, yet says: 'My hope rests on God's bounty. He will be generous to me.' This is wishful thinking! The following example illustrates both these attitudes.

A man occupied a piece of land; cleared it; ploughed it; and did all that was necessary to prepare it before finally sowing his seed. After doing all this he was hopeful that the piece of land would provide the food he needed. This is hope. On the other hand, if someone occupies a piece of land in the jungle, but makes no effort to clear it or sow seed, yet says: 'I am hopeful that this piece of land will provide the food I need,' then this is wishful thinking. In *Kimiya-i Sa'adat* [The Alchemy of Happiness][371] this is called 'foolishness.' Ordinary people also regard it as foolishness." At this stage Qazi Ashrafuddin said: "If some who haunt taverns have a good interior disposition, but outwardly appear bad, then it is said that they have fear and hope, which is a result of serving God.[372] How could this be?" The Revered Master replied: "A person's external reprehensible behaviour is seen in the context of all the prescriptions of the Law—in all its aspects—or at least it so appears in some instances to an onlooker. If this external reprehensible behaviour applies to the Law in all its aspects, then the discussion is not about such a situation. That would be the height of error and absurdity.

---

371. This work is an abridgement of al-Ghazali's famous *Ihya*.

372. Textual discrepancies here, and further on, pose translation problems .

A person in such a situation would be completely deluded. That external reprehensible behaviour might be found in only a few actions, however. If it is meant to conceal the spiritual stature of a person who is given over to a life of loving care, and his whole life is directed towards perfecting his religion, then his behaviour is reprehensible in the eyes of an onlooker, but is essentially deeply authentic. This would be genuine hope stemming from devoted service, not something antecedent to it."

He went on to explain: "This occurs in two ways. One is when a person's external behaviour is quite laudable, while his inner disposition is reprehensible. This is not permissible, because such people are hypocrites. Some people outwardly seem to follow the Law, but are bad at heart. The second way is when a person's external behaviour seems reprehensible, yet his internal disposition is praiseworthy. This is how things should be, because anyone who is good at heart will certainly act in a praiseworthy manner. The measure of a person's laudable behaviour will depend upon the degree of his inner goodness. It is said that the Commander of the Faithful, Umar, was consumed by an inner fear of God and the effect of this was discernible externally. If a demon saw him, it would tremble with fear. Human beings are normally afraid of demons, but when the effect of Umar's inner fear became outwardly discernible, demons themselves would be afraid of him." At this point, he began to discuss the sign of the fear of God. He said: "The sign of this fear is when a person shuns what is forbidden, while the sign of hope is the observance of God's commandments. If someone lays claim to the fear of God by saying, 'I fear God,' take a look and see if he shuns what is forbidden or not. If he actually does shun prohibited things, people will know that he really does fear God. If he does not, then he is a liar."

After a while he quoted: "'Whatever claim is not verified by a person's deeds is a lie.' If a person really did experience the fear of God, he would not be indulging in forbidden things. In a similar way, if someone says, 'I hope in *God*,' and 'My hope is in *God*,' then it has to be seen whether he observes the divine ordinances and commands or not. If he shows himself observant, then we know that he does have hope and his claim is consequently genuine. On the other hand, if he is not obedient and does what is forbidden, he is a liar. This is because hope depends on the precondition of devoted service. Once this is in place, hope would follow."

Qazi Ashrafuddin inquired: "If someone says to himself: 'Every good deed and every evil act that comes into existence through me are all from God,' will a person experience peace because he has attributed everything to *God?*" The Revered Master replied: "This is not the way to feel secure. Fear of God and a sense of security stem from one's deeds. Each has its own place, yet nothing more can be extracted from the above understanding than that peace is found. This is because whenever a person sees both good and evil as originating from *God*, he will have no contest or quarrel with anyone, because attributing everything to God results in peace.[373] This is because we realized that, if a person performs a thousand acts of devotion, it could happen that he does not attain union with God. On the other hand, if someone commits a thousand sins which cut him off from God, it can happen that *God* Most Exalted bestows union with himself upon that person. He becomes one of those in privileged union with God. Devotion is no more than the reason for union with God, while sin is no more that the reason for being separated from God. The cause of union or separation depends on the Will of God. Thus it is said that hell, if one is united to the Friend, is heaven." The Revered Master at this point recited this couplet:

> If His tresses were entwined around the denizens of hell,
> In all five prayers I myself would plead for hell!

Qazi Ashrafuddin objected thus: "Since there is no union with God in hell, how can this truth be set aside?" The Revered Master replied: "Although it is true that hell is not the place of union, nevertheless their large-heartedness is such that, if union did occur in hell, then hell would become heaven." After a while, he added: "What they are really after is not heaven but union with God, because that is what will constitute heaven. The comprehensive

---

373. It seems that Qazi Ashrafuddin is operating at one level of conscience—as his next question confirms—while Maneri is operating at a much deeper level. The question implies that there is no difference between good or bad acts. Maneri disagrees. They are quite different. At a deeper level of consciousness, however, when a person realizes that no single being or action can occur separated from God, the Source and Sustainer of all beings, this realization brings peace. God's all-embracing, providential care includes, so to say, the detritus of sin, otherwise there is no freedom to love. "He loves them and they love Him" (Q5:54). Maneri goes on to insist on God's unfettered freedom of choice and action.

meaning of heaven is nothing more than this. Consider this verse, 'They pray to their Lord in fear and hope' (Q32:16). Some externalist scholars interpret this to mean that they are afraid of hell and hope to go to heaven. Sheikhs, however, interpret it as meaning that they are afraid of separation from God and hope to be united to Him. Both interpretations are correct. One applies to ordinary people, while the other applies to the specially chosen." The Revered Master thereupon recited the following:

> The selfish soul inhabits a lust-filled abode,
> While the heart's abode is that of a pearl.
> A life passed with any other than the Beloved,
> Will know no peace, even if filled with others.

Qazi Ashrafuddin again inquired: "How can it be true that 'The saints of God experience no fear, nor are they sad?'" The Revered Master replied: "This denial of fear does not mean an absolute denial, but a restricted one. In other words, God's saints do not feel the fear that others experience. Their fear stems from the sight of their own sins. They become afraid of the pain and torment that lies in store for them. Saints do not experience this pain, however, since they are not guilty of sin. They are fearful of the glory, greatness and total self-sufficiency of *God*." Again he asked: "Do those who are afraid of pain and torment experience this fear on the Day of Resurrection or in this world?" The Revered Master replied: "They experience it both in this world and on the day of Resurrection. This is because *God* Most Exalted visits people with some of the consequences of their deeds also in this world. Whatever a person does is accompanied by its reward or punishment also in this world. Whenever other people do something against God's Law, they are afraid that, as a consequence, some calamity might befall them. It is in this situation that consequences have to be faced. Moreover, the world to come is also a place of reward or punishment where there is also the fear of pain and torment. *God's* saints do not experience either of these two fears, but they are fearful of *God's* glory, greatness and utter self-sufficiency. In heaven they will not be afraid of pain and torment, or of separation from God, yet they will still be fearful of the glory and greatness of *God*. This will remain. Yet it must be added that we realize that fear brings unhappiness, so how could it be a blessing? Moreover, heaven is a place where nothing brings unhappiness. In answer to this difficulty, it has to be pointed out that there is a reason for being fearful of the glory and greatness of God, and that a person should not be rendered miserable." Afterwards he added: "Fear of *God's* utter self-sufficiency arises within saints precisely on account of His utter self-sufficiency. If someone performs a thousand acts of devotion, how does it profit Him? In what way is He harmed if someone commits a thousand sins? Union or separation depends on the Will of *God*. It could happen that He drives away someone who is adorned with a thousand acts of devotion and worship, yet grants union to someone else who is loaded with a thousand sins." At this point, the Revered Master recited the following couplet:

> How does it profit or harm the Lord of Glory
> If you memorize the Quran or worship idols?

He also said: "When their gaze is fixed on the Will of *God*, in this world also they are fearful of being separated from Him. No one has any knowledge about what will happen. That is why they are fearful of being separated."[374]

---

374. Maneri teaches that sinners have every reason to be afraid of what lies in store for them unless they repent, while those earnestly seeking God can humbly look forward to union with Him, but never presume it is theirs, granted God's untrammelled freedom.

CHAPTER 28
WATCHFULNESS AND MEDITATION[375]

A discussion arose about watchfulness. Qazi Ashrafuddin inquired: "What is watchfulness?" The Revered Master replied: "Watchfulness is keeping a careful watch over one's heart. It should be realized that God Most Exalted is keeping watch over me. His gaze penetrates to the inner recesses of my mind which lie hidden from others. It is the custom of some spiritual guides to enjoin this practice on their disciples. If at all times they are aware that God is watching them and His gaze penetrates to their innermost secrets, then, if they are tempted to commit a sin, they immediately thrust the temptation aside. They are fully aware that God is watching them and is aware of that temptation. It can even happen that the inner workings of the Sufi Path are revealed. For example, it is related that a sheikh had a number of disciples. One of them was considered special. The sheikh was more interested in him and paid more attention to him than he did to the others. He was asked to explain his behaviour. He said he would explain the matter to them. He gave each of his disciples a knife and a chicken and told them to go somewhere where no one could see them and kill the chicken. He also gave a knife and a chicken to his favourite disciple and told him to do the same. They all went away, did as they had been instructed, and brought back the dead chickens. The favoured disciple, however, returned with his chicken still alive. The sheikh asked him why he had not killed the chicken. He replied: 'You told me to kill the chicken somewhere where no one could see me. Wherever I went, however, God Most Exalted was watching me, so how could I kill the chicken?' The sheikh turned towards

---

375. *Muraqaba* and *tafakkur* are the terms used. The more standard translation for the former is 'contemplation,' and 'meditation' for the latter. 'Watchfulness' has been chosen for the former in this chapter taking into account the use of the word in this particular context. On the other hand, 'meditation' seems to acquire a broader meaning towards the end of the chapter. It is important to try to grasp what is being said rather than to focus on a particular word. Maneri himself will call meditation 'many-faceted.'

his disciples and said: 'This is why I have been especially attentive towards him.'" When the Revered Master finished this story, he recited the following:

> Along this Way you are not able to bind or loose:
> You see other things because you are not squinting.

He continued: "It is authoritatively related that Gabriel one day came to the Apostle in the appearance of a man. He said: 'O Muhammad, what is faith?' The Messenger replied: 'It means believing in God; in His angels; in His books; in His messengers; in the Day of Resurrection; and that whatever good or evil has been ordained is from the Lord.' He commented: 'You have answered correctly.' He then asked what Islam was. The Messenger replied: 'Betaking yourself to daily prayer; paying the poor tax; going on pilgrimage to the Ka'ba; and observing the fast during the month of Ramazan.' He answered: 'Correct.' He then asked him about doing good. The Messenger replied: 'Doing good means worshipping the Lord as though you were seeing Him. Even though your do not see Him, He sees you.' He commented: 'Correct.'" Afterwards the Revered Master recited the following:

> How can anyone behold the entire ocean?
> Can an ant's gaze take in the entire Pleiades?
> As long as you draw breath, you are not of one breath:
> As long as a hair of yours remains, you are not intimate.

"When the Apostle said, 'You do not see Him, but He sees you,' he was hinting at this state of watchfulness. This is because watchfulness refers to the knowledge that a devotee has that the Lord is keeping a careful eye on him and on his deeds and actions. This knowledge is the origin of all good. It is said that a devotee does not reach this stage until he has succeeded in bringing his selfish soul to heel. Once it is under control, he moves ahead and, in a state of spiritual enlightenment, is endowed with a right disposition and feels compelled to embrace the Path to *God*. Then it is that *God*—may He be glorified and exalted—becomes his guardian. He is aware of the states of his soul; sees what he does; and hears what he says. He also notices any negligence in these matters. How could someone who is himself far from the beginning of union know the realities of watchfulness?" He thereupon recited the following:

245

The inattentive are asleep and ascetics are foolish:
An ass is hurt more by a groan than a packsaddle.
Man is not meant to be free from sorrow:
Man's lot is to have one foot in trouble.
I see nothing but brambles along your path:
How can you keep on dreaming, O foolish one?

He related this story of one of the dervishes: "There was a certain king who paid more attention to one of his slaves than to the others. He had not cost much, nor was he handsome. On one occasion, people asked the king for an explanation. The king wanted them all to see his merit for themselves. One day he set out on horseback with his attendants and servants. They came to a hill. The snow on it had turned to ice. The king looked up at the hill and then brought his gaze back down again. He did not say a word. That particular slave put spurs to his horse and galloped towards the hill. No one knew why had had gone. After a short while he returned with a lump of ice. The king said to him: 'How did you know that I wanted some ice?' The slave replied: 'Because you had looked at the hill, and kings do not look at things unless they have something in mind.' The king turned towards his attendants and servants and said: 'This is why I pay so much attention to him! All have some particular work and occupation to which they devote themselves. This slave is fully occupied in being alert to any danger to me and in being attentive to my needs.'" The Revered Master thereupon recited the following:

Travelling along this Path requires the whole man:
You have to give up everything to reach this Threshold!
Whoever knows tells the secret to the sun:
How can even a particle remain?

He commented: "Watchfulness and calling to account have a similar meaning. First you have the calling to account, and then watchfulness, as explained above." Later on, he explained: "Calling to account refers to a person's very life-situation. He takes a thorough look at his situation. 'What are the things I have done? What acts of worship have I accomplished? What sinful habits have I acquired?' He looks within himself to see what was done correctly and what was not done correctly. When he has thus taken an account of himself, you could say that he was reading an account of his actions and was doing so out in the open. The tradition, 'Call yourself to account before you are called to account' is applicable here."

Qazi Ashrafuddin again put a question: "What is the difference between watchfulness and meditation?" The Revered Master replied: "Watchfulness is paying assiduous attention to your heart, as I have said, namely, 'A devotee's knowledge is revealed to him by God Most Exalted.' On the other hand, meditation involves thinking, according to the dictionary meaning. According to the terminology of this group, however, it is many-faceted. Because of this it is said that, if a disciple wanted to enumerate how many things meditation applies to, he could not do so. Some have said that meditation applies to 'from all eternity' and 'to all eternity.' A traveller should take time to ponder about 'from all eternity' by thinking 'I do not know whether from all eternity the pen has inscribed my name for union or for separation.' He then looks at his own actions and reflects thus: 'Let me see whether the qualities of men of union are found within me, or those of men of separation.' The qualities of men of union are such as are linked to promises, while the qualities of men of separation are such as are linked to threats. If he sees the former qualities, he rejoices, but if he sees the qualities of men of separation, he will do his best to change them so that the qualities of men of union appear in him. Now he wants to worship God. Every act of devotion that he performs in this frame of mind will be specifically for the love of *God*. When this happens, both the desire of heaven and the fear of hell will evaporate. A person's gaze rises above both desire and fear. Otherwise, before meditation, a person would have prayed out of fear of hell or the desire of heaven. Now a person prays out of fear of separation and a longing for love. Externalist scholars explain 'fearing and desiring' (Q32:16) as 'fearing hell and desiring heaven.' The sheikhs, however, explain it as 'fearing separation and longing for love.'"

Afterwards he said: "This is also why it is said that 'an hour's meditation is better than a year's worship.' If you do not meditate, it would be easy to perform a few cycles of prayer, yet what enlightenment would that produce? On the other hand, when a person meditates, there is no end to the meaningful insights that can come to him. With meditation he can cover in one hour what would otherwise take him a year. In other words, previously the motivation for devotion and worship was either fear of the fire or the desire of heaven. Now a longing for love and a fear of separation motivates a person. This hour's effort is better than a year of the other kind. *God* Most Exalted has referred to meditation in innumerable places in His precious Book and praised those given to reflection. For example, He speaks of 'Those who remember God, standing and sitting and on their sides, and ponder over the creation of the heavens and the earth, saying: Our Lord, You have not created these in vain' (Q3:191). Those who remember God Most Exalted do so to acquire a greater insight into them and say, 'O You our Nourisher, You have not created these in vain. This is a proof of Your wisdom and complete power.' It is mentioned that the Apostle said: 'Give your eyes a portion of worship!' People inquired: 'O Apostle of God, what is this portion of worship?' He replied: 'Examine the Book; reflect on what is in it; and profit from the wonders it contains.' The Apostle restricted meditation to the actions of the Lord. He said, 'Meditate on *except God,* but do not meditate on *God.*'[376] Moreover, 'Whoever meditates on the Lord would soon fall into unbelief.' This is because such meditation would end up in idle speculation, or in making God resemble something else. Meditation is focussed on something circumscribed and limited. This means that meditating on God would be impossible, because *God's* pure essence is not circumscribed or limited, so how could meditation be a path to God? The necessary result would be either idle speculation, or making God resemble something else." He thereupon recited the following quatrain:

> If someone sees the reflection of Your beauty in a mirror,
> He is seeing either a playful wink or a glance from You.
> He exclaims: "I have attainted that Impossible Being!"
> How could a mere particle, of itself, see the light of Your glory?

He also recited the following:

> There is no path to things beyond those near you:
> The very limit of your thought is you, not God.

---

376. The reference is to the first part of the profession of faith—*There is no god except God.* There is, as it were, a verbal sleight of hand, but the meaning, in the given context, is clear. Moreover, 'meditation' in this context clearly refers to thoughtful reflection.

A discussion arose about the benefits of meditation. The Revered Master said: "Meditation involves knowledge, states and actions, but its fruit is knowledge. Yes indeed, when the heart obtains knowledge its state changes, and when this change occurs, the actions of a person's limbs also change. When a person's behaviour changes, as a result, this changed behaviour makes a person more attractive. It is said that 'an attraction which comes from *God* is equal to the work of jinn and men.'" Afterwards he said: "Holy men have said that there are two kinds of journeys, because there are two kinds of goals. One journey is that of the body in the lower world. It involves bodies, people, acts or worship and the corporeal world. This journey involves moving oneself bodily. It requires the use of one's feet. The second journey involves the heart in the higher world. Its whole aim is to seek signs of God's power, wisdom, ingenious art and the hidden world. That journey involves meditation. It is accomplished by means of insight. Just as an external journey requires food, provisions and camels to reach one's destination, in a similar way, meditation, which is an internal journey, requires knowledge of the Law and of the Way in order to attain one's goal. One who meditates can obtain in a short time what men take years to accomplish through good works and worship. The Apostle has said that an hour's meditation is better than sixty years of worship. A person meditates on his religion, the states of his soul and on creation. He seeks profit from the wisdom of his endeavours. This type of meditation is worth sixty years of activity because actions are movements of the body, while meditation is a movement of the heart, which is swift because it is delicate and agile. The distance a body travels in sixty years of activity can be accomplished by the heart in one hour on account of its swiftness and slenderness." At this point, he recited the following:

The soul has sublimity, the body, dust's lowliness:
Lowly dust and pure soul have been united.
Since high and low came together as friends,
Man became a wonder, filled with secrets.
No one has become aware of his secrets:
What he does is not the work of a beggar.

Afterwards he added: "A time comes during meditation when it becomes clear to a traveller that the power of movement leaves him. With a great effort he takes himself off to prayer. This is found in the Quran: 'On the day when secrets will be tested, and he will be without power or supporter' (Q86:9-10). When a traveller is engaged in meditation, all those things within him that were hidden become clear to him. In that state he reaches a point when he no longer has the power to move forward. You could say that this also was in a wide open expanse."[377] At this juncture Qazi Ashrafuddin inquired: "If in this very state a person misses some litany or prayer he has voluntarily undertaken to recite, what should he do? Should he recite what he has missed at some other time or not?" The Revered Master replied: "He is free to recite or not recite what he has missed. This is because meditation is superior to prayer, litanies and other such things, which are of a lower order. It is a case of something lower giving way to something higher."

Sheikh Mu'izzuddin asked: "What should he do if he fails to carry out an instruction of his guide?" He replied: "The same thing applies here also. When a guide orders a disciple to do something, he does so in order that he might act in an appropriate manner. If a disciple finds something else that is profitable for him and sets aside an instruction of his guide, there is nothing to fear.[378] A guide keeps on giving instructions to his disciple as long as he sees that he is a beginner. After that a disciple will do whatever he sees will be appropriate for himself. This presupposes, however, that every single day the disciple weans himself away from the customs and habits of worldly people. As a result of this, his reputation suffers in the eyes of the people, and the people suffer a similar fate in his eyes. When that happens, if comprehension comes to him, he will put it to good use. If not, he will become absorbed therein. The comprehension that has been granted to him will not have been

---

377. From the context it seems that thoughtful rumination has given way to a higher form of prayer marked by a seeming passivity on the part of the devotee, but commonly attributed by spiritual guides to greater divine activity within a person

378. This is a significant statement. Perhaps his main point is that a disciple should remain under the direct care of his guide for the commonly accepted period of three years. Once he has 'matured,' he should be able to decide for himself what is more appropriate for him. He can, of course, always visit his guide for guidance or correspond with him. What seems to be rejected is a disciple's 'clinging' to his guide, or a guide's 'clinging' to a disciple, for that matter.

put to good use."[379]

The Helpless One inquired: "Are there particular times fixed for watchfulness and meditation, or can they be practised at any time?" The Revered Master replied: "Meditation can be practised at any time. The same applies to watchfulness. The examination of conscience, however, should be done after the evening prayer." Qazi Ashrafuddin inquired: "In the Discourse of Sheikh Nizamuddin, it is mentioned in the discussion about watchfulness that the head is placed upon the knees, which are used as a cushion, and a person devotes himself to watchfulness." The Revered Master replied: "There are several ways of practising watchfulness. This is one of them. The Apostle used to place his head on his knees while engaged in watchfulness. But actually, God knows best!"

---

379. The commonly accepted general principle is that transformative spiritual experiences are not to be "wallowed in," so to say, but gratefully accepted and acted upon as a stimulus for doing good to others.

CHAPTER 29
SERVANTHOOD
AND SERVITUDE

A discussion arose about servanthood and servitude. The Revered Master said: "Servitude simply means carrying out orders, while servanthood means being totally given over to service. It is said that Satan spent many years carrying out orders, but not for a moment was he able to be a genuine servant. Master Abu Ali Daqqaq[380] is reported to have said: 'Servanthood is better than servitude. First of all, there is servitude. Then comes servanthood, and finally whole-hearted service. The first is for ordinary believers; the second is for special believers; while the third is for the most privileged of all.' This has been explained thus: 'Servitude applies to the person who has trustworthy knowledge; servanthood to the person with certain knowledge; and whole-hearted service to the person whose certainty is based on experiential knowledge.' Another holy man put it like this: 'Servitude applies to those given over to struggle with self; servanthood to those intent on serving; and whole-hearted service to those with mystical knowledge.'" At this point he recited the following:

> It is not possible, for privileged or ordinary believers,
> To have a higher station that that of service.

"Khwaja Muhammad bin Khafif[381] was asked: 'When does servanthood become perfect?' He replied: 'When you entrust all your efforts to the Lord and endure patiently with Him the trials He sends you.'" Maulana Nasiruddin was reading an abridged version of *Ihya* and came to these words: "The hearts of noble souls are the graves of secrets." The Revered Master said: "This has been said about the sheikhs. In reality, they are the noble souls intended. We have been ensnared in a hundred ways and enslaved by every desire."

---

380. Abu Ali Daqqaq, reported to have died in 1015 or 1021, was the father-in-law and spiritual guide of Qushairi.

381. This is Abdullah Khafif of Shiraz, who has already been mentioned. His full name is Abu Abdullah Muhammad ibn Khafif.

A discussion arose to the effect that in the next world verifying the truth of claiming to be a servant of God would prove endless. The Revered Master said: "As long as a person is attached to something, he is fettered by it. Indeed, he is enslaved by it, because slavery means being fettered by something. The Lord the Law has correctly said: 'The slave of *dinars* will perish and the slave of *dirhams* will perish.'[382] When he saw people enslaved by the love of *dirhams* and *dinars*, he said: 'The slave of *dinars* will perish, and the slave of *dirhams* will perish'—and what the Messenger says cannot be false. The meaning of 'perishing' here does not refer to dying and thus perishing, but refers rather to eternal destruction, namely, with reference to those who lament and are consigned to hell. As long as a person is in quest of something he desires, he is a slave to that particular thing. That becomes the focus of his life, whether he desires ten or twenty things. The greater the desire, the more complete the enslavement. This is in accord with what is indicated by the blessed saying of the Prophet regarding "the slave of *dinars* and the slave of *dirhams*." This is why experienced masters of mystical insight do not allow themselves to be fettered by anything. They banish from their sight anything to which they experience a growing attachment so that the thrust of their lives might remain focussed and not distracted. This applies especially to those who, in love, whole-heartedly seek *God*." At this point, the Revered Master recited the following:

Adorn the garden of paradise, for we don't know what is written:
The secret of that is not something we can pull from our skirt.

"It is said: 'You are the slave of the thing that is destined to enchain you.' If you are enchained by your selfish soul, you are a slave to self. If you are enchained by the world, you are its slave. Khwaja Abu Yazid saw a man and asked him what he was doing. He told him he was the slave of an ass. 'May God kill that ass of yours so that you can become a slave of God, not the slave of an ass!'" Afterwards the Revered Master said: "This is why it is said that there are two journeys. One is within oneself, and the second is from oneself. The inner journey refers to the things surrounding a person, such as the people who depend on him and those he loves, as also his familiar surroundings. These are all other than *God*. He puts them

---

382. A *dinar* was a gold coin, and a *dirham* a silver one.

at a distance from himself. His single-mindedness carries him beyond them. Such a person is said to have escaped from the world, even though he still lives in the world." He quoted the following:

> Be like Joseph, escape from the prison of the well:
> In this way you will acquire kingly honour in Egypt.
> If you become a Muslim in such a country,
> You will become just like Righteous Joseph.

Fixing his attention on those present in the assembly, he said: "In your study of the Way, whenever you read that such and such a dervish has escaped from the world, this is what is meant. This is because the whole point of being in the world is to make use of it and enjoy its delights. For him, however, since the world has been cut off from him, you could say that he is not in it. He only appears to be in the world, nothing more. After this comes the second journey. This means that, when a person has emerged from the hold of all those he loves, familiar things, and his dependants, he has thereby freed himself from his very own wishes and desires. He is now firmly established in doing what *God* wants. This has not come about through acts of devotion, or by shunning forbidden things. By embracing acts of devotion and shunning forbidden things, however, he is clearly doing what *God* wants. I am not talking now about acts of devotion or forbidden things. There is no need to spend time on such things in order to find out what God wants. We have reached the stage where one category of actions remains, namely, those that are indifferent. There is no difference between doing them or neglecting them. Here a person should put aside his own inclinations and choose what *God* wants. For example, even though health or sickness, as well as poverty or riches, are alternatives, they are in the category of indifferent things. A person should accept whichever state he happens to be in. He should not want to change his actual condition. If the will of *God* for him is health, that should also be what he wants, not because he likes being healthy, but because this is *God's* will for him. The same applies to sickness. If this is *God's* will for him, sickness should be what he wants. He will not try to get rid of it, because by doing so he would be seeking his own will. A person whose will has been totally conformed to what *God* wants does nothing, not even for a fraction of a second, of his own will. At this stage it is said that his deeds are God's deeds. In this situation whatever he gives, God gives; whomsoever he accepts, God accepts; and whomsoever he rejects, *God* rejects. This is because his own will does not intervene. Whatever happens is the will of *God*. This is because it is clearly accepted by Him."[383]

The Helpless One inquired: "In the very qualities themselves, such as sickness or health, poverty or wealth, knowledge of the will of *God* becomes clear in so far as *God* Most Exalted, without giving the person a choice, has chosen a specific situation for him. On the other hand, how can the will of *God* be discerned in things such as eating and clothing oneself?" The Revered Master replied: "In such a situation *God* makes it known to them. This is because *God* Most Exalted enlightens the hearts of such people. It occurs to them that they should acquire a particular thing and even hear, 'Do this!' or 'Don't do this!' They act accordingly. For example, if something is presented to them and they sense within their hearts that *God* Most Exalted is telling them to accept it, they do so immediately. If they sense He is prohibiting them from receiving it, they immediately desist from doing so. But God knows best!"[384]

---

383. This is an important passage. This is indicated at the beginning by the indication of Maneri's intense look, or gesture towards, those present in the assembly. This is most unusual. The second indication of its importance is the use of the Persian word, *man*, meaning 'I.' Maneri scarcely ever uses this word, as it draws attention to the speaker. Here the actual phrase is *sukhun-i man*, meaning, literally, "the word of I." The translation offered, "I am not talking…" is meant to highlight the importance of Maneri's use of *man*. Maneri's words are yet another indication of his profound level of personal experience.

384. This is a further revelation of Maneri's inner life of docility to the inspirations he receives.

CHAPTER 30
FREEDOM AND WHAT IS CONGRUENT WITH IT

The Helpless One was reading the *Mathnavi* of Maulana Rumi.[385] He came to this couplet:

> A mere fistful from *God* would satisfy a free man:
> Even if you load him with treasures, he'd still be free.

The Revered Master told a story related to this couplet. "I have heard a story related by Sheikh Zada Chishti.[386] 'Once I was on my way to Egypt. There is a mountain near Egypt. It is called *Jabal ul-Fath* [The Mountain of Victory]. Dervishes go to that mountain in search of enlightenment. Every dervish who reaches that mountain and sets to work is enlightened. This is the origin of its name, *Jabal ul-Fath*. Nowadays ten to twenty dervishes spend one or two years in residence there. As I approached Egypt I mentioned the story I had heard and expressed my desire to see the mountain and visit the dervishes who happened to be there. This was my plan. I reached a nearby settlement and asked the inhabitants if there were any dervishes on the mountain, and how I could meet them. They told me that there was one dervish there at that time. It was his practice to come to the mosque for the Friday prayer.

---

385. Neither this work nor its author needs any introduction. It is often referred to as "The Quran in Persian." Maneri's copy of the work was a treasured possession. Rumi died in Konya in 1273 and is buried there.

386. Sheikh Zada Chishti visited Maneri while he was still in his cave at Rajgir. The details of the visit are found in the sixteenth chapter of *Khwan-i Pur-Ni'mat*. It was a significant event in Maneri's spiritual development. Maneri simply wanted to be alone with the Alone, but the local people were pestering him to write petitions on their behalf to the local military governor. He got annoyed while Sheikh Zada Chishti was with him. Upon seeing this, he commented: "So you are annoyed. Be careful not to get annoyed. Take upon yourself the affliction of the people." He thereupon accepted his new role of "bringing comfort to hearts"—*rahat bedilan rasanidan*.

After the prayer, he would ascend the pulpit and deliver a religious discourse. He would then return to the mountain. Friday was close at hand, so I stayed and went for the Friday prayer. The dervish also came. When the prayer was over, he ascended the pulpit and gave his discourse. I knew several languages—Turkish, Persian and Arabic—and tried my level best to understand what he was saying, but was unable to do so. I could not work out what language he was using. Moreover, the people to the left and right of me listened to what he had to say, experienced consolation, and began to cry out aloud. I also began to grasp something here and there and became deeply moved. I said to myself that there was nothing meant for me in the dervish's words, as I did not understand them. After finishing his discourse, he came down from the pulpit and returned to the mountain. People in the mosque were kissing his hand.

I went to that mountain. Every dervish that had resided there was remembered by some sign of his sojourn. I looked at them all and then set out in search of the dervish. I came across him sitting in the shade of a rock. I greeted him and placed some gold coins in his lap. He returned my greeting and inquired where I had come from. I told him I was from Chisht. He said that I had come from an important place, and repeated this comment a couple of times. He then recited the opening chapter of the Quran and stood up to leave. All those gold coins fell from his lap and lay scattered on the ground. He was oblivious to what had happened. When I saw this attitude of his I was amazed and realized that he had made great progress. He had reached the stage where, for him, there was no difference between a piece of gold and a pebble. He did not distinguish one from the other. I saw something else in him, which also astonished me. In the middle of his discourse a louse began to bite him. He stopped speaking; took off his upper garment; hunted for the louse; found it; picked it up between the tips of his fingernails and killed it. He then put back on his unwashed garment. From this I understood that he did not care what people thought of him. If even the slightest trace of concern about what people thought of him had remained in him, he could not have acted in this way. Both of these traits that I witnessed in that dervish gave me much consolation.' The point of this story is that the dervish showed no interest whatsoever in those gold coins." The Revered Master then recited the following:

Whoever strays from the Way will remain lost:
If his feet are bound, how could he remain there?
If your coarse robe has become a thing of dreams,
Bundle it up and you will be comforted.
If you burn your robe here out of fear,
What will remain tomorrow on the broad path to hell?
Be a man of depth, for there is nothing to appearance,
That is true meaning, for appearance is nothing, nothing.
Gold is colourful to look at, but is really a stone:
Because you are an infant, you are tempted by its colour.

A dear soul said: "Since those gold coins fell from the lap of the dervish and he did not gather them up, this is clearly a waste of goods, and such wastage is forbidden." The Revered Master explained: "He had gone beyond that stage and had attained to the reality of things. He saw gold for what it really is. It is a stone. Here the prayer of the Apostle comes to mind: 'O God, show me things as they really are!' He compared the appearance of gold to moulding wax. A person who moulds wax can produce a hundred thousand extraordinary shapes when he skilfully moulds the wax into some particular object. Nevertheless, it remains wax. The same applies to the external appearances of the world. Their reality is of the very same clay. The penetrating gaze of that holy man had passed beyond external appearances and settled on that dust." When the Revered Master reached this point, he recited the following couplets:

Open your generous eyes and gaze upon the Way:
Set out along the Way and see what happens!
Whatever is accomplished in love appears as a trial:
It seems like being afflicted with a thousand trials!

He continued: "It is said that freedom means that a servant does not remain caught up with the appearance of creatures, nor has the Creator Lord passed him by. The sign of the complete freedom of such a man is his discernment. As far as his heart is concerned, both great and contemptible things are equal for him, as Harisa reported concerning the Messenger: 'I turned my soul away from the world and, for me, its stone and gold became one.' Ustad Ali Daqqaq is reported to have said: 'Whoever has come into the world and passed beyond it is a free person, and if he also passes beyond the next world he would be free of that as well.'" He recited the following:

Anyone who has faintly sensed this mystery,
Has had his head turned by the Lord of both worlds.
For an experienced person, there is now no other,
Since at this stage there is neither Ka'ba nor convent.
Whoever has not become lost in that unique Ocean,
No matter who he may be, has not become a real man.

"Khwaja Junaid was asked: 'If nothing of this world remained to a person except some date-stones for boiling, would he be free?' He replied: 'A man remains a slave if he is short of securing his manumission by one silver coin.'"[387] He then recited the following:

On the tree of love there is neither leaf nor fruit:
Each tree that has leaves is where the head comes in.
Whoever is not completely dead to the world lives not:
Die, for on becoming a confidant, there is no veil.

Ghalbak,[388] an Afghan dervish, was present in the assembly on the Day of Ashura, the 10th Muharram. He asked the meaning of "whatever a Sufi owns is common property, and his blood can be shed lawfully." The Revered Master replied: "If someone makes use of something belonging to a Sufi without his permission, he won't make a fuss about it. He will consider it to be the same as if he himself had made use of it. Similarly, he will not hold it against anyone if he sheds his blood, neither in this world, nor in the next. Indeed, he will imagine it is the moment appointed for his death and will consider it as coming from *God*. The manner of his death does not bother him at all."

Again he inquired: "According to the Law, it is not allowed to make use of something belonging to someone else without his permission. It is similarly not allowed to kill a person without a just

387. In some places it was possible for a slave to earn money and buy his own freedom. It needs to be recalled that some slaves were highly trained and became army commanders. Qutbuddin Aibek was the general in charge of Delhi when his master, Sultan Mu'izzuddin Ghuri, was assassinated in 1206. He immediately assumed control and was formally manumitted and recognized as Sultan in 1209.

388. This same Ghalbak came to inquire about Maneri's health when he had a bout of fever, as is recorded in the first assembly in *Khwan-i Pur Ni'mat*. This took place on 8th November 1348. He also posed a question to Maneri about the necessity of knowledge.

reason, yet both are considered lawful with regard to a Sufi. To all appearances, the Law is against the Sufi way of acting, but both form a unity. Why is there an apparent contradiction?" The Revered Master replied: "In this instance, and in all instances, they are coherent. Moreover, they say that it is allowed to use what belongs to another without permission in the sense that there was no prohibition before the thing was made use of, neither was there any search for it, or claim to it, afterwards. Clearly, no permission was granted, yet it was obtained by default. Since permission was presumed in this way, it became lawful. With regard to non-culpable murder, the meaning is that, in lieu of a life, the Law has two provisions—retaliation or compensation. Since a Sufi does not seek retaliation or accept compensation, you could say his murder is covered by the Law and is not in conflict with it."

Afterwards he added: "This emerges from the principle enunciated by those masters who believe in One God: 'There is no dominion except that of God.' A slave has no dominion because a slave is himself the possession of someone else. How can someone, who belongs to anther person, possess dominion? Slavery and dominion cannot co-exist in one and the same person! In all this one question needs to be addressed: 'What is this making use of one's own possessions, while it is not allowed to use the goods of another?' The answer is given like this: 'The Law says it is allowed to make use of slaves. A person can possess slaves according to the Law. By making use of them according to the Law, they become permitted. This is because a person might entrust his goods to a slave who can make use of them for himself, even though they do not belong to him, and such usage is allowed—but God knows best![389]

---

389. This convoluted argument highlights the difficulty of fitting what is essentially a free waiving of one's rights into the framework of the Law, which is based on the twin pillars of rights and duties.

CHAPTER 31
CONVICTION[390]

A discussion arose about conviction. The Revered Master said: "The strength of faith depends on its conviction. Its strength or weakness varies accordingly. Whoever is firmly convinced has a stronger faith, while a person whose conviction is shallow has a weaker faith." In connection with this comment he told the following story: "Ja'far Haddad[391] said: 'Khwaja Abu Turab Nakhshabi[392] appeared to me as I was sitting beside a pool of water in the desert. I had gone for sixteen days without eating or drinking. He asked me what I was doing sitting there. I told him that I was caught between knowledge and conviction, and was waiting to see which would be victorious so that I could side with it. This means that if knowledge were to win, I would drink some water; but if conviction were to win, I would pass on. He told me that I had undertaken a difficult task.'" When the Revered Master reached these words, he recited the following:

> When you are advancing, strong in your convictions,
> Expect dust from the sea, and moisture from fire!

He said: "It is related that Khwaja Abu Bakr Tahir said: 'Knowledge is replete with doubts, while conviction admits of no doubt.' This saying is indicative of the fact that knowledge is an acquisition, and that something that flows along a particular course fluctuates. It can become firmly established.[393] The same thing applies to the knowledge of this group. In the beginning is knowledge which then becomes firm conviction. This is why some have said: 'Con-

---

390. *Yaqin* is usually translated as 'certainty' or 'true faith.' Perhaps 'conviction' conveys adequately what is meant in the discussion that follows.

391. Abu Hafs Haddad (d. 879) is meant. The story is well known, with slight variations.

392. Khwaja Abu Turab Nakhshabi was a well-known Sufi who died in 859.

393. The image is of water flowing and gradually etching out a fixed water-course and becoming a river.

viction is the knowledge which is deposited in hearts.' This is also an indication that any knowledge which has become conviction is not acquired."

The Helpless One objected: "How could this be, because doubt is opposite to knowledge and is not conviction?" The Revered Master replied: "It is like being apprehensive about the riches of tomorrow. In spite of the fact that a person knows about the Lord's providential care regarding tomorrow, yet he may be apprehensive about tomorrow's riches today, not knowing whether he will receive the necessary divine assistance or not. This is a doubt, and is the opposite of knowledge. On the other hand, conviction means that today he has no apprehension about tomorrow. He knows that he will be granted life tomorrow. This good fortune has been promised him. Without doubt it is going to be received." At this juncture, he recited the following:

> Abandoning control is happily believing in One:
> Banishing control is unalloyed solitude.

The Helpless One inquired: "What is the object of conviction?" The Revered Master replied: "*God's* promises are the object of conviction, as also His threats. He knows that whatever He has promised exists, as well as whatever He has threatened. As an example, *God* Most Exalted has promised whatever is needed for our sustenance in this verse: 'There is no creature on the earth whose sustenance is not provided by God' (Q11:6). He has undertaken to provide daily sustenance for His servants. When a person becomes convinced of this, he does not act greedily, nor does he rely on any human being. The strength of the conviction of some people has become so strong that, it one of them is seated in front of a bazaar filled with different kinds of food and goods, nevertheless, his heart would remain at peace and undisturbed. If he then gets up and goes to some deserted place, he would experience the same peace and tranquillity as he had in the bazaar. Such a person is called a man of conviction. Most holy men who choose to live in a deserted place are enabled to do so on the strength of their conviction.[394] Similarly, those who retire to the jungle for about twenty days or a month are able to do so on the strength of their conviction." Afterwards

---

394. Maneri himself had lived in the jungle of Bihiya for at least a year, and then in a cave in Rajgir. He therefore speaks from experience.

he recited this couplet:

> Men of conviction are a different breed:
> If they are the head, all of us are the feet.

A discussion arose about the knowledge of conviction. The Revered Master said: "There are these three things: conviction based on knowledge; conviction based on truth; and conviction based on seeing.[395] An example of conviction based on knowledge would be that a person hears a sound coming from behind a wall. He is convinced that an animal is there and it has made the sound. This is because there cannot be such a sound without an animal to make it. This is an example of conviction based on knowledge. If that same sound has a certain refinement and conveys meaning, he knows for certain that this is the voice of a human being, because a refined, meaning-laden sound can come only from a human being. This is an example of conviction based on truth. Another degree, however, remains, namely, that it is the voice of Zaid or Umar, because he goes behind the wall and sees for certain that the voice is that of this particular person. This is an example of conviction based on seeing." Later on, he continued: "Examples of these three kinds in matters of belief are like this. A person who believes in heaven and hell on the basis of the Book and the Traditions has reached the stage of conviction based on knowledge. A person who establishes the existence of heaven and hell by means of demonstrations and proofs has reached the stage of conviction based on truth.[396] A person who sees them in this life with the eyes of the heart, as through a veil, has attained conviction based on seeing."

At this point, he distinguished three types of conviction: "Conviction is of three kinds, stemming from something heard; or proved; or based on seeing. As examples of conviction based on something heard, we could take Samarqand, Bukhara, Egypt, Syria and other similar cities. We have not seen them with our own eyes. We have no other proof than that we have heard about them. With regard to conviction based on proof, imagine that I am sitting here

---

395. *'Ilm ul-yaqin; haq ul-yaqin;* and *'ain ul-yaqin.* The point of these categories is to indicate a gradation of conviction.

396. All Maneri's listeners and readers accepted the existence of heaven and hell. They formed part of their faith-based worldview. Unlike some moderns, who do not share this worldview, they assumed their existence could be 'proved.'

and smoke begins to rise nearby. I suddenly see that smoke. Arguing from seeing the smoke, I conclude that there is a fire over there. This is because there can be no smoke without a fire. An example of conviction based on seeing would be if I were to go and see the fire with my own eyes. This I call witnessing in the world of dominion. The same thing applies to the angelic world." He then explained: "What can be attained by enlightened perception is dominion, and what cannot be attained by enlightened perception is hidden from our gaze. That is the angelic world."

Qazi Sadruddin inquired: "Perceptible things are perceived by the senses, but how can we attain something imperceptible in the angelic world?" The Revered Master replied: "There are two kinds of senses, external and internal. The external senses attain to what is externally perceptible, while the internal senses attain to what is internal. An indication of this is found in these words of the Apostle: 'But for the ever-present satanic influence on the hearts of the sons of Adam, their gaze would be directed towards the angelic world.'" Afterwards he added: "Our conviction regarding matters of religious belief which cannot be attained by sense perception is of three kinds. It is based on something heard; or proved; or seen. Those convictions, based on the teaching of *God* Most Exalted and His Apostle, are based on hearing—such as heaven is like this, and hell is like that—and so many other things. Hearing about them has led to conviction. As for convictions based on proof, we have the existence of the Creator through the existence of creatures. By arguing from the existence of creatures, the existence of the Creator is convincingly established without recourse to the Book or Traditions. Our conviction with regard to religious beliefs is based either on proof or on what we have heard. This latter comes from the Book, the Traditions of the Apostle, or the consensus of the community. If we want to acquire a conviction based on seeing, we cannot do so unless *God* Most Exalted removes the veil from our hearts. Then we will see and acquire by means of the eye of our heart. Our conviction will be based on that seeing, namely, through the 'seeing' of contemplation. After death, we shall see face to face with our bodily eyes. Mystics also experience a conviction which is based on 'seeing,' namely the vision of contemplation. This is because seeing something other than God is the type of seeing that is associated with external vision. This does not occur except in the world to come."

He said: "It needs to be established whether the seeing with one's bodily eyes that will take place in the world to come, and the seeing of mystics in this world with the eyes of the heart, are different, or whether both are the same. If there is a difference, then the contemplation that will occur tomorrow is not what takes place today. If it is the same, however, of what profit is tomorrow's contemplation?" He himself proffered this answer: "Tomorrow's vision will be by means of our bodily eyes. It is what mystics witness today by means of the eyes of the heart, yet tomorrow's vision will have a superabundance that is not found in that of today. This is because, even if people see with their bodily eyes today, nevertheless they do so through a thin veil.[397] Tomorrow, however, there will be no sort of veil, neither thin nor otherwise. Consider, for example, if someone today sees the sun reflected in water or in a mirror, he would be seeing the sun, but as though through a thin veil. If he looks up at the sky, however, and sees the same sun, but without any veil at all, in both examples it is still the same sun. Another example is that of a person who sees someone very early in the morning. He sees that it is a human being, but does not make out the person's colour and external form in detail. As soon as the sun rises, he sees the person's colour in great detail. In both instances, the very same person is involved. There is a firm belief in both instances. The difference is in the greatly increased conviction."[398] He then recited:

The special ones are in the world of beholding:
They are like quicksilver in front of a mirror.

Afterwards he said: "The difference among these three levels of conviction is that, in conviction based on what is heard or proved, there is room for anxiety, while there is no room for anxiety in conviction based on seeing. It is in this context that we can understand the question put by the eminent Abraham, the Friend, to the Most Eminent: 'My Lord, show me how you raise the dead.' The response came: 'Have you no faith?' Esteemed Abraham, the Friend, replied: 'Yes, but I want to set my heart at rest' (Q2:260). Two or

---

397. One would have expected "the eyes of the heart" and not "bodily eyes" according to the thrust of the argument.

398. In *Khwan* Maneri gives a metaphysical argument he heard from Amir Fazil Balkhi which carefully distinguishes between 'seeing' God in this life and the "vision of God" for all eternity in the life to come (p.105).

three issues are at stake in this dialogue. The first is that *God* Most Exalted said to esteemed Abraham, the Friend: 'Have you no faith?' *God* Most Exalted, however, knew that the esteemed Friend did believe, so what did the question mean? A second point is that the esteemed Friend said: 'Yes, but I want to set my heart at rest.' Now a composed heart is a precondition for a healthy faith. Moreover, he himself was a messenger. He could not say that his heart was not at peace over that. In the commentary of Imam Zahid the reply explains why the esteemed Friend put this question, 'My Lord, how do you raise the dead to life?' If he had not put this question, then the reply would not have been given. Some unbelievers may have thought, 'Does he doubt the power of God Most Exalted?' They would consider him a doubter, because he did not believe in God's power. This is why he put the question. God replied, 'Have you no faith?' This enabled the Friend to reply, 'Yes!' This removed all doubt."

"With regard to the second point that arose, namely, that he did not enjoy tranquillity of heart, the response is that tranquillity of heart and conviction, which are preconditions for a healthy faith, were found in him. It was a conviction based on hearing and proofs. He possessed both, yet he did not have that tranquillity which results from actual seeing. Naturally, he experienced a certain hesitancy regarding his nature and state. He asked the question in order to remove that doubt and be granted a conviction based on seeing. He wanted to experience the tranquillity and reassurance that comes from seeing, not the type he already experienced. However, God rightly knows best!"[399]

---

399. Problems arising from textural variations are reflected in the translation.

CHAPTER 32
LOVE[400]

Qazi Sadruddin and Qazi Ashrafuddin put this question: "Is the love of a slave for the Lord, and of the Lord for a slave, permitted?" The Revered Master replied: "This is a controversial matter. Some scholars deny the possibility of mutual love. They define love as being nothing more than a slave's assiduous devotion and the Lord's providing him with enabling grace. This is their interpretation of 'He loves them and they love Him' (Q5:54). They say that real love, however, which is something mutual, is impossible, for that can occur only when there is similarity and compatibility of kind, which is not found between the Lord and a slave." He then recited the following:

> How could the Simurgh be my rest?
> Paradise is my exalted abode!
> Although I cannot attain union with Him,
> Let me at least cling to this Way!

He continued: "The truth is what the majority of sheikhs and scholars hold, namely, that it is correct. They say so because the consensus of the community is that the love of God and His Apostle is divinely enjoined. How can God enjoin something if it does not exist? How otherwise could love be correctly explained in terms of devotion which follows love and is its fruit? Inevitably, love must come first for devotion to make its appearance. This is the usage of the Arabs, as a poet has put it:

> A lover certainly does what the beloved wants:
> Undoubtedly love means obeying your command.

Passionate love[401] is also a controversial matter. Whoever says love is not permitted says the same about passionate love. Those who say that love is permitted also consider passionate love as lawful. Passionate love is considered to be intensified love. If love is permitted, so also is intensified love." He then recited the following:

---

400. *Muhabbat.* This could also be translated as "affectionate love."
401. *'Ishq.*

267

> Only the intoxicated know the secrets of the tavern:
> How could the prudent know there is mystery in the lane?
> You want to walk jauntily in the sacred realm of love:
> Sit at ease in a tavern, for the way to the Ka'ba is long!

Qazi Sadruddin inquired: "Intensified love means an increase of love, and this involves an alteration. How is it possible for the Lord's love for a slave to be intensified?" The Revered Master replied: "Two possibilities have to be examined to determine whether the saying concerning the Lord is acceptable or not. If it is not acceptable, it is because it necessarily entails a change. If it is acceptable, there would be an interpretation befitting the Pure Lord. Perhaps an explanation would be that the Lord, in pre-eternity, changed the servant in a special way into a diligent person through a special quality which was given to no one else. Perhaps there is a different interpretation—but God knows best!"[402]

Afterwards he said: "The servant's love for the Lord is the absolutely highest of all stations and the most eminent of all stages. After attaining the love of the Lord, no further station remains. Any other station would be one of the fruits of the station of love, such as yearning, familiarity, being intent on pleasing God, docility and suchlike things. Similarly, there is no station prior to that of love that is anything other than a preparation for love, such as repentance, patience, asceticism and other things. The love of the servant for the Lord is the origin of all happiness and spiritual wealth, and results in abundant goodness."[403]

> Whoever has experienced a taste of love for Him
> Should soon receive the key to both worlds.
> Whoever has experienced the world of intimacy
> Becomes the king of all the people in the world.

He said: "It is related that Khwaja Sari Saqati said: 'Tomorrow, on the Day of Resurrection, all communities will be called according to their messengers, such as, 'O community of Moses!' and 'O community of Jesus!' The friends of the Lord, however, will be called thus: 'O friends of the Lord, hasten towards Him!' At that moment

---

402. This disclaimer is particularly apt in this instance. Maneri's main concern is to defend God from any change in Himself.

403. This paragraph itself is one of the fruits of Maneri's personal experience.

their hearts will be so filled with joy that they will feel like jump-
ing out of their bodies!'" Afterwards the Revered Master recited
the following:

> When You seat Your friends upon the throne of union,
> Do not exclude me, but dust, from Your royal company!
> When You drink a draught of wine with Your friends,
> Do not exclude the dregs at the bottom of the cup!

He said: "All believers in principle are partners in love by virtue of
their participation in the root of mystical knowledge. Nonetheless,
the strength of love and its untrammelled predominance, so that
one becomes totally enamoured in passionate love, is not the lot of
most human beings. Two things are necessary for its acquisition.
The first is to sever all attachments to the world and to expel the
love for anything other than God from one's heart. The second is
to foster intimate knowledge of the Lord and nourish its hold over
one's heart. This would be after purifying one's heart of all pas-
sions." He then recited the following:

> When your heart is purified of qualities
> It will shine forth with the Lord's pure light.
> When that light shines forth brightly from your heart,
> The single quest it holds will become a thousand.

Khwaja Khizr[404] was going through the *Lawami'*[Flashes of Light] of
Qazi Hamiduddin Nagori[405] until he came upon these words: "Stay
there in shame and do not plead with me" (Q23:108)! Moreover,
Imam Shibli expressed this wish: "O that these words had been addressed to me!" The Revered Master said: "This verse refers to the
inhabitants of hell. They cried out for four hundred years, saying,
'O Beneficent One! O Most Compassionate One!' After four hundred years this reply was given to them: 'Stay there in shame and
do not plead with Me!' In other words, 'Go far away! Remain where
you are! Keep quiet!' When Arabs shoo a dog away, they customar-
ily say, 'Base creature!'" Afterwards he said: "Whether a beloved
utters an angry word or a gracious one, a lover takes delight in either saying of the beloved, for the simple reason that it is the word

---

404. Khwaja Khizr was the Deputy Governor of Bihar.
405. Hamiduddin Nagori was an early Chishti Sufi of Nagore, Rajasthan,
who died in 1274.

of the beloved. This is because his attention is not on whether it is an angry word or a gracious one, but rather on the fact that his beloved has said it. As to what sort of thing has been said, ignore it! What is important is that it is the word of the beloved!" He then recited one of Sheikh Sa'di's[406] couplets:

> Whatever comes from those lovely lips and slender limbs
> Evokes no distinction, whether it be a prayer or a taunt!

"Imam Shibli paid no attention to what was said but focussed on the fact that it was his Friend who had spoken." Afterwards he said: "In the topic under discussion, this group has one firm principle, namely that a holy man applies himself to this task, which is extremely subtle. Apart from men of insight, few people pay attention to it. Most of the sayings of the sheikhs, as well as their hints and verses written about love, can be well understood from this principle, and misunderstanding will be avoided. The principle is that a lover, in the presence of his Beloved, has no choice. This is because it is love that chooses and desires. If he loves the Beloved for his own sake, then his love would be something accruing to himself, not to his Beloved. When a lover has completely set aside his own choices and desires, which would be his due, in order to ensure that whatever he wants is what the Beloved wants, and whatever he does is what the Beloved does, then such a person would be called a lover. You will have heard that when Khwaja Bayazid was experiencing a mystical flight he heard: 'Bayazid, what do you want?' He replied: 'The desire not to desire.' This is a hint about this matter." The Revered Master then recited the following:

> A lover is a person who seeks nothing,
> Provided his entire being is united to the Friend.
> To prevent regret at your passing away,
> How fully alive becomes your astonished heart!

"The investigators of Reality say: 'Thou-ness belongs to you, while his-ness belongs to Him.' On this foundation, anything your thou-ness intends seeks what you choose and desire, while anything His

---

406. Sa'di was born in Shiraz but travelled extensively. He finally ended up in Shiraz where he died in 1292. His beautiful tomb is situated on the outskirts of Shiraz. His *Bustan* and *Gulistan* have been staple texts for Indian students of Persian.

his-ness intends seeks what He chooses and desires. It is said: 'As long as your thou-ness remains in you, it is you-you and He-He. When your thou-ness is completely removed from you, it will all be He. This refers to what is willed, not to an essence." At this point, he recited the following:

> Inevitably at this stage words utterly fail:
> Neither guide nor wayfarer remains, only the Way.
> They become lost in Him, with heads spinning,
> As all shade is lost in the Sun, and all is peace.

He said: "Men of insight have said that, whoever has attained the stage when all personal choosing and desiring have been completely removed from within him and, ensconced in their place, is the will of *God*, then such a servant has emerged from the world of control. This is because a servant exercises control because of what he wants, chooses and desires, as well as because of his disposition. When none of all this remains, everything would be according to what *God* wants. The servant would have no control whatsoever. The saying, 'I am His hearing and I am His seeing' is interpreted along these lines." At this point, he recited the following:

> If fully intoxicated, how could I distinguish a church from the Ka'ba?
> If self is set aside, how could I talk of union or separation?

The Master's son was going through *Siraj ul-'Arifin* [A Lamp for Mystics] and reached these words: "If a person keeps long fasts and spends nights in vigil, but does not love in God and does not hate in God, he reaps no profit." The Revered Master explained: "Loving for the sake of God means that a person loves someone because *God* loves him. In other words, he loves him in God's love. He does not love everyone for the sake of God. If there is someone for whom *God* has no love, and he were to love that person and say that he loves him for the sake of God, this would be personal desire—indeed, it would be lust. A similar argument applies when considering a person as an enemy for the sake of God. This would refer to anybody whom *God* considers an enemy, not anyone against whom he himself has a personal grudge. That is forbidden. Loving for the sake of God would be like this, and would provide the basis for what some people say about love: 'Love is the conformity of the lover with the one He loves and with the one He hates.' The Lord loves everything that is lawful. A believer should also love all such things. The Lord detests everything that is unlawful. Hence, a believer should also detest such things. This is the explanation why lovers accept all lawful things and reject everything that is unlawful, namely, in so far as there is conformity.[407] Indeed it has been said that the most intimate degree of love is conformity, not the desire of heaven or the fear of hell, as is true for ordinary people." At this point, he recited the following:

> For us there is neither the sorrow of hell nor the desire of heaven:
> Remove the veil from Your face, for we yearn to meet You!

Qazi Ashrafuddin inquired: "How do people know that *God* loves some particular person but hates someone else?" The Revered Master replied: "Believers, by virtue of their faith, are friends of the Lord. As it is said: 'God is the friend of those who believe' (Q2:257). Wherever a believer finds himself, he should realize that he is a friend of the Lord by virtue of his faith. Wherever a believer may be, he loves, just as *God* Most Exalted loves, while he considers all unbelievers as enemies of the Lord on account of their unbelief, as it has been said: 'God is the enemy of unbelievers' (Q2:98). Realize that all unbelievers, by virtue of their unbelief, are enemies of the Lord. Wherever a believer encounters an unbeliever, he is his enemy, just as *God* Most Exalted considers all of them enemies."[408]

Again he inquired: "If a believer is a sinner, what would happen?" The Revered Master replied: "By virtue of his faith, he loves him, but, on account of his sin, he considers him an enemy, just as a believer who is a sinner is loved by the Lord because of his faith, but loathed by the Lord because of his sin." Again he inquired: "This pertains to ordinary love. With regard to special love, however, how can it be determined whether it has been bestowed upon a particular person?" The Revered Master replied: "This is indicated by a person's state and sublime way of thinking. For example, people see that a person's external behaviour is in conformity with the Law. They also find him adorned with the qualities

---

407. The whole thrust of the argument is the desire of the lover—the devotee—to be entirely conformed to whatever the Beloved wants. This is something very personal and existential. It should be understood at this level.

408. The Quranic basis for these remarks is clear, as is the need for further theological elaboration.

of special lovers, as well as with their exemplary behaviour. In this way they perceive that someone is an example of special love—but God knows best!"

A discussion arose about "He was two bow-lengths away or even closer" (Q53:9). The Revered Master explained: "These words have been interpreted in various ways. One explanation is that the Arabs have a custom that is followed by two people bound together in love. They align their bows together at the notches for the bowstrings. This serves as a confirmation of the bond of love between them. *God* Most Exalted expressed His love for His Apostle in this verse according to this custom of the Arabs, namely, that His love for this particular person was of such a nature." Qazi Ashrafuddin recited this Tradition, "God has made dear to me three things: perfume and women, and my consolation is in prayer," and opined: "The Apostle loves each of these, yet they are all other than God. How can this be explained?"[409] The Revered Master replied: "This did not come from him, because he said, 'made dear.' This love was poured into his heart. This would not be something he himself had added. If he had said, 'I love,' in that case the answer would be that this is not something essential, but rather a consequence, and is lawful."

A discussion arose about loving one's wife and children. The Revered Master explained: "If someone loves his mother and father, then this love would not be a defect in his love for *God*. On the other hand, if his love for them were to become greater than his love for *God*, then harm would result. The same thing applies to his love for his wife and children, and for anyone else it is lawful to love. If he loves them all in a lawful way, then his love for *God* would in no way be defective.[410] In a similar way, if someone likes gold and silver because he knows that, if he has some, his heart will be at ease and he will be able to perform his devotions without anxiety or apprehension, no harm would result. Thus it is said that a particular holy man, who had abandoned the world, did not think it proper for himself to have anything except *God*. When the time for him to die arrived, his disciples were all present. He took out a purse from the folds of his garment and gave it to his disciples. They were dumbfounded at this turn of events! They were on the

---

409. The context of this question is the repeated prohibition of loving anything other than God.

410. This clarification needs to be kept in mind.

point of losing faith in him when the holy man spoke up: 'Believe what you want, but you should know why I kept this purse. I did so because, if this had not been with me, Satan would have come every time I began to pray and tempted me by asking me what I was going to eat that day, and what was I going to wear. I kept the purse so that, if he came with unsettling suggestions like these, I would immediately be able to reply: 'Look! I have all this silver! I'll be able to eat.' Satan will not be able to disturb me. This is why I kept the purse.' The disciples were satisfied with this explanation."

A dear soul inquired: "Would not this love for wife and children according to the Law be a partnership in the love of *God*?" The Revered Master replied: "This would not imply partnership. The reason for saying this is that a beloved by nature is one, and anything else would be loved because of the beloved. For example, if someone is in love with learning, he will also love books and paper. This does not imply partnership in his love for learning. It is similarly related that Majnun kissed the paw of a dog that used to roam in the lane where Laila lived. No intelligent person would say that this is a partnership in his love for Laila! On the contrary, this shows how much he loves Laila, as it has been said:"

> One day Majnun saw a dog in the desert:
> He began to caress it and was cheered by it.
> He was asked: "How could you be enamoured of a dog?"
> He replied: "One day it had passed along Laila's lane!"

"On the other hand, loving something other than God for its own sake is very damaging. It should not be done. That is why lovers love everything that has been made and created because it is all the result of the creative activity of the Friend. This would be the very epitome of love for the Friend, not of love for any particular thing for its own sake. Nevertheless, if it happens to be the good pleasure of the Friend to efface a letter that He has written; or destroy a house that He has built; or spoil a painting that He has made, it would be necessary to do so, because this is what the Friend wants. This is fidelity to love of the Friend. Killing infidels, destroying idol-temples and whatever is related to them are in this category. This means that no one can say that he has despised something created or made by the Friend, or has shown some sign of opposition."[411]

The Helpless One put this difficulty: "Abu Huraira related that the Apostle said, 'Come one day, but not the next!' This prohibits visiting repeatedly. This necessarily makes people feel out of sorts." The Revered Master replied: "This feeling of despondency was not the intention of the Apostle. On the contrary, it was meant to obviate any slackening of love resulting from too many visits. This is because an abundance of seeing leads to diminishing respect. The Apostle remedied this situation by forbidding daily visits. It is only human for an abundance of visits to lead to diminishing respect. If a person has been overwhelmed by love for someone, however, daily visits would not lead to satiety. That daily seeing would not be 'seeing' for him. Every time he sees, his love would increase. He would consider daily seeing as a restriction and a rarity for him." At this point, he recited the following:

> He beholds beauty, yet remains filled with desire:
> If the whole world is given to an ass, it's still an ass.

He said: "This couplet is indicative of the state of such a person. It is also a sign of his sublime magnanimity that, although it[412] is present and he has obtained it, he does not fix his gaze on it. It has been acquired, but he does not think of it as such. Even if he has attained a stage that is superior to that of others and is praiseworthy, he does not rest content therein, for it is possible that there is even a higher stage of union. He does not rest content in any stage on account of the saying, 'The person who looks at his station veils his Leader.' In other words, anyone who gazes at his station becomes blind to a station which is superior to it. This means he will not attain the higher one."

The Helpless One asked: "What does it mean to say, 'He does not consider acquired what he has acquired?'" The Revered Mas-

---

411. Many people would nowadays question whether God ever directly intends the slaughter of human beings or whatever is precious to them. Such people have anthropological interpretations for such passages, for example, in the Old Testament portion of the Bible. In the present instance, it is best to focus one's attention on Maneri's basic teaching of loving the entire creation because it is the handiwork of God's creative and sustaining power. This 'degree' of love is the fruit of a combination of steadfast endeavour and the grace of God.

412. The reference is to a person's somewhat advanced spiritual stage.

ter replied: "It means that, if a traveller concentrates on what he has in hand and has obtained, his state is not one of emptiness. Because of this, it happens that he has attained all that he was aiming at and desiring. At that moment, all his efforts cease. If this is because of what he has in hand, it means he has acquired something that he was seeking and desiring. To this extent, his quest falls short and slackens. He settles down comfortably in what is other than God." At this stage, the Revered Master recited the following quatrain and couplet:

As long as you are preoccupied with heaven and hell,
How can you possibly become aware of this secret?
Whoever has inhaled His fragrance here on earth,
Can never be bribed to turn away from His embrace!

And:

As long as your saddlebags contain all you need,
I will not become a touchstone for young seekers.

Maulana Karimuddin commented: "When I was in Delhi I wanted to leave the city. I went to Qazi Umda and said: 'Give me leave to go!' Qazi Umda replied: 'What am I, and who am I, to sermonize and command you?' Because of my importunity, he eventually told me this story: 'It is said that Majnun was weeping one day, for Laila had died. At that time, someone came up to him and asked him why he was weeping. He said that he had had an intimate friend who had passed away. He was weeping over the death of his friend.' This indicates that it is better for human beings to love someone than to refrain from doing so, and so fail to experience their loss." The Revered Master commented: "This saying is a pointer towards the love of *God*." He expressed his approval by saying: "It was very well put!" He went on to say: "This is known as the very heart of meaning. Masters of the Word say that, of all the meanings that arise there from, the very heart of meaning is that, when a person loves *God*, everything accrues to him: 'The person who has the Lord has everything.'" At this point he recited the following couplet:

If I have nothing, either in this world or the next,
Yet I have You, I have all, even if naught else besides.

A discussion arose about the aim of noble people. The Revered Master said: "Noble souls are not aiming for heaven. They are seeking love and intimate knowledge, as well as witnessing. If a person is in love with someone, he visits his beloved's home. If he does not find his beloved at home, he considers the house no more than a desert. For the most part, the members of this group do not consider going on pilgrimage to Mecca as the most pressing task. They say that a person should first love and have intimate knowledge of someone, and then go to their home. This is the right way to act. If you have no love or personal knowledge of someone, and you go to the person's house, what profit would that be?" At this point, he recited the following:

> If heaven were without You, I would sit in a turret,
> But if hell were with You, I would hang from a chain.

The Helpless One asked: "What is the sign of the love of *God*?" The Revered Master replied: "The sign of the love of *God* is when the love of *God* is all that is found in a person's heart. He thus realizes that he loves *God*. Such a person is also known as one who has attained union. For example, when Rabi'a Adawiyya[413] was asked if she considered Satan, the enemy of God, to be her enemy as well, she replied: 'I love *God*. I have no time for him!' This would be an inner sign. With regard to external matters, he should carry out what is commanded and refrain from doing what is prohibited. His behaviour also serves as a sign."

Afterwards he told this story: "It is related in the *Sharh-i Ta'arruf* that there was a very committed dervish. One night a wide-eyed damsel of paradise, who was destined for him, appeared before him. She stood there. The dervish longed to gaze at her. To be sure, he had not lost his human nature! Thus it was that, when he grew emboldened, restraint became impossible. His human nature reasserted itself. He wanted to gaze at her. If a beautiful woman presents herself to a man, he loses himself and becomes infatuated with her, and wants to look at her, especially if she is stunningly beautiful. His human nature undoubtedly asserts itself. He could not stop himself from looking furtively at her out of the corner of his eye. When morning came, what happened? All

---

413. Commonly known as simply Rabi'a, this extraordinary woman of Basra is the only woman to be given an entry of her own in the standard Medieval Sufi anthologies. She embraced celibacy and is credited with introducing the love of God as the sole aim of her life. She died in 801. Maneri refers to her several times in his letters.

that pleasure and delight that he used to experience in his devotions simply evaporated. Afterwards he occupied himself in begging forgiveness. Moreover, he did things which members of this group would do only at times when they acted disrespectfully. He also prayed and cried out for help. For forty days he was bereft of the former pleasure and delight he used to experience in his devotions. Nevertheless, he continued to beg forgiveness, pray and cry for help. After this, he was granted the pleasure and delight he had previously experienced. After all this, a voice from heaven said: 'Do you know why you were bereft of your customary pleasure and delight for forty days? It was because you looked out of the corner of your eye and set your heart on that damsel of paradise.[414] It is said that the Path to *God* is difficult and demands penury. If all the kingdoms of this world and the next were brought together before someone, he should not pay any attention to them. In addition to this, he should consider himself a person who has nothing. He will not even realize that he has acquired anything. His whole endeavour should be focussed on *God* and on loving Him. This is the origin of the saying, 'A faqir is a person who pays no attention to anything except God.'"

Later on, he continued: "Mystics explain that this means that people become lost in astonishment. This is something special to them. Many books have been written in an attempt to explain all this. They say that, when there is profound faith, people think that they have no faith; when completely obedient, that they are lacking in obedience; when intimately close, that they are at a distance; and when given over to asceticism, that they are dilettantes. They do not pay attention to anything they have accomplished. In fact, if they perform any act of devotion or worship, they consider it defective."[415] Afterwards he added: "In these matters the first thing to do is to become firmly established in poverty and profess sincere belief in the oneness of *God*. This results in a detachment from anything other than God. A person no longer pays attention

---

414. Stories get changed in the telling. The story given here is the version found in the most reliable text.

415. The actual word translated as 'defective' is *ma'siyat*. This means 'disobedience,' 'rebellion' or, more generally, 'sin.' The translation offered conveys the sense that a Sufi is never satisfied with his acts of devotion or worship. He is aware that they fall short of what he would like them to have been.

to any particular thing. His whole focus is on the grace of *God*." At this stage, the Revered Master recited the following couplet:

We do not worship knowledge, asceticism or mysticism:
We travel along every path buoyed up by hope.

The Helpless One inquired: "How could it be that, when there is profound faith, people think that they have no faith; when completely obedient, that they are lacking in obedience, and so on?" The Revered Master explained: "With regard to all that has been said, one point to note is that a person's attention is on the faults and defects of what he does, as well as on the grace and purpose of *God*. Because all this involves his total attention, he is unable to see his own faith and obedience.[416] It seems likely that this is what is meant by the story about the renowned Truthful One. Even though the Apostle had said of him, 'If the value of Abu Bakr's faith was weighed against that of the community, his would be the heavier,' nevertheless, he asked this question of the Apostle: 'What is faith?'"

A discussion arose about the love of the sheikhs. The Revered Master said: "When a person has love for this group, and something important crops up and he says: 'If I obtain what I want, I shall offer such and such a thing in honour of his soul, or I shall bring such and such a thing for him,' what does this mean? In other words, 'What has happened to me I am entrusting to him at the appropriate time.' That work involves a severing. If this does not happen, however, there is no defect from that side. Rather, it would be due to an insufficiency of love, or to a deficiency in its preconditions, or that some hindrance has arisen. Moreover, if anyone claims to love, yet neglects to put in place the conditions of love, he is simply making an unsubstantiated claim to love. Of what value is such a claim?" He told a story to illustrate this:

"One of the companions passed away. The Apostle was informed that the particular companion had died and left behind a gold coin. The Apostle commented: 'He will have a scar on the Day of Resurrection!' Another companion also passed away. The Apostle was informed of this and that he had left two gold coins

---

416. A person, of course, actually sees what he does. The heightened awareness of God, however, leads to a realization of the imperfection of what he does. This makes it impossible for him to make claims about what he has done, as this would draw his attention away from God and towards himself.

behind. He commented: 'He will have two scars on the Day of Resurrection!' When the companions heard all this, they approached the Apostle and said: 'Some of the companions have many possessions. For example, Uthman, the Leader of the Faithful, and Abd ur-Rahman bin Auf. Moreover, a number of the companions who have died left possessions behind them.' The Apostle replied: 'These two people had claimed to be Sufis, and Sufis renounce everything. In spite of their claim to renunciation, they had hoarded gold coins. The others, however, had never made such a claim.'"

INDEX

polytheism 21, 22, 23, 72, 105, 141, 238
poverty 70, 71, 72, 150, 254, 255, 278
praise 1, 2, 19, 24, 32, 52, 74, 78, 85, 100, 112, 123, 128, 130, 145, 147, 154, 155, 159, 160, 162, 188, 201, 214, 229
prayer ix, xv, 8, 12, 13, 18, 33, 36, 39, 49, 51, 54, 70, 72, 74, 82, 86, 100, 101, 102, 103, 104, 106, 107, 108, 109, 110, 111, 112, 113, 114, 115, 116, 117, 118, 119, 120, 121, 122, 123, 125, 126, 127, 128, 130, 131, 135, 143, 144, 145, 146, 147, 148, 149, 150, 151, 152, 153, 154, 155, 159, 160, 161, 166, 179, 182, 185, 192, 200, 201, 202, 203, 205, 208, 210, 212, 213, 214, 218, 219, 222, 231, 233, 235, 245, 247, 250, 251, 257, 258, 270, 273
Prophet 13, 26, 42, 43, 44, 45, 56, 57, 65, 90, 107, 108, 118, 125, 208, 235, 253
prophethood 59, 72, 78, 79, 81, 116, 207
prostration 24, 112, 115, 122, 124, 125, 127
Protected Tablet 61
purity 44, 102, 103, 104, 105, 106, 142, 180, 222

Q

Qamaruddin 8, 59

Qazi Khan 86, 149, 155
Qazi Safi 54, 126
Qazi Umda 216, 276
Qeyamuddin Zafarabadi 128
qualities 8, 15, 68, 69, 83, 93, 94, 102, 105, 106, 128, 136, 142, 167, 187, 188, 190, 216, 220, 222, 238, 247, 255, 269, 273
quality 14, 15, 25, 44, 62, 63, 68, 69, 75, 105, 165, 190, 196, 217, 224, 268
Quraish 21, 49
Quran xiv, xv, xviii, 8, 13, 20, 21, 26, 27, 31, 33, 36, 37, 41, 43, 44, 45, 48, 49, 50, 51, 52, 53, 56, 57, 58, 60, 61, 62, 63, 82, 90, 102, 110, 117, 121, 122, 127, 129, 130, 147, 148, 149, 152, 153, 155, 160, 161, 163, 166, 171, 186, 191, 196, 197, 198, 233, 236, 238, 243, 250, 256, 257
Qut ul-Qulub 154, 155

R

Rabi'a Adawiyya 277
Rajab 155
Ramazan 36, 120, 121, 122, 132, 133, 135, 137, 152, 153, 209, 245
Rauh ul-Arwah 63
Rauzat ul-'Ulama 121
reality/Reality xix, 2, 3, 6, 8, 9, 28, 31, 32, 47, 68, 71, 76, 77, 90, 96, 118, 144, 186, 208, 217, 227, 229, 230, 235, 236, 252, 258, 270
reflecting xv, 162, 197

religion xix, 10, 20, 21, 61, 72,
   75, 89, 97, 107, 114, 118,
   120, 165, 167, 168, 193,
   196, 200, 202, 207, 213,
   214, 215, 217, 218, 232,
   238, 240, 249
remembering 6, 74, 75, 112,
   113, 147, 157, 158, 159,
   160, 161, 162, 166, 188,
   211, 212, 229, 233, 238
renunciation 44, 134, 219, 221,
   228, 236, 280
Resurrection 24, 56, 60, 61, 76,
   82, 110, 112, 136, 145,
   157, 168, 242, 245, 268,
   279, 280
retribution 136
revelation 21, 49, 50, 61, 79,
   121, 125, 144, 145, 171,
   192, 238, 255

S

Sadruddin 27, 45, 71, 73, 96, 99,
   121, 129, 130, 146, 154,
   174, 198, 199, 211, 238,
   264, 267, 268
Sahl Tustari 218
saint(s) xvii, xviii, 44, 45, 62,
   70, 76, 77, 84, 94, 129, 156,
   184, 185, 187, 188, 191,
   192, 194, 238, 242, 243
Samarqand 263
Sari Saqati 184, 205, 268
Satan 9, 11, 38, 39, 45, 46, 62,
   63, 80, 107, 108, 118, 132,
   160, 161, 183, 185, 214,
   215, 230, 252, 274, 277
scholars xvi, xix, 5, 14, 21, 38,
   40, 41, 42, 44, 45, 47, 48,
   49, 52, 56, 60, 66, 67, 84,

   91, 105, 107, 111, 112,
   113, 114, 119, 120, 121,
   124, 135, 186, 198, 199,
   242, 247, 267
seclusion 54, 63, 158, 164, 179,
   186, 230, 231, 232, 233
self 23, 27, 38, 39, 72, 75, 76,
   77, 82, 106, 170, 179, 193,
   209, 211, 212, 214, 215,
   218, 224, 227, 242, 243,
   252, 253, 271
servant xii, 2, 4, 24, 33, 106,
   122, 129, 149, 159, 161,
   169, 171, 172, 220, 229,
   231, 237, 252, 253, 258,
   268, 271
Seth 179, 180
Shamsuddin Kharizmi 36
Shamsuddin Samir 223
Sharafuddin Sabuni 7
Sharh-i Ta'arruf 128, 229, 277
Sheikh Ahmad 121, 175, 177
Sheikh Alauddin 199
Sheikh Ali Zada 203, 204
Sheikh Haidar Zada 204
Sheikh Ladhu 73
Sheikh Nizamuddin 84, 85, 124,
   125, 175, 178, 190, 191,
   193, 196, 251
Sheikh of Sheikhs 49, 56, 134,
   137, 157, 193, 230, 237
Sheikh Ruknuddin 73, 119, 198,
   212
Sheikh Zanjan 204
sheikh(s) 3, 29, 35, 39, 48, 102,
   104, 126, 130, 132, 134,
   135, 137, 138, 139, 169,
   170, 175, 176, 177, 178,
   179, 187, 189, 194, 205,
   211, 219, 222, 232, 242,

244, 247, 252, 267, 270, 279
Shibli 30, 150, 164, 201, 208, 232, 234, 236, 269, 270
Shu'aib 150
Shuniziya 184
signs 1, 8, 46, 79, 81, 103, 232, 249
sin 24, 27, 33, 66, 70, 74, 85, 95, 102, 125, 136, 156, 165, 183, 186, 208, 232, 241, 242, 244, 272, 278
Siraj ul-'Arifin 85, 124, 129, 160, 233, 271
sister 8, 52, 59, 97, 125, 153, 187
slave 88, 152, 154, 246, 253, 259, 260, 267, 268
solitude x, 170, 229, 230, 231, 232, 262
Solomon 36, 37, 83, 187, 220, 221
Sonargaon ix, xvi, xvii, xix, 53, 54, 168, 231
sorrow 50, 87, 118, 144, 170, 183, 228, 246, 272
soul 1, 13, 22, 27, 33, 68, 69, 77, 81, 82, 90, 91, 95, 96, 100, 105, 130, 132, 138, 140, 142, 166, 171, 173, 178, 179, 181, 186, 193, 194, 195, 198, 199, 203, 208, 209, 213, 215, 216, 218, 220, 221, 222, 223, 224, 229, 231, 236, 237, 242, 245, 249, 253, 258, 274, 279
stage 3, 12, 16, 19, 25, 26, 29, 32, 39, 40, 44, 45, 71, 75, 76, 77, 84, 102, 112, 115, 116, 137, 142, 152, 157,

158, 160, 167, 173, 179, 191, 192, 200, 211, 212, 213, 214, 218, 221, 222, 223, 226, 228, 230, 239, 245, 254, 257, 258, 259, 263, 271, 275, 276, 279
state ix, xiv, 3, 6, 7, 19, 22, 23, 27, 40, 42, 43, 44, 45, 46, 61, 62, 63, 74, 80, 86, 90, 91, 106, 130, 133, 134, 142, 157, 165, 177, 183, 189, 190, 192, 195, 197, 199, 201, 202, 208, 211, 228, 245, 249, 250, 254, 266, 272, 275, 276
steadfastness 83, 228
Sufi x, xi, xv, xvi, xvii, xix, 6, 22, 23, 30, 32, 40, 45, 47, 48, 74, 85, 90, 91, 102, 103, 106, 119, 129, 130, 133, 142, 150, 158, 175, 176, 178, 179, 180, 181, 182, 184, 186, 194, 199, 201, 210, 211, 214, 218, 231, 244, 259, 260, 261, 269, 277, 278
Sufism 90, 117, 121, 137, 175, 188, 193
Sufyan Thauri 67
Suhail bin Abdullah 134
Sultan Shamsuddin 54
Sunami 128
Sunni 7, 10, 84, 93
Syria 18, 124, 263

T

Tabuk 144
Tamhidat 136, 140, 193
Tamimi 129, 155
Taqiuddin 53, 54, 130, 131